SEXUAL PEACE

SEXUAL PEACE

Beyond the Dominator Virus

MICHAEL SKY
Introduced by Riane Eisler

BEAR & COMPANY
PUBLISHING
SANTA FE, NEW MEXICO

LIBRARY OF CONGRESS CATALOGING-IN-PUBLICATION DATA

Sky, Michael, 1951–
    Sexual peace : beyond the dominator virus / by Michael Sky.
    p. cm.
    Includes bibliographical references (p.   ) and index.
    ISBN 1-879181-08-8
    1. Sex role—History. 2. Social evolution—History.
3. Patriarchy—History. 4. Social history. I. Title.
HQ1075.S565 1993
305.3′ 09—dc20   93-12172
                                                                          CIP

Bear & Company, Inc.
Santa Fe, NM 87504-2860

Cover & interior design & illustration: Marilyn Hager
Author photo: Marie Favorito © 1988
Editing: Jerry Chasen & Gail Vivino
Typography: Marilyn Hager

The poems "Credo" (from *First Credo*. Anacortes, WA:
Stonemarrow Press, 1986) and "Like A Planet"
have been reprinted courtesy of James Bertolino.

Printed in the United States of America by R.R. Donnelley

1 3 5 7 9 8 6 4 2

For Everychild—
may this be your day.

Contents

Acknowledgments

With gratitude:

to Penny, my friend and partner through fifteen years of learning, living, and writing this book;

to Barbara Clow for believing so strongly, Jerry Chasen for firm pushes in new directions, Gail Vivino for her wise and gentle editing, and all my other friends at Bear for making it happen;

to Deborah Martyn, Deborah Sparks, Elizabeth Duncan, Irene Dimitri, Jan and Frank Loudin, Jeanne and Gabriel Olmsted, Lee Kane, Lynn Roberts, Marcy Lund, Mary Parkinson, Michael Johnson, Peta Hackel, Peter Kevorkian, Skip Snaith, Sue Ann Fazio, Sydney Cooke, Terra and Newman Love, Tina Rose, and Winnie Adams for careful reading and helpful insights;

to Walt Whitman and James Bertolino, my favorite poets of the partnership way;

to the many authors and teachers who have inspired, guided, and affirmed my work, especially Riane Eisler, Alice Miller, Frederick Leboyer, Robin Morgan, Merlin Stone, Andrew Bard Schmookler, George Leonard, Gerda Lerner, Niro Asistent, and Da Free John;

and to several generations of feminist thinkers and writers for rising up in the darkest gloom of planetary patriarchy and still believing in the dawn.

Foreword

Sexual Peace: Beyond the Dominator Virus is both a passionate and a practical book, a book that speaks to us from the heart and the mind. It is an intensely personal book. But at the same time, it deals with some of the most important issues of our age, issues that affect us all and for which, as Michael Sky eloquently writes, we must all take some measure of responsibility.

I first began to read *Sexual Peace: Beyond the Dominator Virus* because of its subtitle. A friend phoned me to tell me about a new book using the dominator and partnership models I introduced in *The Chalice and The Blade*. A week later, the publisher sent me the manuscript, requesting that I write the foreword.

From the very beginning, what struck me about the book was Michael's personal honesty. I liked his "With gratitude," for the warmth with which it acknowledged those who had helped and inspired him. I liked his preface, the way he posed his questions in the context of his own life experiences. Most of all, I liked his refusal to mince words when faced with injustice, his commitment to sharing what he had learned with others, and his caring.

In this book Michael Sky deals with a very provocative question about human evolution. In *The Chalice and The Blade* I introduced a new view of our cultural evolution, presenting evidence that the shift in our prehistory from a partnership to a dominator direction has been a five-thousand-year detour from which we are today struggling to get back on course. What Michael does is to take this one big step further, suggesting that this detour has affected not only our cultural evolution, but our biological evolution as well. This is highly speculative, so I imagine *Sexual Peace* will be a controversial book. As Michael writes, some people will find it a disturbing book. But precisely because of this, it is also a very interesting book, not only because of its view of evolution but because, unlike other books that take the position that our problems stem from genetic causes, it does not conclude that this means that human nature is essentially flawed. Quite the contrary, Michael's central thesis is that we can heal ourselves from what he calls the "dominator virus,"and much of this book deals with just that.

I certainly agree with Michael that inner work—in both the emotional and the spiritual sense of the word—is a major force toward both individual and social healing. I further agree with him that to shift from a dominator to a partnership approach toward human sexuality is of critical importance for any realistic hope of fundamental transformation (and I am in fact researching and writing a new book in this area myself). And I fully agree with Michael that without a shift from domination to partnership in the relations between the female and male halves of humanity, talk of a more equitable, peaceful, and harmonious world will continue to be just that: talk.

There are matters on which Michael and I do not agree. I think that "dominator virus" is a powerful metaphor, but I do not think our problems are cellular. Also, unlike Michael, who writes how in 1971 he gave up social activism for inner work, I am still a social activist. So while I strongly believe that the personal is political, I also believe that political and legal action has historically been— and continues to be—essential, as it is only through group action that entrenched institutions can be changed.

But like Michael, I also believe it is essential—and urgent— that we address violence and abuse in our most intimate relations, not only because these relations directly impact the day-to-day quality of our lives, but because these are the relations that pro- vide the underlying foundations for all other relations. For me as a woman, Michael's commitment to "at least attempt a visceral understanding of what it means to grow up female in a male- favoring culture" is particularly meaningful. Even more so is his willingness to frontally tackle male dominance as integral to the habits of violence and abuse that spread the dominator "virus."

Michael's challenge to this critical component of a dominator model of society—one that my findings indicate keeps undermin- ing all our personal and social gains—-is particularly forceful, as he does so in terms of his own life experiences and feelings, including his often tumultuous emotions. And this not only makes the material come to life, but is extremely significant. Because in the last analysis, what transformation is about is the courage to question, not in some abstract way but in very personal and concrete ways, much that we are gradually beginning to recognize is a social sickness.

And perhaps above all, *Sexual Peace* is a courageous book. We may not always agree with what Michael Sky has to say. But what is so important about the book is that it combines a passionate idealism with the equally passionate determination to find cures for the dominator "virus" that has for so long embittered life on this planet and now increasingly threatens its very survival.

I say cures, rather than cure, because completing the shift from a dominator to a partnership world is obviously a multifaceted task. And it is a task in which only challenging the old is not enough. What is needed is that we envision and develop the new. This has been the emphasis of my own work and also what gives this book its power. For as he has done in his own emotional and spiritual quest, which he shares with us openly and unashamedly, Michael is not afraid to venture into even the most delicate and often taboo areas, from child sexuality to the possibility of what Rupert Sheldrake calls morphogenetic energy fields.

I have enjoyed reading this book, getting to know Michael through it, and joining him in his search for personal answers to universal questions. It is a book that gives us hope that, as Michael writes, women and men are increasingly "willing to bravely step, as partners, into a world of peaceful cooperation."

We are still a long way from this world. But books like this can help take us a little closer, opening not only our eyes, but our hearts.

Riane Eisler
Carmel, California
April 1993

Riane Eisler is the author of the international bestseller The Chalice and The Blade: Our History, Our Future, *hailed by Princeton anthropologist Ashley Montagu as "the most important book since Darwin's* Origin of Species." *She is also coauthor with social psychologist David Loye of* The Partnership Way: New Tools for Living and Learning.

Preface

As the twentieth century draws to a close, our world is spinning through a rush of extraordinary change. Things are moving so fast that we almost expect to pick up each morning's paper and read of the next Earth-shattering event. Political turmoil and flux are facts of life in almost every nation, and few leaders or ruling parties feel secure in their power. Local, national, and global economies are beyond prediction and are approaching chaos. Ecological systems everywhere are under assault, and many are near collapse. The most basic social institutions—sexual relationships, families, schools, medical systems, religious practices—are all being questioned, and are in many cases failing; they are surely undergoing radical change.

Yet in the midst of all of this wild upset there have come some stunning movements toward world peace. More than forty years of superpower struggle and an ever-growing nuclear threat have suddenly ended, and the old, cold warriors have decided to become good, if cautious, friends. As is the style of our times, we have so quickly become accustomed to this new reality that the great transformation bears repeating: After forty years of the most intense hatred, of seriously worrying over worldwide nuclear holocaust, and of the two largest economies in history racing hell-bent toward producing ever bigger and more terrible weapons, suddenly there is peace instead.

This event seems to have sent a wave of peace around the planet. In a single weekend, the East German people began leaving their country; like magic, the Berlin Wall came down and all of Eastern Europe lurched toward democracy. In a visit with the pope, Mikhail Gorbachev allowed the spirit of religion back into his long-suffering nation. Nelson Mandela was finally released from prison and the grips of racism were loosened in South Africa and throughout the world. In a meeting in Paris, the countries of Europe and North America declared an end to the Cold War and the nuclear arms race. Long, violent struggles in El Salvador and Nicaragua came to welcome, if tentative, conclusions.

So sudden, monumental, and amazingly peaceful have these changes been that we could hardly be blamed for indulging in a great swell of optimism about our future. Yet even as we dream of peace, the arms industry plunders on, a dozen new ethnic, racial, and religious hot spots have exploded into bloodshed, and it is difficult to shake the feeling that humans can learn no other way than war. The sad message is that far too many people still view violence as the primary answer to human conflict. For all the genuine movement toward peace in our world, we are still an angry, fearsome species, given to fits of stupid aggression.

Is our world *really* moving toward a lasting peace? Or is any apparent movement just a temporary balance of power, a brief respite before the next hateful conflict? Are we really moving toward a lasting peace or are our economies just too tired to build any more bombs? Is all this talk of peace but the wishful dreaming of bleeding hearts and sentimental fools? Is lasting peace even possible for the people of our world?

It is this final question that gives me the greatest pause and provides the impetus for this book. Is lasting peace even possible for the people of our world? Can we the people—women, men, mothers, fathers, daughters, sons, human beings—*become any more peaceful?* Can we people a world of lasting peace?

In 1971, I traveled with a group of antiwar activists to Washington, D.C., for the purpose of shutting down the U.S. government. It was, admittedly, a lot to hope for, and I was not too disappointed that we failed to pull it off. I was crushed, however, by what I observed of the workings of the "peace movement." All of the hierarchical power structures, the sexism, the racism, the blind dogma, and, most disturbingly, *the angry violence* that I had come to protest in my country were fully present in the very movement designed to end all these things. How, I wondered, could such angry, hate-driven men and women possibly be expected to create a world of peace?

It was an abrupt end to outward social activism for me and the beginning of a long period devoted to the inner work of purging myself of violence while helping others to do the same. I leapt whole-heartedly into a therapeutic, human-potential sea of tools, teachings, practices, and experiences committed, each in their own way, to exploring two basic questions: How do we find inner peace in a world filled with violence and abuse, and can we extend such peace outwardly, positively affecting society and its institutions and creating, ultimately, a world of lasting peace?

Eventually, my work focused on a practice of deep breathing called "circular breathing" that I described at length in my book *Breathing* (Bear & Company, 1990). Circular breathing initiates a physio-emotional recall of childhood events, specifically those events from birth through the first few years of life that retain suppressed emotional pain. In reexperiencing unresolved emotional hurts from the past, breathers are able to create positive resolutions, and thus deep healing, in the present.

Through this work I have been able, in effect, to observe the births and childhood experiences of thousands of clients and students. I have witnessed the clear correlation between early conditioning and later behavior and experience. Most importantly, I have found that much early conditioning, in even the best of families, is abusive, sexist, racist, and anti-ecological.

This is a strong statement, I know. But I am hardly alone in this conclusion. The past twenty years have brought a growing awareness of the degree to which physical, sexual, emotional, racial, and environmental abuses permeate civilized culture at all levels. Terms such as child abuse, domestic violence, wife-battering, date rape, dysfunctional families, poisonous pedagogy, and ecocide have made their way into the vocabulary as we wrestle with the psycho-emotional structures of our society. Practices that have been culturally sanctioned for countless generations are now coming to be seen as vile, destructive, and no longer acceptable.

At the heart of this new awareness is one inescapable fact: we learn these abusive practices as children. Our relationships with our bodies, with the opposite sex, with our neighbors, with other races and cultures, and with the environment are all powerfully conditioned during early childhood. The imbalances and abuses of our family structures create the imbalances and abuses of our society that in turn impact heavily upon our family structures. This is the cycle of abuse that must be ended if we are ever to live in a world of lasting peace.

It is no coincidence that the growing movements to end culturally sanctioned physical, sexual, racial, and ecological abuses are arising at the same time as the growing movement to bring about worldwide lasting peace. Indeed, these are all faces of a single movement, and the success of each is critical to the success of the whole. We will never create a world of peace between nations until we stop transmitting patterns of sanctioned abuse to each new generation of boys and girls. We will never birth and raise a generation of peaceful children until we touch, feel, and begin to resolve the patterns of abuse within our own bodies and lives. And we cannot hope to fully heal ourselves unless we are simultaneously ending the culturally sanctioned abuses of our societies.

Ending the cycle of abuse demands a deep transformation of all points of the cycle: the birthing of babies; the raising of children; the relationships among men and women; the family dynamic; the political, economic, and religious structures of society; the interactions among different societies and races; and the relationship between humans and the natural world. It is a Herculean task, certainly; the only thing harder than doing it would be continuing to live with the effects of *not* doing it.

I believe that a vital key to this all-encompassing transformation is human sexuality. All work with early childhood events, family patterns, current relationships, and societal structures eventually takes us to our experience as fundamentally sexual creatures. The first act of abuse inflicted upon almost every new human is the denial and suppression of the vital sexual-energy-awareness that is our birthright. As children we are conditioned to inhibit and suppress the full and free feeling of sexual joy; as adults we create a joyless and all-too-abusive world. Transforming the world requires that we recover our primary state of sexual joy, individually and socially: that we come to a true and lasting peace with our sexual selves and then extend that peace through all our relations.

Toward this goal, I have concluded each chapter of *Sexual Peace* with a series of questions designed to help you explore the issues raised by the book within your own life. I recommend that you read the questions slowly enough for you to *feel* the answers; or, even better, read through the questions and then take some time for meditation or writing in a journal. The notion of *sexual peace* is irrelevant if it remains but an abstraction or a theory. My most sincere prayer is that the material in this book become physically and emotionally *real* for you. I can only ask that you join me in this prayer and that we become active partners in the embodiment of ever-expanding joy and the moving of our world beyond its ancient and chronic habits of violence and abuse.

One cautionary note: This book can at times be disturbing, especially for men. In it, I address the history, structure, and continuing creation of our long violent and abusive world, and I use the term *patriarchy* to describe the primary system of human relationship that prevails in such a world. I stress that this system tends to favor men in fundamental ways and that our world has indeed been "a man's world" for several thousand years. And I catalogue the abusive excesses of this male-favoring system at length.

It may seem at times as if I am indicting men for all the world's problems while casting women as history's poor and pathetic victims. This is not my actual belief nor is it my intention to convey this in writing *Sexual Peace*. Rather, as I hope to make clear, our world has always been and can only be the collective creation of men and women acting together.

It *is* my intention to bring focused awareness to the common abuses of our world. In so doing, it is hard to avoid the conclusion that women have suffered terribly at the hands of men for thousands of years. This is not to say that individual women are never abusive and domineering nor that individual men are never victimized by women. Moreover, there are certain clear benefits to being a woman in a patriarchal world, just as there are specific burdens typically thrust upon a man. The fact remains, however, that

women as a group have been commonly and collectively dominated by men as a group, and this almost universal domination
has run to horrible abuses.

As a man, I have found that coming to a place of *sexual peace*
with the women in my life has required that I at least attempt a
visceral understanding of what it means to grow up female in a
male-favoring culture. This has, in turn, meant facing the harsher
facts of male domination. This process is not a matter of incurring
guilt nor of engaging in self-flagellation; it is a matter of reaching
across a painful divide to gratefully touch another's reality. If I
seem to concentrate too heavily on the story of male domination, it
is because I am convinced that unflinching awareness of *who we have
been* is an essential first step toward realizing *who we could become*.

Women, I should add, tend toward a fairer understanding of
what it means to grow up male by virtue of their constant exposure
to the mostly male voices in history, culture, media, religion, and
leadership at higher levels. Women tend to "get" what it is to be a
man because they have been given a mostly male representation of
reality. And though they have good reason to protest such an
ancient and ubiquitous state of affairs, our challenge now is not to
diminish Everywoman's understanding of maleness but to expand Everyman's understanding of femaleness.

I feel that our world is in the midst of monumental changes that
will alter the lives and relationships of all women and men and will
move us beyond our chronic habits of abusive domination. We are
all called, men and women together, to let go of our defenses and
definitions and to be willing to bravely step into a world of peaceful
cooperation. My hope is that *Sexual Peace* will provide a map, some
tools, and a good measure of encouragement for the journey before us.

SEXUAL PEACE

Credo

We believe in the one message
    like a fever chill
    in each mushroom, inside
    the chanterelle, the morel,
    the rose coral and shaggy mane.
We believe the movement of a lake trout
    takes on the sanctity of number
    as the osprey dives. We believe the towhee.
We believe alpine snow water, when it teases the crags
    and outcrops like clear giggling crystal,
    is memorizing sunlight to help oysters grow.
We believe in synchronicity. We believe when a poem is conceived
    the beloved knows. We believe Jupiter touches us with luck
    as we live and live again, and that Jesus knew.
We believe sod holds. We believe there are
    in each of us particles that once
    were stars, that matter is thought,
    and that this belief is the way
    of breathing in.

                      —*James Bertolino,* <u>First Credo</u>

ONE

The Nature of the Beast

One night, some twenty years ago, I went to the movies alone. The film title escapes me now, but it was typical Hollywood fare. At some point during the movie, in typical Hollywood fashion, there was a portrayal of a rape scene. As I sat watching a young woman suffer violent abuse, I was suddenly appalled to notice that I was becoming sexually aroused.

I got out of my seat and left in a rush, feeling confused and ashamed. I felt somehow complicit in the behavior on the screen. Even worse, I experienced profound self-doubt: Was that the real me? Was I capable of rape, of murder? How could I experience sexual excitement at the sight of such violence? Did I have some evil horror lurking within me, just a momentary lapse of control away? Could I ever be sure that I did not?

My experience that night, and my need to answer the questions it provoked, marked the first step on a personal journey toward what I now call *sexual peace*. I have struggled in my life with the common range of addictive behaviors, abusive relationships, and "inner lurking horrors," while sometimes feeling an overwhelming despair for the collective horrors of our world. I have often thought, despite my better judgment, that humans are born wretched into a wretched world and that there is no lasting solution to our deeply conflicted lives nor to the suffering we so naturally inflict upon one another.

Though I now believe quite the opposite—that we are born for the daily blessing of personal and planetary peace—my own struggle is hardly over: it requires constant vigilance to keep the peace in a world so committed to violence and abuse. Yet it is surely within the power of each of us to do so. An important key, I am convinced, is transforming our sexual experience.

I now view my movie-theater revelation as but a mild symptom of a species-wide, psycho-emotional affliction: the aggressive and abusive domination of women by men, leading to male domination of virtually all facets of human society. For the past several thousand years (with some minor exceptions) life in our world has been controlled by men through the forces of religious doctrine, civil law, family structure, and chronic physical and sexual abuse. A fundamental characteristic of this history of male control has been the aggressive and routinely violent subordination of women.

A second characteristic of the long history of male control has been the spreading of coercive, abusive, dominant/submissive power dynamics throughout all levels of human relationship. The male domination of woman sets the pattern for and gives credence to the strongman's domination of the weak, the wealthy person's domination of the poor, the slave owner's domination of the slave, the soldier's domination of the pacifist, the industrialist's domination of the primitive, and humanity's domination of all animals, plants, and ecosystems.

I will be using the term *patriarchy* to refer to this whole pattern of human interaction. Patriarchy describes the universal rule of men at the state, religious, professional, corporate, and family levels. Patriarchy further describes a basic approach toward resolving conflicts in which power accrues to the most dominant in any relationship—the biggest, the strongest, the wealthiest, the most violent, the most industrially advanced. As we shall see, male control of social institutions has led inexorably to domination as the primary means of resolving conflicts, just as any institution that is committed to dominant/submissive power dynamics is controlled, invariably, by men. Thus, to say that a society, a government, a church, an institution, a corporation, or a family is patriarchal is to assert that it is *usually governed by men* and is done so *through the power dynamics of domination.*

Patriarchal society is rooted in a fundamentally abusive imbalance in the relationship between men and women that extends to systemic patterns of abuse within our religious, governmental, corporate, and social institutions. Now, in the late twentieth century, these patterns of abuse direly threaten all of creation. As historian and theologian Thomas Berry writes, "The term *patriarchy* has now been brought forward as a way of indicating the larger sources of responsibility for what is happening not only with women, but also with the total civilizational structure of our society and even with the planet itself. The sense of *patriarchy* has now evolved as the archetypal pattern of oppressive governance by men with little regard for the well-being or personal fulfillment of women, for the more significant human values, or for the destiny of the earth itself."[1]

This "archetypal pattern of oppressive governance" has left a universally terrible history in its wake. It is a steady tale of brutality and violence, with our planet lurching from one war to the next, year after year, century upon century. Revolutions follow upheavals leading to palace coups and then more wars, and all the while the weapons of mass murder steadily grow in their power to wreak misery and destruction. For all the talk of "new world orders," there is little sign that the men of this world know how to stop aggressively dominating each other and everything else that gets in their way, nor even that most men care to try. For women, life under patriarchal oppression has been an unrelenting experience of beatings, rapes, burnings, veilings, foot-bindings, genital mutilations, enslavements, infanticides, witch hunts, intimidations, molestations, harassments, disenfranchisements, disempowerments and, through it all, unending and dehumanizing subordinations to men.

If *any* of this was getting better, then perhaps we could think of patriarchy as an evolving system and give it time to become kinder, gentler, more equitable, and just. Unfortunately, the wars just get deadlier, our streets grow more violent, and, for all the apparent progress of women's rights, the daily crimes against women are increasing, not lessening. Moreover, while patriarchal society has always been ecologically destructive, these days the magnitude of its threats to the environment have shifted from local to global proportions. It is one thing to destroy an ecological niche through poor husbandry or industrial greed; it is another thing entirely to destroy oceans, rain forests, and the atmospheric ozone layer.

Clearly, we are in desperate need of some other way of structuring our societies. Clearly, the answer *does not* lie in fiddling with the driving mechanisms of the various patriarchal systems of our world. Witness the collapse of communism: While the "free" world celebrates this grand triumph of capitalism, the living conditions for women, children, ethnic and racial minorities, the poor, and the environment in the now "free" nations have only worsened. In fact, the transformation of Eastern Europe and the Soviet Union involved little more than a shifting of power from one group of men to another, the only kind of change that patriarchies ever allow.

This is especially apparent in America. Two hundred years of facing the false and increasingly vapid choice of one group of old, white, wealthy men versus another group of old, white, wealthy men has resulted in a steady increase of nonvoters. While much of the world is braving death to earn democracy, less than half of Americans now choose to exercise it. They know better: voting changes the players, but not the game; the cast, but not the long-depressing drama.

Rather than voting for the Tweedledees and Tweedledums of patriarchal governments, we need to exercise some *real* choice by shifting to fundamentally nonpatriarchal societies. In her revolutionary book, *The Chalice and the Blade*, Riane Eisler precisely spells out our two basic choices: "The first, which I call the *dominator* model, is what is popularly termed either patriarchy or matriarchy—the *ranking* of one half of humanity over the other. The second, in which social relations are primarily based on the principle of *linking* rather than ranking, may best be described as the *partnership* model."[2] As we shall see, humans have lived before in partnership societies. There is every reason to believe that we can do so again.

Eisler's two models of relationship closely correspond to the definitions of power suggested by ecofeminist and writer Starhawk. Starhawk writes of *power-over*, the power to dominate and control others; *power-from-within*, the force of our own personal abilities and potentials; and *power-with*, "the influence we wield among equals."[3] For our purposes, *power-over* is a clear description of patriarchal domination, while *power-from-within* and *power-with* together give the full sense of any genuine linking partnership.

I am using the term *patriarchy* to refer to all power-over, domination-controlled relationships and systems, from the micro-patriarchies of the common nuclear family through the larger patriarchies of businesses, schools, religions, and governments to the all-encompassing macropatriarchy that has been human life on planet Earth for the past four to five thousand years. In any patriarchal relationship or system, power accrues to an individual or group of individuals according to specific hierarchical means of ranking, with the ability to exert force against or over another (domination) given highest priority. Moreover, where control by domination is the norm, men inevitably subordinate women.

This is not to say that male governance must of necessity be dominating. Nor, I might add, must female governance necessarily be *non*-dominating. Rather, any system of governance in which power accrues to those able to exert the greatest force against others tends to favor men as a group. Once such a dominant/submissive power dynamic is set in motion, power invariably shifts away from women as a group. Historical exceptions, such as Golda Meir and Margaret Thatcher, merely prove the rule: rarely, if ever, is such a powerful woman followed in office by another woman.

Instead, the power shifts back to men, as it will always do in a patriarchal system.

I am also, following Eisler, using the term *partnership* to refer to power-with relationships and systems that are essentially egalitarian in nature and practice. In any true partnership, emphasis is placed on *linking* and *connecting* and *sharing power* for the common good rather than on *ranking over* for individual advantage. Eisler writes that partnership systems strive "for the resolution of our problems through the freeing of both halves of humanity from the stultifying and distorting rigidity of roles imposed by the domination hierarchies inherent in [patriarchal] systems."[4] Just as the fundamentally dominant/submissive dynamic between men and women has extended into global systems of patriarchal control, so would a true partnership between men and women initiate a planetary transformation toward more egalitarian societies.

A major result of such a transformation would be a significant lessening in human-caused abuse. Patriarchal society has always been and can only be abusive since domination, however sincerely it may be justified, always abuses. The subordinate within a patriarchal relationship always suffers—whether physically, sexually, emotionally, psychologically, economically, or spiritually. *To be dominated by another is to suffer harm.* This applies to the domination of women by men, of children by parents, of students by teachers, of clients by therapists, of workers by bosses, of the poor by the rich, of small nations by stronger nations, and of ecosystems by human beings. Any dominant/submissive relationship is by definition and necessity an abusive relationship.

This concept is so critical to our understanding that it bears repeating: Patriarchal rule—within a family, a church, a school, a society, a government, an environment—always abuses; domination, however one might justify it, always injures the one being dominated. Believing that domination of another is God's will, or thinking that domination is just and legally correct, or considering domination of others to be "for their own good," or asserting that domination is biologically ordained are the fundamental doctrines of patriarchy. All have been used to support the continuing patriarchal rule of our world, and all are abusive. Anything less than a true linking partnership—between any two people, or between groups of people, or between a person and the environment—inevitably abuses the subordinate in the relationship.

Finally, I must stress that in speaking of patriarchy in this way I am not strictly and solely blaming men. Women play a part in this ancient dance of abuse. They are not merely victims any more than men are outright winners. Indeed, many women are themselves patriarchally abusive of subordinate men, women, and children in their lives, just as many men spend their entire lives as abused subordinates to other men *and* women. Our task is not to "bash" men or presuppose some "womanly perfection." Though men hold many advantages over women, and though women are subjected to terrible abuses at the hands of men, in truth everybody loses under patriarchy, for everybody is demeaned, lessened, and abused. Everybody is breathing the same foul air; nobody is reaching his or her full human potential.

Likewise, both sexes share in the continuing creation of our patriarchal world. We are equally born into and conditioned for this self-sustaining system in which each generation of patriarchal fathers and mothers indoctrinates the next generation of boys and girls When we consider the power of this childhood conditioning, assigning malicious intent or fixing blame for patriarchy is pointless. We have been for a long time, and thus currently are, a patriarchal people. The important question is what we *as partners* will become and how we will get there.

First, I will delve deeper into the roots of patriarchal culture, paying special attention to the ways in which it defends and perpetuates its own existence. There are four basic doctrines of patriarchal inevitability: the religious, the social, the biological, and the historical. These four doctrines give patriarchal culture its perennial explanations and justifications for continuing abuse. Not surprisingly, each assumes that patriarchal domination is the only way of ordering society and ignores any evidence that humans once lived in partnership cultures or could ever hope to again.

God the Father

> But ye shall destroy their altars, break their images and
> cut down their groves, for thou shalt worship no other god,
> for the Lord whose name is jealous is a jealous God.
> —*Exodus 34:13-14*

> The rulership of men in the church, by divine determi-
> nation, assured the relegation of women to subordinate
> status in the religious community, the denial of integral
> participation in religious ritual, and the identification of
> women with seduction and moral evil.
> —*Thomas Berry*[5]

The religious doctrine of patriarchal inevitability begins with
"God the Father." In the Bible, the father or male principle is the
active, initiating force and the sustaining presence throughout all
aspects of the human experience.[6] There is little reference to a
mother or female principle anywhere in the Old Testament. As
Merlin Stone points out in her superb book *When God Was a Woman*,
"The Old Testament does not even have a word for 'Goddess.'"[7]
The New Testament does, of course, have the Virgin Mary, but she
is a mere mortal in the company of the divine Father and Son.
Clearly, the men who wrote the Bible went to great lengths to
establish that God is masculine. Though they tell us that he created
us in his likeness, in fact quite the opposite was the case.

Above all, the first few pages of Genesis leave no doubt that
woman is a subordinate, indeed, an afterthought, to man. Eve is
created from Adam's rib as his "help meet" and to keep him from
his loneliness. She promptly engineers the supreme foolishness of
listening to the snake and its sexy talk. For her sin, all of humankind
is thoroughly damned (until the Son comes along to make things
right), childbearing is forever painful, and it is deemed that a
woman's desire should be only for her husband, *her ruler.*

This biblical story has profoundly affected all of the Jews,
Christians, and Moslems who have ever read the Old Testament
and considered it to be the word of God, as well as all of the other
people of the world who have found themselves under the domination of one of these three Old Testament religions. In the first

few pages of the Bible, the nature of woman as a subordinate creature to man is divinely cast and forever justified. Remember, *she asked for it*. For the rest of patriarchal history, she gets it.

The story of women, through both the Old and New Testaments, is such a sorry, sorry tale that it is a wonder how the Bible can be thought by so many to be "the greatest story ever told" or, for that matter, a holy book. Any book written today that contained so much rape, pillage, murder, bondage, and child abuse would be denounced as pornography by the very people who so revere the Bible. We are to believe that because it is God himself, angry and vengeful in the heavens, who is demanding the constant misogy-nous violation in the Bible, that it is somehow sanctified. Brutality in the name of God the Father is holy. Besides, it's all *her* fault, anyway.

God the Father does not stop with the subordination of women to men; he dictates the total domination of *everything and everybody* on Earth by those who obey his laws. Man is given rulership over all of nature, which is divinely cursed in Genesis and which, in any case, is only a stage along the journey to heaven. We can search the Bible in vain for the simple love of nature that so inspires the Tao Te Ching and the mythologies and oral histories of so many Native American and other indigenous cultures. Indeed, it follows quite directly from the Bible that Judeo-Christian culture has grown into an ecological blight upon the entire planet.

But God the Father is not finished. "I am the one and only God," he commands. With this single proclamation, the wholesale genocide of entire races, the rape and conquest of whole civilizations, the violent eradication of all Goddess religions, the burning of temples, holy texts, and sacred groves, the torture and murder of witches and pagans, the brutal conversion of "ignorant savages," and an endless saga of crusades, jihads, and holy wars all thunder into terrible and unrelenting parade. He is a jealous and easily angered God, given to fits of impulsive violence: the ultimate abusive Father. He has caused infinite suffering to the people of this world. The greatest crimes in human history have been those performed in the service of this angry and jealous God the Father; our greatest sin has been in thinking that any abuses are justified when "God is on our side."

There are exceptions to this dominator saga scattered throughout the Bible—moments when God the Father softens and a great love and promise of true partnership shine through. In such passages, the Bible becomes a true holy book, uplifting, inspiring, and wise. The most glorious of these exceptions is the life and teachings of Jesus.

One wonders how the rulers of his time allowed this man to teach for even three years, so revolutionary was his message. He walked the land in the close company of the poor and disenfranchised, preaching an end to all of the dominating hierarchies of his age. He traveled with women, talked with women, and gave every indication that he considered women to be the equals of men. He offered a new commandment—that we love one another—and he demonstrated the simple power of this commandment in his own living and dying.

There is none of the dominator in Jesus' teachings; rather, he reached out and claimed partnership with all others. There is also none of the abuser in any of his words or actions; rather, he turned the other cheek even to those who would do him the greatest harm. There is none of the constant threat of Father-violence. Though Jesus freely expressed his anger, and though he was unyielding regarding the demands of a spiritual life, he was infinitely forgiving, rather than punishing. As Eisler writes, Jesus knew "that the 'masculine' values of dominance, inequality, and conquest he could see all around him debasing and distorting human life must be replaced by a softer, more 'feminine' set of values based on compassion, responsibility, and love."[8]

That so much violence has since been perpetrated in Jesus' name is testament to the cleverness and determination of the patriarchal packagers of his message. However inspired the original writings of the Bible may have been, the end result—the Bible in its current form—reflects a massive editing job by committees of mostly nameless men who were primarily concerned with strengthening patriarchal law and consolidating church power. There are passages and whole books of the Old and New Testaments that were censored and suppressed from cultural awareness. Certain sections of the Bible underwent extensive rewriting over time. Judeo-Christian culture, to the extent that it is based on the Bible, is strongly influenced by the patriarchal biases and agendas of the Bible's editors and interpreters—men who were more interested in preserving patriarchal power than in the revolutionary teachings of the man called Jesus. Indeed, some of Jesus' most important teachings exist only on the fringes of Christianity, and others were no doubt erased for all time. It may be that the editors let just enough of his gentle message come through to encourage a submissive, "opiated" populace that would be easy to dominate.

It is significant, I think, that the angriest passages in the Gospels are those in which Jesus is railing against the scribes and Pharisees—the editors and interpreters of his day. He understood well the power they had and the degree to which they were abusing it. Did he know that centuries after his death such men would use his life to justify the Crusades, the Inquisition, and the brutal and incessant disinheritance of the Earth's meekest people? How would he respond now to the editors and interpreters who use his words to enslave and demean women? Could he have imagined himself, a symbol, raised on a banner marching into war?

Perhaps he knew. He surely knew that his most revolutionary message—"that access to the deity need *not* go through a religious hierarchy headed by a chief rabbi, high bishop, or pope"[9]—would receive no support from that hierarchy. A patriarchal system will destroy anything in defense of itself.

Ultimately, Jesus' teaching was not revolutionary enough, though he probably took it to the limits for his time. He was the first wild-eyed radical to demonstrate the perils of working within the system, but he never questioned God the Father; nor did he lift up and celebrate the Queen of Heaven. With the primal hierarchy left in place and God the Father, the sole Supreme Being, seated firmly upon his throne, the church built upon Jesus' teaching became only another patriarchal system.

Any religion that so posits the father principle as a power-over system invariably becomes a system of domination, of ranking and judging, and of ordained abuse against those who fail to measure up. This in turn gives credence, and the blessings of God, to the many precepts of a dominator culture: only men can be priests, all property is owned by husbands and bequeathed to sons, a woman's body is the source of suffering and sin, man rules over woman and has dominion over nature. Any who believe otherwise are subjected to the wrath of God as expressed through the brutality of his servants. That such God-the-Father religions have entangled our world in four thousand years of constant strife could have been expected given their basic premises. Domination *always* abuses.

Man the Hunter, Woman the Hearther

Women do have the edge here, because we have always seen through the lie of Woman, whereas men are only beginning to see through the lie of Man.
　　　　　　　　　　　　　—Robin Morgan[10]

Like the religious doctrine, the social doctrine of patriarchal inevitability presumes the universal fact of male domination from the very beginning. It describes our early planet as a rough and nasty place, filled with dangerous aggressors all competing with each other for survival. Onto this bleak landscape struts "Man the Hunter," upright, strong, aggressive, and, through his special intelligence, soon to be the top species on the block.

The female in this narrative is at home minding one child and pregnant with another and thus perfectly suited to the role of "Woman the Hearther." She remains with the kids, cooking, cleaning, propagating the race, and totally dependent on her man's protection. Later in the story she takes on further responsibilities such as agriculture, weaving, and pottery—all tasks perfectly suited to her inferior size and strength, as well as to her need to stay close to the hearth.

Meanwhile, the woman's mate must go out and hunt: for food, for suitable living quarters, and in defense against ever-changing enemies and threats. While the woman's role quickly becomes commonplace and repetitive, the man's is always different, more demanding, and ultimately more critical to human survival. With time, he becomes more adaptive, inventive, adventuresome, and creative. Millennia after the hunt is over, the man is still venturing out to provide and protect, discovering a new challenge every day, while the woman is still staying close to the hearth, minding the children and stirring the pot.

Thus, according to this viewpoint, a fundamental hierarchy of social roles and responsibilities was established in the early stages of human culture that has steadily strengthened with the passing of time. There is men's work and there is women's work. There are demands of manhood and demands of femalehood. And there is an obvious recognition of which sex is weaker and which sex is dominant and protective.

From the perspective of this social narrative, because a man's responsibilities demand greater freedom and mobility and more vigorous adaptation to the changing nature of the world, he has naturally evolved in intelligence and talents according to the serious challenges he has faced. He has come to personify humanity at its greatest: the innovator, the explorer, the hero, the sage, the king, the healer, the warrior, the Christ. He has marched off to war to save us all, again and again. He has written *Macbeth*, composed *Ave Maria*, and painted the Mona Lisa. He has discovered America, he fathered the revolution, and conceived of the Declaration of Independence, the Constitution, and the Bill of Rights. He has invented computers, cured diseases, and stepped on the surface of the moon. He has done all of this, and what's more, he has also provided for and protected his wife and family.

Woman, meanwhile, has gone on having babies. This is, after all, her primary responsibility (since men can't do it and somebody has to). She, too, has evolved in intelligence and talent according to the rather ordinary challenges she has faced. Which is to say, hardly at all. Let's face it, any animal is capable of getting pregnant, carrying the fetus to term, giving birth, nursing the infant, and mothering it through early childhood. Unfortunately, mothering has been quite taxing labor nonetheless, leaving little time or energy for anything else. So woman could not have been expected to invent, create, discover, write, paint, compose, lead, or enlighten. Nor could she have been expected to keep pace with man's brilliant evolution: she will always be the weaker sex.

This story of our social development has persisted into the present despite reams of evidence against its authenticity. From the archaeological record, from the observation of existing hunter-gatherer cultures, and from a planetwide mythological record, a rather different story has emerged. As we shall see in chapter 3, there most certainly was a time when women and men were equal partners. During this partnership time (which lasted in some areas for thousands of years), there were clear differences in male and female roles, but there was no weaker sex, no less evolved sex, no dependent sex, and no stronger, more heroic, inventive, and adventuresome sex. Women and men were different but equal partners.

Nonetheless, there is an inexorable logic to Man the Hunter's superiority if the presumption of the world as a hostile and violent place is accepted. Because men have the difficult task of protecting women and children from attackers (sometimes animals, but mostly other men), men are best suited for managing all the details of organized violence (war). Because success in war is vital to a community's survival, the demands of war on a community's resources and energy must be given top priority. If war is of primary importance and men are in charge of war, it follows that men will be in charge of and superior to everything else, including women and children.

Furthermore, women do have babies and mothering does have certain unavoidable demands. As any modern woman attempting to "have it all" will likely attest, there are trade-offs with mothering. Proper mothering requires time and energy that cannot be spent in other areas, most especially the waging of war.

Moreover, while a woman is pregnant and tending other children, somebody must hunt and gather the food, provide protection from any threats, and go to war when necessary. Men are bigger, stronger, and never get pregnant. They are well suited to the tasks of warring and defending, along with much of the heavy lifting of daily life. It does make sense.

What does not make sense, however, is the hierarchical ranking of these two different sets of experiences and expressions. The viewpoint of a "differently equal" partnership would be so much healthier. The special nature and possibilities of women's experiences give rise to a whole realm of learning and self-expression that is quite different from that of men, just as the special nature of men's experiences gives rise to a whole realm of learning and self-expression that is quite different from that of women. These differences should be the source of combined strength, the varied threads of a rich human tapestry. Instead, they have become the foundation of the dominator's continuing self-justification.

Ultimately, the central lie of Man the Hunter's "natural" superiority is the idea that humans are naturally violent. This concept makes individual human survival dependant upon the capacity to commit violence. As we shall see in chapter 4, this lie took hold of the human race several thousand years ago and has darkly determined all of human experience ever since then. Once man's capacity to cause death was considered of greater importance and necessity than woman's capacity to give birth, a self-confirming and perpetuating dominator system was set in motion. Women have become weaker because domination abuses, and they have been the most abused for so very long. Men have become stronger because they have been afforded the advantages of domination for so very long.

Any society so committed to violence of necessity becomes patriarchal. In any patriarchy, men will come to dominate women. And domination always abuses.

It's Only Human

For the female is, as it were, a mutilated male.
—*Aristotle*
Biology is destiny. —*Sigmund Freud*

The third doctrine of patriarchal inevitability is biological. This line of reasoning seizes upon several physiological differences between man and woman and uses them as validation of man's innate superiority. Just as many other species show a dominant sex, the male is naturally presumed to be the dominant sex in the human species, and a range of "purely scientific" observations are offered as proof.

The oldest and most widely spread of these observations relates to the female reproductive system. The simple fact of pregnancy, as we have already seen, is used as a strong argument for women's subordination. The last stage of pregnancy and the act of giving birth can both be debilitating conditions within a dominator value system. To the extent that a pregnant or delivering woman is less effective in meeting the demands of day-to-day survival, and especially the demands of self-defense in the event of violence, she is the weaker sex.

Likewise, menstruation has long been cited as proof of feminine inferiority. Of course, losing blood can make one weaker, so losing blood every month might make one perennially weaker. For some women, menstruation also comes with heavy pain and emotional disruption. And there is the unseemliness of it all, with the blood flowing from the genitals in an apparent loss of control. It is easy, especially for men, to construe this as something wrong, like a wound or injury. Menstrual taboos are thus common throughout the world as men have sought to protect themselves from the monthly curse of the weaker sex.

In modern times, this taboo is expressed most clearly in advertisements for feminine hygiene products. Typically there is no use of the word menstruation, no mention or sight of blood, and the models are either triumphant athletes or successful business women. The not-too-subtle suggestion is that, indeed, menstruation is weakening and debilitating, but modern science has a cure. That it can only ever be a partial cure (short of a hysterectomy) is just further evidence of woman's innate inferiority.

Then there is the act of sexual intercourse, perhaps the ultimate proving ground for male domination. The structural and operational differences in male and female genitalia and sexual experience certainly allow for, and perhaps even encourage, men to sexually dominate women. Some would argue that men's anatomical ability to rape women led inevitably to the discovery of and evolving tendency toward rape, which led in turn to male domination. Certainly the differences between men and women that give sex its wonderful possibilities can easily be turned into a dominant/submissive pattern of relationship.

At the core of these differences is choice. A man can sexually dominate a woman because he wants to, regardless of her desire. His choice overwhelms her choice as his organ invades hers — the essence of power-over domination. The more she resists, the more sexual stimulation he experiences and the more dominating power he attains. A penis can thus become addicted to domination — to rape — very easily: it feels good and it gives a man a sense of power.

Within a dominator value system, rape is in fact adaptive. A man's ability to rape a woman is proof of strength and virility; indeed, it *is* strength and virility, and it brings great dominator rewards. From the violent shaming of the loser's women throughout the history of war to the brutal subjugation of the enslaved to the religiously and culturally sanctioned sexual control of one's wife to the beaming pride of gang-raping fraternity brothers, men have clearly been considered *better men* through the exercising of their organ of domination.

I am not saying that sex must be this way. We can, for instance, as easily speak of a vagina hungrily engulfing and dominating a penis. Or, in the case of true sexual *partners*, of their two astonishingly different sexual organs merging for the equal good of both woman and man.

However, if the game is domination, man has the better equipment. He's been given a hard thruster; she's got a soft yielder. He can force the issue; she can seduce, but not really rape. He can start when he's ready, he can greatly control the pace, and when he's done, it's over; she can say no, mean no, plead no, scream no, and it will make no difference. His choice *and* sexual anatomy overwhelm hers.

Catherine MacKinnon has stated it most precisely: "Man fucks woman; subject verb object."[11] The penis is better suited to an active subject role, the vagina better suited to the role of passive object. The constant story of rape and the threat of rape woven throughout the sexual history of women and men has been used both as proof and justification: women are clearly the biologically weaker sex.

Further biological justifications of male superiority have risen to prominence at different times. The nineteenth century, perhaps in reaction to the emergence of feminism, and certainly with the support of scientific determinism, was an especially fertile time for the generation of such dogma. Brain weight became a great banner for patriarchal justifiers as the supposedly larger brains of white men were used to explain their dominance over both women and nonwhite races. The medical opinion of the day was that women were naturally weaker and more delicate in every way: "It identified *all* female functions as *inherently* sick."[12] It was reasoned that all of a woman's energies were tied up in the activity of reproduction, leaving little for the rest of life. Biologically, a woman was therefore ill-suited for education, leadership, creative expression, or any other outward adventure. She should simply have as many babies as she could before wasting away of consumption.

Around this same time, Dr. Freud was erecting his monument to male superiority: the female burden of penis envy. According to Freud, as both little boy and little girl strive to separate from the mother while at the same time gaining daddy's love, little girl discovers she is missing daddy's dangling thing and a lifetime of inferiority quite naturally results. That he should assume a little girl would leap from an observation of differences to a judgment of herself as a mutilated man tells us more about Freud than about the female sex. Moreover, as Simone de Beauvoir has written, it is far more likely that "if the little girl feels penis envy it is only as the symbol of privileges enjoyed by boys. The place the father holds in the family, the universal predominance of males, her own education—everything confirms her in her belief in masculine superiority."[13] Nonetheless, Freud has had a great impact upon modern culture by lending scientific credence to the notion that women are necessarily inferior due to the unfortunate nature of their own bodies.

One modern addition to the doctrine of biological male domination deserves mention. We now know of a male sex hormone, testosterone, that is far more present in male bodies than female bodies and has been proven to cause aggressive and even violent behavior. Likewise, there is a female sex hormone, estrogen, that is far more present in women's bodies, and does not cause such aggressiveness. These hormonal differences carry the arguments of patriarchal determinism to the most subtle levels of the human body: men are biochemically determined to be more aggressive and dominating and therefore they are just naturally more inclined toward football, rape, and military adventures; women, sans testosterone, are biochemically more compliant and thus are perfectly constructed for lives of submissiveness.

Finally, the most obvious of all biological justifiers of male dominance is, I suspect, also the oldest and most persuasive: men have bigger, more muscular bodies. In any wrestling match for control of the planet, men will win. If the ability to physically overpower another becomes a defining value in a family or society, men will win. When, indeed, people have lost the gentle wisdom of living in partnership, man's superior size and strength can only result in woman's essential inferiority and submission, for she is physically the weaker sex.

There is, of course, a strong current of truth running through all of the biological doctrines of patriarchal inevitability. The biological differences between men and women are for the most part beyond dispute and unlikely to change. However, to the extent that such differences have been advantageous to patriarchal control, they have been turned into proof of the essential nature of man's superiority over woman. "Differently equal" has been reframed into "different and therefore naturally better or worse, superior or inferior."

Once our differences are used as justifications for hierarchical ranking, the true nature of those differences is debased. Birth becomes a medical emergency rather than an awesome display of female creativity; menstruation an unfortunate mess rather than a woman's connection to the planet's rhythms. Sexual intercourse, with its wondrous potential to celebrate our differences, turns into sexual war, with the ever-present threat of man's propensity to force and rape. Man's physical size and strength—the perfect balance to woman's procreative abilities—becomes a blunt weapon, more devoted to destruction than to creation.

Again and again, the self-sustaining logic of the patriarchy is virtually inescapable. Since men are physically stronger and more aggressive than women, men must be the dominant sex. Since men are the dominant sex, society must be patriarchal. Since society is patriarchal, and since patriarchal domination always abuses, women are born into endless abuse. It's only human.

The Price of Civilization

Neolithic society may have seen the domestication of plants, but what the age after the Neolithic sees is the domestication of women by men.
—*William Irwin Thompson*[14]

How did men and women in their society-building and in the construction of Western civilization arrive at the present state? Once we abandon the concept of women as historical victims . . . we must explain the central puzzle—woman's participation in the construction of the system that subordinates her.   —*Gerda Lerner*[15]

The historical doctrine of patriarchal inevitability contends that patriarchal culture has developed as an unavoidable result of the progress of civilization. According to this viewpoint, while the primitive condition of early gatherer-hunter tribes may have allowed for greater egalitarianism (an assertion borne out by many anthropological studies), the transition to more advanced and complex agricultural societies, inevitably made human relationships more patriarchal.

Most historians mark the dawn of civilization some ten thousand years ago when various gatherer-hunter tribes began experimenting with agriculture. It is likely that food scarcity, brought on by population pressures or environmental changes, prompted the discovery of agriculture, since planting seeds and then tending and worrying over crops is more work than gathering and hunting, is somewhat less enjoyable, and does not provide as good overall nutrition. It is also fairly likely that agriculture was the discovery of women, that it initially was the sole responsibility of women, and that, for the short term, it brought greater power and prestige in the community to women as a group.

However, certain tendencies observed in historic agricultural societies suggest that agriculture naturally led to patriarchy. Good, steady crops meant food surpluses, which allowed for the growth of dense population centers, the accumulation of riches, and eventually the development of the concept and practice of private property. Next, bureaucracies evolved to manage all this, leading to stratified hierarchies, class systems of ranking, and, sooner or later, the formation of laws and the means to enforce the laws. The dominator could have shown up at any place along this line of development: to keep the peace among people living in dense populations; to protect the surpluses of wealth and private property from theft within the community or attack from without; to legitimize power dynamics in hierarchies and between classes; or to proclaim law and mete out punishment.

The place of women in such agricultural societies can only be subordination. Marxists argue that with the establishment of private property "men sought to secure it to themselves and their heirs; they did so by instituting the monogamous family. By controlling women's sexuality through the requirement of prenuptial chastity and by the establishment of the sexual double standard in marriage, men assured themselves of the legitimacy of their offspring and thus secured their property interest."[16] Woman, in essence, became part of the private property of man. The nuclear family became an individual economic unit, apart from the good of the whole community and kinship relations, and man became the head of the household, with woman the head servant. The beginning of the dominator-driven class society was, in Friedrich Engels's memorable words, "the world historic defeat of women."

A second problem with the emergence of agricultural societies

was the amassing of wealth. The existence of well-stocked grana-
ries at some point led to a whole new level of gathering-hunting:
taking from other humans rather than from nature. The defense
industry was thus created and, for an array of practical reasons,
men took up the task. This would bode poorly for women. As
William Irwin Thompson writes, "Wealth engendered the need for
defense, and by the time the men were through protecting the
women, they would be talking about protecting *their* women. . . . It
would not happen overnight but . . . the discovery of cereals by
women permitted the discovery of warfare by men."[17] And, of
course, with the discovery of warfare by men, patriarchal culture
became firmly entrenched.

Yet another problem with the development of agriculture was
that it represented humans taking control of nature. In the gatherer-
hunter tribal state, humans lived in close symbiosis with the natural world, neither controlling nature nor being controlled by it.
In agricultural society, a significant change occurred. Crops grew
where humans wanted them to grow. Water was directed to flow
according to human design. Wild animals were domesticated for
human purpose. Permanent shelters were erected in place of
groves and meadows. A timeless series of inventions and innova-
tions was begun, leading to the greatest wonders of our modern
world and leading as well to greater and greater dominion of man
over nature.

Alas, this development would also bode poorly for woman. It
has long been observed, in most all cultures, that women live closer
to nature than men. Or, as Sherry Ortner asserts in a classic essay
that has fed years of feminist debate: "Female is to male as nature
is to culture."[18] Women's bodies, with their lunar-tidal flows and
awesome birth-giving powers, have a connection to the planet that
men can only envy. Women's roles, generally nearer to children,
hearth, and soil, have a continuing course of interest and study
that men have mostly avoided. To the extent that woman *is* nature,
the historic defeat of nature, beginning with agriculture, became
yet further ammunition in the historic defeat of woman.

Some theorists, I should add, would place the subordination

of women prior to the emergence of agricultural society. It has been suggested that patriarchy arose with the "exchange of women" among different tribal groupings, which arose as a way to keep the peace among otherwise warring tribes. By making the "gift" of a sister or daughter to the leader of a rival tribe, new kinship alliances were formed and the power of male leaders grew. With time, this turning of women into commodities would translate into strict male control of the family unit and all aspects of female sexuality.

In *The Creation of Patriarchy*, Lerner considers all of these factors as significant contributions and offers something of a synthesis: "The development of agriculture in the Neolithic period fostered the intertribal 'exchange of women,' not only as a means of avoiding incessant warfare by the cementing of marriage alliances but also because societies with more women could produce more children. In contrast to the economic needs of hunting/gathering societies, agriculturalists could use the labor of children to increase production and accumulate surpluses. Men-as-a-group had rights in women that women-as-a-group did not have in men. Women themselves became a resource, acquired by men much as the land was acquired by men. Women were exchanged or bought in marriages for the benefit of their families; later, they were conquered or bought in slavery, where their sexual services were part of their labor and where their children were the property of their masters."[19]

Just as the biological doctrine of patriarchal inevitability twists specific male and female differences into good reasons for the dominator culture, so the historical doctrine looks to the known record of male and female social evolution as proof that we can progress in no other way. We are again faced with a line of reasoning that makes great sense and that is supported by thousands of years of human history. It is a history of untold and excessive abuse that is unfortunate but, it is assumed, inevitable: it is the nature of the beast.

A Hangman's Rope

The system of patriarchy no longer serves the needs of
men or women and in its inextricable linkage to militarism,
hierarchy, and racism it threatens the very existence of life
on earth.
                                   —*Gerda Lerner* [20]

There are other doctrines of patriarchal inevitability that I
have not addressed directly, and there are always new ones being
created to fit the needs of a particular time. For instance, in a society
in which financial and computer skills are growing sources of
power, women—wouldn't you just know it—are presumed to be
inherently weaker in math. The converse also applies, with
"women's" skills such as nursing and teaching young children
being absurdly undervalued in our present society.

As we have seen, the doctrinal justifications of patriarchal
culture all contain strong appeals to reason. For those who believe
in the Bible, it's right there in black and white, in the Lord's own
words, that men always have and always will dominate women.
For the more secular minded, our natural gender roles—hunter
and hearther, warrior and mother—stem from and reinforce male
superiority. For the purely scientific, the biological necessity of
male domination can be logically deduced from any number of
physical differences in men and women and from the unavoidable
demands of civilization. For the historian, patriarchal culture is
natural human evolution, whatever its abuses. For those who want
to defend the past and the continuing male rule of our world, there
are a host of good reasons, just causes, and holy laws to draw upon.
Male domination may not always be fair, it certainly has run to
terrible excesses, but men are men and women are women and
patriarchy is just the natural way of ordering human society.

If I have seemed through much of this discussion to be stating
patriarchal arguments as if they are perfectly true, it is because
right now in our present world they are true—and have been for
several thousand years. The Bible is *causing*, right now, men to
dominate women. The violent nature of our world is causing men
to dominate women. The natural course of pregnancy, childbirth,

and mothering is causing men to dominate women. Our most ordinary and sublime sexual and psychological differences are causing men to dominate women. The demands of civilized culture are causing men to dominate women. The world is patriarchal, with all its abuses, and can be justified as such with utter and unequivocal conviction.

However, continuing cause is not the same as original cause. While all of the doctrinal justifications of male domination have been cited as original causes of patriarchy, the simple fact (as we shall explore in depth in chapter 3) that humans have also lived in true partnership without male *or* female domination proves otherwise. Our differences do not *of necessity* lead to domination; rather, a dominator culture of necessity turns differences into just cause for further domination. Likewise, our attempts to evolve toward a new partnership society require not that we somehow eliminate the differences between men and women; rather, we must end the self-sustaining habits of body, relationship, and society that give patriarchy its power.

I will later attempt to answer the question of original cause, of why the world ever turned patriarchal. Frankly, there may not be one satisfactory answer, nor any answer that could be effectively proven. What matters most is to understand that the present causes of our dominator culture are ultimately mutable. They are of human creation; therefore we can discover new justifications for the way we are and for the people we desire to become. *Life does not have to be so abusive.* Dominator culture and its abuses are not spiritually ordained, socially indispensable, biologically determined, or historically destined.

Moreover, the underlying logic of patriarchal culture—one half of society forever at war with the other half—is ultimately suicidal. Our world is suspended in the noose of a hangman's rope; the doctrines of patriarchal inevitability tie the knot. If we do not resolve the knot—if we do not learn to live as partners now—we may never get another chance.

Personal Reflections

I recommend that you read the questions following each chapter slowly enough to *feel* your own answers. You might even take some time for meditation or writing in a journal.

Consider the patriarchal relationships in your present life. When and where does the domination of another person or group of people seem justifiable to you: within your family? at work? with clients? with poor people? with sick people? with children? with people of other races? with women? with men?

Is it right and necessary to exercise power over criminals, rapists, war-lords, and other "bad guys?"

With whom do you feel submissive: with your parents? with employers? with the police? with your teachers? with your doctor? with rich people? with those who are physically stronger than you? with women? with men?

Do your religious beliefs give you power over those who believe differently? Do you believe that there is only one God and that he demands the conversion of all nonbelievers? Do you believe in a single faith that is destined to overtake all other faiths?

Is each of the human races naturally inclined toward specific strengths and weaknesses? Are rich people more worthy than poor people? Are poor people more worthy than the rich? Is technologically-advanced culture more evolved than primitive culture? Are primitive cultures more spiritually evolved than technologically-advanced ones? Is any race, nation, or culture manifestly destined to dominate our world? Should might make right?

Do you believe that "men just are" and "women just are" certain ways? Are men just naturally more aggressive? more logical? more extroverted? more independent? more goal oriented? more inclined toward anger? more dominating? Are women just naturally more passive? more intuitive? more introverted? more nurturing? more process oriented? more inclined toward sadness? more submissive?

What about individual men and women, or perhaps entire cultures, who do not fit these categories? Are they different and unequal? Do they deserve to be dominated?

What are your "masculine" traits? What are your "feminine" traits? Do you have difficulty embodying traits that are identified with the opposite gender?

Have you ever or do you often feel afraid of men? Do you believe it is safer, perhaps better, to simply submit to an aggressive man's will? Do you find it sexually stimulating to fantasize that you are being aggressively dominated by a man? Do you believe that your personal power derives from your physical attractiveness to men?

Do you ever fantasize or engage in violence against women? Do you think this is just the way you are, or that women prefer aggressive sex, or that you just naturally must be more dominating during sex? Do you think it is sexy to demonstrate your superior strength to women?

Do you believe it is possible for humans to live in peace? Can men and women live as partners? Can men live peacefully with men? Can women with women? Can people of all races and creeds develop egalitarian cultures that embrace and celebrate individual differences? Can we grow beyond patriarchal patterns of violence and abuse?

TWO

Sins of the Father

The patriarchal history of human society is a straight, rather phallic, line of progress from the primitive and unevolved to the many wonders of contemporary civilization. The repeated image in so many history texts is that of ape-man turning into caveman, turning into agricultural man, turning into modern man—a constant, natural, and perfectly adaptive growth in intelligence, physical beauty, technological ability, and societal structure. Every human accomplishment lays the foundation for further accomplishments, leading to the perpetual betterment of the race.

Interestingly, this patriarchal view of social evolution is in direct contrast to the patriarchal view of human nature. For patriarchal theology and philosophy hold that human nature is inevitably wretched, violent, and abusive. Patriarchy presumes that, though the elements of culture have undergone constant improvement, we the people are still the fundamentally sinful and animalistic brutes we have always been. This belief, in turn, justifies the dominating hierarchies of patriarchal society.

This basic dichotomy underlies much of the enduring thrust of patriarchy. One part of us is considered to be splendidly evolving, while the other part remains forever primitive. Human intellect—our knowledge of the natural world and the way things work—is always progressing, whereas human emotion—the wild, unruly part of us that is forever erupting out of control—never changes. Our tools, technologies, and methods for controlling reality to our advantage are always progressing, while our visceral perception of the natural world as distinctly separate and threatening never changes. Our legal, educational, financial, and governmental systems are always progressing, but our primal experience of being solitary individuals in constant competition for our survival never changes. Our ability to kill others is always progressing, while our tragic inability to simply live in peace never changes.

As might be expected, this dichotomy extends to the relationship between men and women. Thus, the ways and means of Man the Hunter are always progressing, while the daily grind of Woman the Hearther never changes. The steady recognition of women's rights—by men—is always progressing, but the utter absence of true egalitarianism never changes. Our scientific understanding of human sexuality is always progressing, though our fundamental confusion regarding virtually all aspects of the sexual experience never changes.

There is, I believe, a consistent evolutionary mechanism at work in this contradictory flow of progress. Evolution favors adaptation to the prevailing environment, and for the past several thousand years, the prevailing environment has been one of patriarchal human relationship. Therefore, human evolution has favored the means and methods of domination.

All the ways of a dominator culture have continually evolved and improved, while all the essentials of a partnership culture (unadaptive traits in a patriarchal world) have atrophied. Weapons, tools, technologies, symbols, scriptures, tales, practices, habits, and laws that increase the power and effectiveness of the dominator elite have made the most evolutionary sense and thus have drawn the greatest force of human intellect and creative effort.

More cooperation-based traits are sadly undeveloped in human beings because they have been disadvantageous for humanity to develop. They include: an unquestioning faith in one's brothers and sisters; a compassionate sharing with all others; a boundless joy in discovering and creating as equal partners; an empathic capacity to feel the suffering of other living creatures; a mutual, unashamed, bodily thrill in sexual play; and the simple emotion of unconditional love.

I must add that the human social evolution I describe here is a somewhat twisted version of the evolutionary process found in nature. Natural evolution, it is being discovered, favors cooperation as well as competition. As Guy Murchie explains, "Evolutionists seem to have completely accepted the natural law of Survival of the Fittest, which many interpret as meaning 'kill or be killed.' But all too few realize that nature also has an opposite principle at least as strong and potentially much stronger: the natural law of cooperation."[1] In nature, evolution has favored those species that are best able to synergistically merge or cooperate with their environment: any thriving ecosystem is in essence a complex, multi-partnership culture.

Human evolution has gradually lost its cooperation component and has come to strictly favor domination-based competition. "With the coming of civilization," observes social historian Andrew Bard Schmookler, "an ancient intricate pattern of wholeness began systematically to be demolished and replaced by a new pattern governed less by the needs of life than by the dangerous logic of power."[2] This "dangerous logic of power" is the dominating, power-over pattern of patriarchal relationship. It assumes that humans are natural and inevitable competitors—for food, land, resources, money, privilege, and power—and then it ranks all participants in relationship as to whether they are winners or losers, strong or weak, or the dominator or the oppressed.

As human social evolution has come to be governed by the competition-driven demands of the dominator culture, humans have inevitably become more competitive. Inherent tendencies toward cooperative relationship have been devalued and derided as weak, naive, romantic, and unrealistic and thus have tended to atrophy. The dangerous logic of power has forced all of human society toward ever greater systems of domination, even as our world so obviously suffers from the unending abuses such competition-driven systems create.

I strongly believe that we can grow beyond lives driven solely by competition and domination and that we can purposefully evolve toward relationships and societies that are cooperation-based and power-sharing. However, before exploring this potential, I would like to examine more deeply the stark realities of our present-day, patriarchal world, paying special attention to the ways in which our daily lives are driven by the dangerous logic of domination.

Patriarchy Embodied

> And so I walk the streets, aware of the pervasive ugliness of the people . . . the lines of hurt and anxiety and greed around their eyes and mouths, the imbalance of their walk, the deformation of their bodies. Oh no, it is not genetic. Civilization has twisted and scarred those bodies as surely as it has damaged and tortured the face of the planet.
> —*George Leonard*[3]

The greatest victim of the past several thousand years of planetary patriarchy has been the human body. Though I may be overstating the obvious, it would be a more serious mistake to pursue a neat and academic trail of mental abstractions that would lead away from the purely physical and all too personal. For all the arguments, opinions, facts, and theories regarding patriarchy and its historic causes and abuses, the essential story that we must finally grasp is of individual bodies suffering pain, hardship, and senseless limitation.

A single phrase such as "clitoral circumcision," spoken and defined and then framed with statistics—"more than *eighty million* women have undergone sexual surgery in Africa alone"[4]—can sweep us right past the reality of a terrified twelve-year-old having her clitoris torn away with a piece of broken glass and then lying in pain, her vulva sewn together with catgut and her legs bound so that she will not move until the scars have formed. We may theorize at length about the cultural reasons for her mutilation without ever perceiving her chronic urinary tract infections, her possible infertility, or her appallingly dangerous delivery of oxygen-starved babies. We may intellectually reject such a barbarous practice but never actually *feel* her lifetime of painful intercourse, her violently circumcised sexual nature, or the passing on of such nature to her young.

We can speak of "patrilineal descent" as a simple and nearly universal legality that gives financial and political power to husbands, sons, and brothers and overlook the profound impact of this system on countless generations of female bodies and souls: the lifelong feelings of poor self-esteem from being the "wrong" sex; the anatomical effects of forever lowering one's gaze in the presence of men, of cutting off one's voice, or of stooping lest one be too tall; the basic malnourishment from getting less food than spouses and brothers; the deep-seated, visceral anxieties from having no control over money and property, nor any rights to take such control; and the tragically degraded sexual experience that one's body must feel and, inevitably, pass on to children.

In modern America, we have taut statistical phrases such as "a woman is battered every fifteen seconds," "a rape is committed every six minutes," "one in three women will suffer rape," ("Your Sister, Your Mother, or You," warns a poster) and "four million women . . . are beaten in their homes each year by their husbands, ex-husbands, or male lovers."[5] Again, these phrases might allow us—men and women alike—to glide right past the physical reality of such abuses and the daily experience of growing up in a female body. What is the breath, the posture, the purse-clutching tension, and the gait of a woman walking alone on a dark city street? What are the physical sensations and anatomical consequences of forever anticipating the next angry curse or blow to the face? What does the body experience as it is forced into violent sex and what does it carry forward into each new relationship and each new moment of sexual arousal? Do blackened eyes, broken bones, and bruised thighs ever forget? Should they?

The male body has fared no better through the many centuries of patriarchal relationship. It has been equally, though differently, brutalized by the ways and means of domination. The young boy who is bred and conditioned for warfare loses most of the living, tingling joy of his body before the battles ever begin. And if he is

not killed or physically maimed—another young, male body for
the ever-hungry war machine—he will likely be left a psychoemotional cripple for the remainder of his life. To the extent that
organized violence has been a primary preoccupation of patriarchal civilization, the male body has paid with dehumanizing
training, dreadful deeds forever remembered, and inevitable suffering, win or lose.

When men are not marching off to war—for the good of
country and family and usually with the approval of the women
in their lives—they are marching their bodies off to work, for the
very same reasons and with equal encouragement. "Making a
living" is the essence of being a man. However, as the bodies of
miners, lumberjacks, truck drivers, and white-collar workers will
all painfully proclaim (if anyone is listening), the muscle-wrench-
ing, bone-weary truth of work is that it makes a slow but steady
dying out of every day. Oh, there is much pride for men in their
working lives: the healthy sweat of honest labor, the rough and
calloused hands of a man's job, the strong but aching muscles of a
good day's work, and the weary satisfaction of having provided
for one's family. But so much of a man's labor is externally forced,
and his body pays dearly for every ounce of such effort. Not only
women have sacrificed themselves for their families.

How do men really feel about their primary duties as protectors
and providers? It is a fair enough question, but one that is rarely
answered. For, basic to man's training as cannon fodder and/or
cog in the wheel is a profound loss of somato-emotional feeling. The
little boy learns to reign in his emotions, to suppress his tears, to
never show any weak or *womanly* loss of control over his internal
experience. There is no adaptive value in bodily feeling for the
warrior/worker, so he chokes it off instead. Sadly, such denial of
bodily feeling is nothing less than slow suicide and, tragically,
such living-dead men are universally inclined toward senselessly
aberrant behavior.

Naturally, the sexual experience of those who are at constant
war with all bodily feelings and sensations is something of a
quandary, to say the least. Sex can be a great healing balm for men,

if it brings them home to the simple pleasures of physical embodiment and intimate connection with others. Sex is more often an ordeal, an unfulfilled aching, an empty, driven conquest, or a brief, explosive moment of something so sweet, but so quickly gone again. It is no wonder that male bodies, conditioned from early childhood for the lifelong competitions of war and work, so compulsively turn sex into yet another competition against all other men. Nor is it a surprise that male bodies, inculcated from early childhood with the normality of violence, so often and so easily cross over the line from making love with women to waging war against them.

Some women may protest that I am trivializing the enormous and unrelenting suffering that the female body has sustained, so much at the hands of men, by suggesting that the suffering of the male body is of equal gravity. Consider, however, that in most of the world women outlive men despite the violence and inequities women everywhere endure. As bad as any male-inflicted suffering of the female body clearly is, the culturally-ordained loss of feeling that men endure is surely every bit as bad. (Malcolm X once wrote of America's historic subjugation of black people: "But I want to tell you something. This pattern, this 'system' that the white man created . . . has done the American white man more harm than an invading army would do to him."[6]) In the same way that women have been patiently pointing out that "men just don't get" the special nature and problems of women's reality, I would suggest that women—who may never lose the innate human capacity for feeling life—just don't get the terrible price of growing up numb in a male body.

On the other hand, some men will surely protest that I have not stressed enough the extent to which women have been partners in so much of the body's suffering: in the socio-sexual conditioning of sons and daughters; in the glorification and lustful encouragement of warriors, soldiers, policemen, outlaws, "bad boys," and the like; in joining in the mythologizing of the "good provider" while coming to expect that men effectively manage the external world; and in often finding genuine pleasure in sexual submission. At the very least, the modern man, fed up with being blamed for all of the world's sins, will gripe that women must admit to some self-serving complicity in the varied abuses of patriarchy.

All such complaints, from men and women both, are quite beside the point. The point is not in assigning blame but in understanding and learning to feel the fundamental pains of all human bodies so that we may finally heal them. The point is that the flesh and blood reality of all women and men tells an equally sad story of unending hurt.

For thousands of years, human beings have been born into all-encompassing patriarchal relationships; for thousands of years, the human body has suffered the unnecessary abuses of dominator reality. This has been the primary human condition: being born into lifetimes of giving and receiving unwarranted pain. However we may have philosophically or religiously explained the human condition, the body has gone on suffering abuse. More important-ly, however we now choose to think about this state of affairs, we are thinking within deeply wounded and scarred bodies that neg-atively bend and refract all of our thoughts.

It will never be enough to change the sexist, racist, and class-based laws of patriarchal culture, nor to prevent species and biosystem extinctions, nor even to eliminate all weapons of mass destruction. (Though this would be a fair enough beginning.) *Healing our world means healing the body*—your body, my body, his body, and her body. Changing the world entails nothing less than changing ourselves (our*cell*ves) as living, breathing, human organisms.

Again, I may seem to be belaboring the obvious: of course the suffering of humans is the suffering of bodies; of course the abuses of patriarchal culture are experienced as physical and emotional pains; and of course each of us is now living in, as, or through a body that has been injured and scarred by the harsher realities of this world.

What is not always so obvious is the degree to which people, especially in the West, separate mind from body and spirit from flesh and then live as if the body's reality is of secondary importance. The hierarchical ranking of patriarchy, applied to the individual, deems the spiritual and mental as superior to, more relevant than, and more real than, the physical. In patriarchal culture, thoughts, prayers, dreams, and visions, the wise and ethereal abstractions of theology, philosophy, and mathematics, the ideal forms of Plato, and the heavenly realms of Christianity all acquire greater significance than the daily human trials of aching muscles, bowel movements, pregnant bellies, and tired bones.

The spirit is willing but the flesh is weak, we say, and then we turn all attention and striving to the life of spirit. The streets of heaven are lined with gold, we say, and then we turn our eyes away from the more mundane streets where the body lives. From such bodily disregard, it is a short step to the denial of simple, earthly pleasures, and thence to sexual repression, to mortification of the flesh, and to the utterly inhumane punishments and tortures of pedagogues, psychotics, and religious fanatics. Moreover, century upon century of scorning the body has developed into a dense cultural myopia regarding all things physical: witness the growing environmental crisis and the inability of most people to feel the ecological damages we are inflicting. To the extent that the experience of the human body has been ignored, invalidated, distrusted, and denied, all aspects of human culture have been fundamentally impaired, and indeed crippled.

Finally, in disregarding the body we are disregarding a history of our species more relevant and more precise than any we may hope to find in stones and bones and yellowed manuscripts. For the body was there when sexual play first twisted into rape, and when brotherly conflict first twisted into murder. The body *knows* the whip and shackles of slavery, *knows* the empty belly of drought and famine, *knows* the long and hopeless trek of forced migration, and *knows* the infinite stupidity of armed violence.

The body has been there for all of human history, and the body forgets nothing: all of human history is engraved within the cells and sinews of human embodiment. All of the ancient and continuing abuses of patriarchal culture are carried forward in each living body and are passed along as blood and breath to every new body conceived and born. Our efforts to understand and positively affect the flow of history will be greatly enhanced by our ability to understand and positively affect our own bodies.

Animal Sexuality

The Darwinian revolution in biology, which demonstrated that man was part of the animal world, encouraged the search for the animal in man, and found it in his sex.
—*Jeffrey Weeks*[7]

The patriarchal crippling of human beings and societies is especially apparent with regard to our common sexual experience. No subject is more charged with emotion, more difficult to talk about, and more resistant to substantial personal and cultural change. And in no area of our lives is it more critical that we question the supposed inevitabilities of human nature, that we grow beyond the abuses of dominant/submissive relationship, and that we explore, as partners, the further reaches of joyful human embodiment and transcendent sexual play.

When two lovers come together for the simple purpose of sexual play, they rarely *simply* meet. Most sexual encounters, and even the merest fantasies of such encounters, are overlaid and burdened with the long human history of dominant/submissive patterns of abuse; with ancient religious doctrines and priestly recriminations; with the underlying themes and hidden messages of a thousand fairy tales, fables, stories, and mythologies; with society's notions of correct gender roles and the laws that enforce such notions; with the varied confusions of Freud and other "sexual experts"; with mommy and daddy's sexual reality and manner of relationship; with every physical abuse and pleasure of childhood; and with, for the modern man and woman, the reams of sexual misinformation that are ubiquitously spread by the popular media and mass advertising. Truly, it is something of a miracle that we manage to "do it" at all, much less derive any pleasure in the process.

Most of the psycho-emotional burdens that we carry into our sexual encounters are held in place by a single, mistaken, and utterly patriarchal belief—the idea that sexuality derives solely from our animal nature, as apart from and in opposition to our higher human nature. As Jamake Highwater writes, it is the "belief that 'sex' is an obsessive natural force, a biological imperative focused entirely in the genitals (particularly the male organ) that dominates our decisions and actions."[8]

Thus, theologians look at sex and see earthly passions (animal instincts) that are forever interfering with more heavenly pursuits (free human will). Conservative moralists look at sex (reluctantly) and declare that men have penises, women have vaginas, and that the sole purpose of sex is to bring the two together to make babies. Even the more scientifically-minded of theorists, building on Darwinian connections between the animal and human worlds, tend toward conclusions of "anatomy as destiny" and of sexuality arising purely from genetics, biological necessity, and the demand for procreation. Popularly stated, "Birds, bees, and educated fleas do it," and we humans, animals that we ultimately are, do it also, and with as little real freedom, understanding, or conscious creativity as any other animal.

This is a further consequence of the patriarchally imposed split between the spiritual and the physical. To rigidly constrain sexuality to genetics, biology, and animal instincts requires humans who rarely experience and forcefully deny any meaningful merging of spirit and flesh—or the "heavenly sacred" with the "earthly profane." Having falsely divided culture and the human body into these two forever conflicted realities, sex is consigned to our baser "animal nature" and thus becomes, not surprisingly, an eternal human torment.

The problem with such an approach to sex is that it fails to acknowledge and embrace the creative effects of human consciousness, especially where the body and its vital energies are concerned. It is simply impossible to separate human sexuality from the thoughts, beliefs, memories, attitudes, visions, desires, dreams, myths, emotions, and consciousness of the human organism, not to mention the broader forces of history and society. As Highwater writes, "Far from being the most natural force of our lives, [sex] is, in fact, the most susceptible to cultural influences."[10] And, I would add, the most susceptible to the full spectrum of human subjectivity.

Once the notion of compulsive, subhuman, antispiritual sexuality is presumed, culturally codified, and rigidly enforced, the common and collective sexual reality of a society is restricted, damned, and painfully bound toward continuing degradation. Given several centuries of Christian missionaries tirelessly spreading the sex-is-animalistic-sin gospel, there are now few cultures on our planet that remain sexually innocent and free. Indeed, there are few *bodies* on our planet still capable of feeling—simply and without guilt—the deeper pleasures of conscious, human-spirited sexuality.

The effects of such long-term sexual degradation have become mere "facts of life" for the modern human. Consider the mind-numbing statistics on rape, incest, and domestic violence; the pandemic growth of AIDS and other sexually-transmitted diseases; the legitimization of pornographic themes in popular movies; the twisting of body image and gender roles by the advertising industry; the mean and often vicious polarization of quarrels over abortion, homosexuality, and sex education; our seeming inability to forthrightly address the issue of birth control, with the resulting tragedy of millions of unwanted babies; and, above all, our clear inability to forthrightly discuss *any* of this without splitting into hopeless confusion and rancorous debate. One can hardly be blamed for looking at the whole mess and saying, "It is all unbridled animalism and must be brought under control! Just say no!"

This is typical patriarchal thinking: suppress, inhibit, damn, and abuse the very essence of joyful human embodiment and then point to the dark and sickly results, blame the victims, and prescribe a course of further suppression, inhibition, damnation, and abuse. In the long litany of patriarchal foolishness, this has been, I believe, the greatest sin of all. We will never inhabit a world of lasting peace unless we first grow beyond the patriarchal degradation of the human sexual response.

Initiation into Abuse

In 1979, the State of California . . . appropriated $750,000 for the first scientific study ever made of the root causes of crime and violence. Two years later a first paper was issued, listing the ten principal causes of crime and violence in our nation. At the top of the list was the violent way we bring our children into the world.

—*Joseph Chilton Pearce* [10]

Its traces are everywhere—in the skin, in the bones, in the stomach, in the back. In all our human folly. In our madness, our tortures, our prisons. In legends, epics, myths. In the Scriptures.

—*Dr. Frederick Leboyer* [11]

Given the great cultural dysfunction that sex has become, it is not surprising that the result of much sexual interaction—the birthing of babies—has degraded into similar dysfunction. However healthy the first nine months of life in the womb may be, the passage of birth for modern humans is often a harsh, crude, and unnecessarily rude transition into a seemingly hostile world.

This is, I realize, thoroughly irrelevant to many people. "That was then and this is now," they will say. "Whatever we may have experienced during birth surely was outgrown and left behind many years ago. We are no longer infants, we have not been for a long time, and there can be no meaningful comparison between the life of an infant and the life of an adult. Nor are there any lessons from our primal existence that could matter to us now, nor any good reasons to even think about our birth."

This point of view finds a fair measure of authoritative support in the modern world. Many biologists, obstetricians, and child-development experts assert that infants (up until the age of two) are fundamentally different creatures from older children and adults, with quite different needs regarding treatment and relationship. The central supposition of such thinking is that infants are preconscious—that just as they have undeveloped bodies, so must they have undeveloped attributes of human consciousness, such as intelligence, emotion, memory, and learning. Thus, they are not affected by events in the same way that adults are.

If, for instance, somebody is physically abused as an adult, it is natural to expect that the person will remember his or her abuser, will be emotionally impacted by the abuse, and will probably alter behavior (though not always for the best) as a result of the event. Many believe that an abused infant, on the other hand, will neither remember, nor be emotionally affected or behaviorally conditioned by even the most staggering of abuses. Any mistreatment is presumed to pass through the infant without a significant trace. Thus, "it does not matter how you treat such creatures, so long as you are tending to their bodily survival. Since they are not yet fully conscious beings, they will not take offense or draw any conclusions from your behavior."[12]

This terrible misunderstanding—the belief that there is a clear and indisputable discontinuity between the experiences of early infancy and the people we later become—has given rise, in America especially, to an abusive style of obstetrics that I call "techno-birthing." As Joseph Chilton Pearce describes it: "What happens is quite simple: the infant is exposed to an intelligence determined to outwit nature, an intelligence with a vast array of tools at its disposal with which to outwit and, in fact, supplant nature entirely. And in that outwitting and supplanting, damage is done that is incalculable."[13] Since infants are thought to be preconscious and unimpressionable, and nature is considered to be basically insufficient to the task of bringing new humans into the world (better living through modern chemistry), the tools of techno-birthing have grown ever more complex, with ever more negative impacts upon the newborn.

Here is yet another logical dysfunction in any culture that splits humanity from the natural world, as well as the mind from the body, and the spirit from the flesh. The excesses of techno-birthing can only seem reasonable to people who have themselves been split from the natural world, from the inherent wisdom of the body, and from the ineffable relevance of all fleshy pains and pleasures.

Moreover, it must be noted that the vast majority of obstetricians are men: techno-birthing rose out of "the burning times," a period of Western history from A.D.1500 to 1650 that condoned the brutal suppression of midwives and all other female practitioners of the healing arts. Estimates of the number of women murdered for the "practice of witchcraft" during this time range from one to nine million. While it is common to remember the Inquisition for the great religious madness that it was, there was also a strong political subtext to the period: power-mad men engineered the elimination of women from all positions of social authority, focusing especially on the practice of medicine. Extreme patriarchy, applied to medicine, has since meant that almost all doctors are men and almost all doctoring is based on the study of male bodies. Nowhere has this damaged us more than in the inherently female domain of pregnancy and birthing babies.

The specific procedures and long-term consequences of techno-birthing have already been thoroughly documented by myself and many others.[14] Suffice it to say that when a culture invalidates the conscious awareness of a birthing infant, it can seem eminently reasonable to shock the infant with labor-inducing drugs; to impatiently circumvent normal labor with forceps or Caesarian section; to greet the infant with bright lights, cold temperatures, harsh surfaces, loud noises, and masked faces; to prematurely cut the umbilical cord, sending the infant into brain-killing oxygen deprivation; to swing the infant upside down and strike it; and, lest exposure to the mother have some insidious effect, to send the infant off into prolonged isolation and a diet of man-made food. "This is birth," writes obstetrician Frederick Leboyer, "The torture of an innocent. What futility to believe that so great a cataclysm will not leave its mark."[15]

But of course it does leave its mark; the notion that infants lack the requisites of meaningful memory and thus are not affected by any physical and emotional abuses could not be further from the truth. Though access to early memories is complicated by an innate ability that humans have to suppress and deny traumatic events, a number of therapeutic modalities have proven successful in stimulating recall of early childhood, infancy, birth, and even fetal memories. The findings of such therapies are fairly unanimous: At some level, *we remember everything*, and the relevance of our primal experiences to our adult lives is significant. As the infant is bent, the adult grows; the child is parent to the man or woman.

When we accept that infants are indeed conscious, aware, intelligent, and highly-impressionable, then the excesses of techno-birthing (however well-intended) must be seen for what they truly are: the self-immolation of an entire culture through the senseless violation of its young. The systematic mistreatments of techno-birthing are nothing less than an initiation into violence; when human beings are introduced to the world through abusive and isolating conditioning, then we can only expect an abusive and isolating culture to result.

Poisonous Pedagogy

Almost everywhere we find the effort... to rid ourselves as quickly as possible of the child within us—i.e., the weak, helpless, dependent creature—in order to become an inde-pendent, competent adult deserving of respect. When we reencounter this creature in our children, we persecute it with the same measures once used on ourselves.
—*Alice Miller* [16]

Birth is a passage into family; however violent or peaceful our births may have been, the most critical work of understanding and undoing patriarchal patterns of relationship begins within our primary family systems. The dangerous logic of domination is most seriously perpetrated and sustained in our more intimate relationships. It is through our family systems that we so thoroughly condition one another to dominant and submissive behavior, and it is through our family systems that any true progress out of patriarchy and into a partnership world must be made.

This is not to say that domination is only spread and supported by the family. Indeed, the most horrid tales of human history describe the large-scale infliction of dominator reality by monotheistic religions, empire builders, colonizers, slavers, and predatory capitalists upon total strangers, foreign nations, and alien cultures. The fastest way to spread patriarchy is through massive, inhuman, and decidedly unfamily methods.

However, most (if not all) of the world's invaders, aggressors, tyrants, and oppressors, both male and female, past and present, share one trait: they grew up in patriarchal families. The tendency toward dominant/submissive relationship is neither natural nor inevitable. It is learned behavior, and the primary learning takes place in childhood and within immediate family systems. Children are taught to dominate some people and submit to others: they are taught to believe in inequalities and to distrust cooperation and partnership.

The Spanish inquisitor, imperiously torturing pagans, witches, midwives, and other nonbelievers, was himself the end product of a patriarchal family system. He had been conditioned from birth by his primary caregivers, in alignment with the extended family of his culture, to accept the dominator's ideology and the angry dictates of God the Father. As with the young in any abusively dominating culture, he himself had been abusively dominated as a basic part of his early upbringing. By the time he rose to church-based power, he was a festering plague of patriarchal abuse, obsessed with putting to the stake any semblance of partnership reality.

When, several hundred years later, an American president decides to bring a tiny Central American nation to its knees simply to prove that America is the dominant force throughout the hemisphere, he too is acting as the product of a patriarchal family system that conditioned him to the colonizer's values, the slaver's means, and the missionary's high moral ground. He too was bred for dominant/submissive reality from the beginning—first through interaction with his parents and later within the patriarchal systems of preppie clubs, the military, and government service. By the time he struggled to the position of commander in chief, he was psycho-emotionally incapable of even grasping the concept of partnership relationship, much less living it.

People are not born patriarchally abusive, and we do not easily take up the bit of human cruelty. Nor, despite the assertions of Freud, are we naturally born into dominant/submissive patterns of relationship. We must be conditioned to all such behavior by those who are already so conditioned; we must be contaminated by those who are already infected. The most powerful of the conditioning happens when we are children, within the confines of our primary family systems.

Much of this conditioning is expressly intended to perpetrate patriarchal reality. Little boys may be beaten so they will be tough enough to survive, or commanded not to cry when they hurt, or motivated with the necessity of winning at competitive games. Little girls may be sexually used and abused, or sternly prohibited from specific "male" activities, or trained to be happy servants of fathers, brothers, and mothers. In many cultures and families, there is no question that learning to be a dominant male or submissive female is the whole point of growing up.

At the same time, children are subjected to equally forceful but mostly unconscious conditioning. Observation of adults, especially parents, communicates to a child the "whole truth" of human relationship. If father uses physical size and strength to dominate mother, or if mother is the dominant power within the domestic sphere, or if father is the final authority in all important matters ("Wait until your father gets home!"), then son and daughter have been taught eons of socio-sexual history before they ever learn to speak. The sins of the father and mother are visited upon the son and daughter: people locked in patriarchal patterns of behavior can only teach the same to their children.

The most significant of childhood conditioning occurs within the relationship between parent (or older caregiver) and child. To the extent that this primary relationship expresses patriarchal values and means, the child is being patterned for a lifetime of such relationships. A child dominated by his or her parents—physically, emotionally, psychologically, or sexually—is psycho-emotionally programmed for dominant/submissive relationship and will forever have difficulty approaching others in the spirit of partnership. And, sadly, when the child grows to have his or her own children, the cycle will be repeated.

"But," countless generations of parents might fairly ask, "isn't it correct to dominate one's child? Isn't it the parent's role to make rules and set limits? Spare the rod and spoil the child: Don't children need to be firmly guided and disciplined? Isn't it a parent's duty to teach good manners and to help the child properly meet society's expectations? Don't the child's spontaneity and free expression need to be reigned in, controlled, and left behind? And don't parents do it all, especially the hard parts, for the child's own good?"

Psychoanalyst and writer Alice Miller has shown, much to the contrary, that such child-rearing attitudes and practices, however common and well-accepted they may be, produce a "poisonous pedagogy" from which most children never recover, to society's great detriment. "I now believe," she writes, "that there is a universal psychological phenomenon involved here that must be brought to light: namely, the way the adult exercises *power over the child* [my emphasis], a use of power that can go undetected and unpunished like no other.... There is a whole gamut of ingenious measures applied 'for the child's own good' which are difficult for a child to comprehend and which for that very reason often have devastating impacts later in life."[17]

As Miller describes the actual practice of poisonous pedagogy, it is striking how normal it all seems: "An enormous amount can be done to a child in the first two years. he or she can be molded, dominated, taught good habits, scolded, and punished—without any repercussions for the person raising the child and without the child taking revenge. The child will overcome the serious consequences of the injustice he has suffered only if he succeeds in defending himself, i.e., if he is allowed to express his pain and anger. If he is prevented from reacting in his own way because the parents cannot tolerate his reactions (crying, sadness, rage) and forbid them by means of looks or other pedagogical methods, then the child will learn to be silent. This silence is a sign of the effectiveness of the pedagogical principles applied, but at the same time it is a danger signal pointing to future pathological development."[18] The adult so thoroughly dominates the child that the child's spontaneous and entirely human responses to events are controlled by the adult; with time, the child stops expressing any painful feelings and, indeed, may stop feeling altogether.

Miller stresses throughout her writings the utter insanity of a culture that casually accepts such practices as good child-rearing: "It is unlikely that someone could proclaim 'truths' that are counter to physical laws for very long (for example, that it is healthy for children to run around in bathing suits in winter and in fur coats in summer) without appearing ridiculous. But it is perfectly normal to speak of the necessity of striking and humiliating children and robbing them of their autonomy, at the same time using such high-sounding words as chastising, upbringing, and guiding onto the right path."[19] The rarely-questioned assumption, simply put, is that children must be dominated "for their own good."

And, it follows, parents must be dominators. As John Bradshaw puts it, "The 'poisonous pedagogy' is based on inequality—a kind of master/slave relationship. The parental authority is vested by virtue of being a parent."[20] What puts the "poison" in any pedagogy is the dangerous logic of dominator relationship being passed from parent to child. When parents act as masters of their children—when children are forced into dominant/submissive relationship—another generation of patriarchal abuse is born into the world. However well-intended an adult's exercising of power over the child may be, it is domination nonetheless and produces a terribly different effect from the power-with of partnership.

The Family of Man

> I finally understood that men, who own all laws—since they make, interpret, and enforce them—will never manipulate their legal systems in a way that threatens their privilege.
> —*Sonia Johnson*[21]

Those who react to our current crises by calling for a return to traditional family values have the right idea, almost. It is true that the unhealthy state of the modern family—as evidenced by escalating divorce rates, a growing recognition of widespread wife-battering and child abuse, and alarming numbers of adolescent dropouts, runaways, suicides, pregnancies, and substance abusers—is at the core of many of today's problems. The family is the ground from which society grows; the modern family is a stressed-out, love-depleted, and abuse-contaminated field of malady and sorrow.

Some would turn this equation around, saying that the state of the modern family is but one more symptom of larger societal problems and that the breakdowns in the family are caused by the breakdowns in society. I am content to say that both are true: the family is the primary building block of society even as society powerfully conditions the family; the family is the ground from which society grows, even as society returns the nutrients to the family soil. If we want to understand, affect, and positively change the world, we must work at the level of societal structures, and we must work with our most intimate family patterns. "The personal is political," runs the feminist mantra, telling us there really is no difference. Work with both.

So it is that our exploration into the nature of patriarchy brings us to an examination of the family. The family is the primary medium through which the dangerous logic of domination is spread. With the historical evolution of patriarchal social systems came a complementary evolution of family systems governed by patriarchal laws, customs, and patterns of relationship. The concern here is not with original causation—Which came first, the family or society? It is enough to understand that each inextricably involves and reflects the other and that the dangerous logic of domination is equally sustained through both.

Thus, transforming dominator culture into partnership culture must eventually entail a fundamental transformation of the family. This is the good sense behind the call for a return to traditional family values—somewhere in our past is a family tradition that gave rise to partnership culture. We would do well to return to it, to whatever extent we can.

However, the lost, lamented "traditional" family of conservative politicians and television evangelists—with its strong provider-protector head-of-the-castle father, its perky pre-feminist stay-at-home mother, and its ever-dutiful son-like-father and

daughter-like-mother children—is hardly the family of partnership culture. Like the "Ozzie and Harriet" and "Father Knows
Best" sitcoms of the fifties, this traditional family is but a patriarchal fantasy springing from a deep craving for greater control
in a rapidly changing world.

When men call for a return to traditional family values they are
really asking for more coercive power over others, beginning with
their wives and children. Claiming to be "pro-family," they are
profoundly antifemale. They are trying to get the uppity women
quietly in line again, while suppressing any semblance of healthy
debate or positive social evolution. They ultimately hunger after a
tradition of family fiefdoms, with husbands enthroned as absolute
lords and masters, ruling with the full backing of church and state.

When women themselves urge the strengthening of patriarchal family structures (for it was women, really, who defeated
the E.R.A.), they are desiring a futile retreat into the false sanctuary
of marriage. Ironically, the more dangerous and threatening a
world male domination creates, the more women must seek the
relative protection of male domination. Rape in the bedroom seems
a better deal than rape on the street; economic subservience in the
home seems better than the abject poverty of abandonment. "Of
all the horrid brutalities of this age," wrote Victoria Woodhull in
1874, "I know of none so horrid as those that are sanctioned and
defended by marriage."[22] Most women would disagree. They see
submission to patriarchal marriage as preferable to the dangers of
feminist rebellion. As Andrea Dworkin put it, "They hide their
bruises of body and heart; they dress carefully and have good
manners; they suffer, they love God, they follow the rules."[23]

For both men and women, the call for a return to the traditional—that is, patriarchal—family structure is attractive because
it promises simple security, gives clear instructions on the purpose in life, and comes with God the Father's blessing. The more
unstable and threatening society becomes, the more safety the
patriarchal family seems to offer. We are compelled toward
strengthening patriarchal family structures by the greatest a-
buses of patriarchal society. This is a truly vicious cycle—one that

power-maximizing men have learned to exploit, even as long-oppressed women have lent their support. Bring back the traditional family, they say, alluding to those good old days when men and women knew their proper places in life. We must return to the way things "used to be," with wife as helpmeet and husband as ruler—God's own happy little family.

This call for a return to the traditional family is a universal phenomenon: Christian, Muslim, and Hebrew fundamentalists, with their stern objections to women's liberation, are after a common goal. It is the same goal that motivates Hindus arguing in favor of the continuation of bridal dowries and widow burnings, and Chinese aborting their female fetuses, and African mothers dutifully performing clitoral circumcision on their daughters, and authorities in almost every country in the world who refuse to prosecute wife-batterers because it would intrude on the "sanctity" of the family. *The call for a return to the traditional family is the siren song of the dominator.* When patriarchal society is even slightly challenged, and especially when women begin to assert their power and aspire to basic human rights, a tightening of suppressive social mechanisms invariably occurs, with the family as the primary means of and arena for the worst of the suppression.

Obviously, no man or woman, young or old, can be faulted for wanting the simple happiness of a functional home and loving family. Nor can anyone be faulted for thinking that society would best be served if everybody lived in such families. The desire for a return to some mythic, ideal family is understandable. But a profound and comprehensive transformation of our family systems is called for now, not a frightened and reactive rigidifying of the fundamental family structures that have caused so many centuries of patriarchal abuse. The family is the ground from which society grows: when human families embody a freely chosen working partnership between all members, then and only then will we have made a significant shift toward partnership culture.

The Linchpin Lie

The warfare system has formed the eyes through which
we see war, which means we are encompassed within the
myth of war. We assume war is "just the way things are."
—*Sam Keen* [24]

Truth, according to Winston Churchill, is the first casualty of
war. Though his observation created a concise, pithy, and widely-
quoted statement, Churchill actually got it backward: it is not war
that murders truth, but the murder of truth that causes war. Any
time two nations take the final, ugly step into armed conflict,
whatever capacity for honest dealings ever existed in their relationship is already long dead. More than anything else, it is the
foul and rotting carcass of murdered truth lying between potential
adversaries that finally drives and emboldens them toward humankind's most horrid inhumanities.

This is the way it has been for humans since the dawn of
patriarchal civilization. Dominating and competition-bound societies come into contact with other societies and, rather than honestly reaching for the fruits of cooperation and partnership, some
essential lie is maintained. "*They* threaten *our* survival," declares
the dominator culture, "We must have their land and food; they are
not to be trusted; God the Father demands their ruination"—and
barbarous slaughter is the only possible outcome. The dangerous
logic of domination, sustained by personal and political dishonesty,
can only bring forth bloodshed and abuse, as the long violent
history of patriarchal civilization so miserably recounts.

If there is one linchpin lie that holds the whole sordid business of war in place, it is the idea that humans are fundamentally unequal. Under the guise of this lie, one people looks across
the divide at another people, notices obvious differences, and
decides that the others are unequal and something less; thereby
they are deserving of mistreatment, abuse, enslavement, displace-
ment, and death. The concept of "differently equal" is twisted into
dif-ferently weaker, smaller, poorer, dumber, or less evolved; the
myriad shades and colorings of diverse cultures become the

grounds and justifications for the thief, soldier, empire-builder, colonizer, industrialist, and predatory capitalist: "Our needs are worthy. If those differently unequals get in the way, kill them."

"Look carefully at the face of the enemy," writes Sam Keen. "The lips are curled downward. The eyes are fanatical and far away. . . . Nothing suggests that this man ever laughs, is torn by doubts, or shaken by tears. He feels no tenderness or pain. Clearly he is unlike us."[25] They are different, less human, less holy, and less successful at surviving, and we do well in ridding the world of them and their kind. This is the millennial-old lie, told with perfect sincerity by each side in every war that humans have ever fought: We are different, they are less than us, and—the crux of the matter—their pain, hardship, and death does not count for as much as ours.

They are less than us and their suffering does not count for as much as ours. Their religious practice, economic system, or governmental structure is less than ours; their claim to and feeling for the land is less than ours; their primitive manner of pursuing happiness is less than ours; their rights are less unalienable than ours—every variation of this linchpin lie sets people moving toward war while providing the intellectual and emotional cover for the coming horrors.

Some will say: "But what about Hitler and his ilk? Aren't there many examples of truly subhuman, destructive cultures that deserve, even demand, eradication? Surely it is not dishonesty but a rational assessment of the facts that justifies such wars. Aren't there many examples of righteous wars fought for the greater good of humankind?"

Within the all-encompassing system that is patriarchy, it is true that some (if not all) wars are justifiable: diverse cultures rank each other as different and unequal, the linchpin lie is maintained, and war invariably comes to make terrible sense. Patriarchy, with all of its abuses, is self-perpetuating, self-sustaining, and self-justifying. As long as we are trapped in the vicious cycle of patriarchal dishonesty and abuse, we can only meet history's villains with superior villainy. "Though the sheep may proclaim the virtues of vegetarianism," warns the soldier, "it does little good if the wolf does not agree." As long as there are killers loose in the world, we seem to have no choice other than to become the very best at killing. Thus have we devolved.

Even worse, the patriarchal foundations for war—the beliefs that humans are essentially different and unequal; that humans must compete with one another for the basics of life; that domination is the inevitable and justifiable result of such unequal competition; and that violence and abuse is unfortunate but necessary—set the foundations for all other systems in a society. Thus, it makes sense (within patriarchy) to speak of a war against cancer, a war against poverty, a war against illiteracy, and, of course, a war between the sexes, even though resolving such problems is clearly unlikely through militaristic means. To accept the doctrines of patriarchal inevitability is to accept war as basic to human nature; *to accept war as basic to human nature is to project the exigencies of war into all of human society.*

Modern society is now one vast and treacherous battlefield, with casualties strewn everywhere. Victor and vanquished, we are all the walking wounded in this war-crazed patriarchal world. As long as we continue to buy the linchpin lie and conclude that humans are inevitably bound for endless competition and hostile struggle, we sentence ourselves and future generations to a prison built upon the bloodied soils of war.

Man Over Nature

> The "control of nature" is a phrase conceived in arrogance, born of the Neanderthal age of biology and philosophy. . . . It is our alarming misfortune that so primitive a science has armed itself with the most modern and terrible weapons.
> —*Rachel Carson* [26]

The linchpin lie of "different and unequal" extends beyond human relations to dangerously affect our relationship with nature as well. Patriarchal culture is inevitably antiecological: "Since humans are obviously different and better than mere plants and animals," says the dominator, "and human needs are of more compelling importance than the needs of any other species, then domination of nature, abusive though it may sometimes be, is always justifiable."

After all, the Bible says that nature exists to serve the many needs of human beings. Man, commanded God the Father in chapter 1 of Genesis, shall "have dominion over the fish of the sea, and over the fowl of the air, and over every living thing that moveth upon the Earth." The modern gods of mammon, with their short-term visions and bottom-line demands, all agree: Any degradation of the Earth, including the wholesale elimination of other species and entire ecosystems, is justifiable if it serves the greater needs of humankind (and brings profit to the dominator elite.)

Since nature is considered the property of humanity, any abuse of nature is considered worthy (if even acknowledged) as long as (some) humans somehow benefit. Like all patriarchal abuse, the human abuse of nature has become so addictively self-serving that it seems both necessary and inevitable. And even though much sincere effort is now being given to environmentalism, when the necessities of a sustainable environment seem to conflict with human needs, patriarchal reality still pushes most people toward continuing environmental abuse.

I say "seem to" since, as we are discovering, the necessities of a sustainable environment are in fact primary human needs, more important even than our televisions and automobiles. We abuse nature with flagrant disregard for our own genuine needs and with shameful disregard for the needs of future generations. And indeed, if we could just ask the question "Is this *really* necessary?" before we in any way impinge on the freedom of another life form, we would positively alter the course of modern civilization, for so much modern eco-abuse *simply is not necessary.*

Is it really necessary to raze the few remaining old-growth forests of our world? Is it really necessary to continue spewing ozone-depleting chemicals into the air? Is it really necessary to fish with driftnets? Is it really necessary to encourage large-scale, fertilizer- and pesticide-dependent agriculture? Is it really necessary to pursue nuclear power? Is it really necessary to remain so rigidly committed to energy policies based on fossil fuels? Is it really necessary to so emphatically underinvest in solar energy? Is it really necessary to ignore and resist a wide range of currently existing energy-conservation technologies?

Granted, in each of these cases there are select groups of humans—clear-cutting loggers, driftnet fishermen, chemical producers, oil barons, purveyors of energy-wasteful technologies—who financially depend upon the continuing abuse of nature and who, along with their families and local communities, resoundingly answer, "Yes, *this* is really necessary." I do not mean to denigrate the value of hard labor and personal investment, nor to diminish the terrible fear of seeing one's livelihood and way of life threatened by a bunch of do-gooder environmentalists. Still, as a conservative biologist might put it, the lesson of the ages is "adapt or die."

The most eco-abusive practices and industries humans engage in are especially and eventually *unadaptive*: they violate any standard of genuine necessity, taking more of the resource base than can ever be replenished, and/or generating more waste than can be ecologically absorbed. Even worse, such practices and industries, and the humans most deeply committed to their continuance, tend toward rigid resistance to any healthy evolutionary growth. They cling to the status-quo clamor for "jobs!" and "the economy!" while ignoring the simple yet unavoidable dictates of environmental common sense in a rapidly changing world. There is no question that all eco-abusive human practices and industries are unadaptive and dying out; the question is—how much of the planet will they take with them?

We must come to collectively recognize "financial necessity" as but a selfish cover-up for ill-thought and irresponsible behavior. To abuse the environment in pursuit of personal wealth is a crime against all of humanity. To remain rigidly attached to occupations and lifestyles that are intrinsically unadaptive is to force others to participate in one's own myopia and suicide. Even the very poor, who often have no choice other than to cause immediate environmental degradation, are only ensuring their impoverished demise: There is no full and healthy life along the path of environmental abuse.

However compelling our personal or political reasons for (unnecessarily) abusing nature may be, such abuse strengthens the dangerous logic of domination and the inevitable grip of patriarchal reality. Like all the many sins of patriarchal reality, the abuse of nature is only inevitable for those who have given up hope of ever knowing something better.

Personal Reflections

How has the dangerous logic of power-over poisoned your body and life? What childhood experiences forced you to suppress your primary feelings of joy and sexual aliveness? Were you mistreated "for your own good?" Were you physically punished? Were you sexually abused? Were you circumcised? Were you ever badly injured or seriously ill as a child? Were you ever hospitalized? Were you left physically alone and untouched for long periods? Did you blame yourself for these pains? Do you still?

Do you know or remember anything about your birth? Was it ever talked about as you were growing up? Could you talk to your mother about it now? How do you feel around babies?

Can you remember feeling sexual as a child? Did you receive any positive encouragement for such feelings? any simple explanations? Or were you taught to suppress the feelings? Were you punished for them?

Did you ever see or hear your parents making love? How would they have reacted if they had known you were observing? Did your parents ever talk to you about sex? Did your parents easily show affection to you? hug you? hold you? kiss you?

Did you ever "play doctor" with other children? Were you forced into such sexual play by an older child? Did you ever force a younger child? Did you like to look at pornographic magazines? Did you ever secretly observe another person undressing? When did you first masturbate? Did you feel guilty and wrong for doing so?

How do you feel now as you read through these questions? Are you feeling uncomfortable? angry? hurt? depressed? bored? Is your body tense? Are you holding your breath? Does the notion of "childhood sexuality" seem unthinkable to you? irrelevant? threatening? sinful?

Do you feel sexually determined now by the experiences you lived through as a child? Do you feel sexually driven, compelled, and unfree—as if you have no choice other than to exhibit certain preferences and behave certain ways? If you had absolute choice in the matter, what sexual reality would you choose for yourself now?

THREE
When God Is a WoMan

If we accept the patriarchal explanations for human origins, we have good cause to feel pessimistic about our future. The idea that we are naturally violent, original sinners and that, as a consequence, we have only ever known dominator culture, is a severe and depressing indictment of the human spirit. To surmise that our earliest intelligence was quickly turned to improving our capacity for killing others is the worst of insults. To suggest that our sexual interactions have been, from the very beginning, drag-the-woman-across-the-cave-floor-by-her-hair rapes, leaves a feeling of awful hopelessness.

If that is how we began, how can we talk of evolution? Sexual assaults against women are a worldwide epidemic, and they are growing. Has anything changed? The greatest intelligence and industry on this planet is dedicated to building weapons of mass murder. Has anything changed? Men dominate women everywhere, and the countries most capable of killing dominate weaker countries everywhere. Has anything changed? If this has been the essential nature of human beings for the past hundred thousand years, then, given the ever-expanding technologies of military destruction and industrial poisoning, what hope is there for us now? Why should we change now? More to the point, *can* we change now?

It is gospel within patriarchal culture that however much

human society may evolve, basic human nature never improves. Patriarchal religious doctrine stresses that we are born sinners, that the world is an evil place, and that only through the acceptance of God the Father's laws can we hope to improve. Even then, we only do so in the hereafter. Human nature, at least until the sweeping changes of the Second Coming, does not change. The demons of weakness, violence, hostility, and abuse are born within all humans; our only hope is in submission to patriarchal rule and salvation.

The secular defenders of patriarchy are every bit as convinced of the notion that human nature is basically weak and essentially unchanging. They claim that our most primal, "animal" instincts derive from the "kill or be killed" reality into which early humans were born. Such being our true nature, the world would be a wild and dangerously anarchistic place, a savage existence, if not for the civilizing influence of the dominator's laws and punishments. The worst excesses of dominator culture are taken as proof of basic human failings—animal instincts run amok—and create a hue and cry for greater domination. The great unwashed masses, including all but the occasional woman, need to be dominated; it's really for everyone's own good.

This is, again, a hopelessly depressing vision of reality. If human nature is essentially weak, violent, hostile, and abusive, then we have lived under male domination from the very beginning, since the strongest, most violent, and abusive men are favored in such a world. If dominator culture is all that we have ever known, there is little reason to hope that we will ever know anything else. The patriarchal explanations of human origins cast a dark, dominating shadow far into humanity's future. The dominators are adamant: this is God's way, this is human nature, this is all we've ever known, this is the best we can do—get used to it. Fortunately, the dominators are wrong.

The Once and Future Goddess

There can be no doubt that in the earliest ages of human history the magical force and wonder of the female was no less a marvel than the universe itself; and this gave to women a prodigious power.
                                        —*Joseph Campbell*[1]

It was an exquisite long period of nonseparative, erotic, fusional living that was primarily peaceful. . . . Birthing and a sense of all things coming from the feminine was at the center of this culture.
                                        —*Barbara Hand Clow*[2]

Western civilization, according to patriarchal doctrine, evolved out of barbarism some five thousand years ago in the fertile valleys of the Near East. Though the data on this early history has constantly shifted with new archaeological technologies and fresh interpretations, the patriarchal version of the story has remained basically the same: There was a gradual growth of male-dominating social systems—powered by steady improvements in military weaponry—that vigorously spread the good news of civilization to primitive pagans everywhere.

However, it is now becoming clear that this version of history is grossly inaccurate and, from our present perspective, tragically misleading. A wealth of recent archaeological findings are substantiating that a vital and thriving human culture existed for *thousands of years* before the coming of the all-encompassing patriarchal civilization. Moreover, the emerging picture of this prehistory suggests that the coming of the patriarchs was more a crippling of civilization than a birth.

Riane Eisler has beautifully and thoroughly documented this new story of human origins in *The Chalice and The Blade*. She begins in the cave sanctuaries of the Paleolithic era (ca. 30,000–10,000 B.C.), with a fresh examination of the wall paintings, stone carvings, and burial sites of the period. Although the prevailing, patriarchal interpretations of Paleolithic findings invariably point to Man the Hunter and the constant chore of killing, Eisler and a growing body of scholars look at the same evidence and see a vastly different human culture.

"These cave sanctuaries, figurines, burials, and rites all seem to have been related to a belief that the same source from which human life springs is also the source of all vegetable and animal life—the great Mother Goddess or Giver of All we still find in later periods of Western civilization. They also suggest that our earliest ancestors recognized that we and our natural environment are integrally linked parts of the great mystery of life and death and that all nature must therefore be treated with respect."[3] There is, then, a feeling of cooperation in living, rather than the bloodthirsty competition of the dominator's reality; and there is a vital presence of woman beyond the mere submissive sex object and breeder.

The presence of woman comes through most vividly in the carved figurines of the period. They are typically round female representations, with overly large breasts, buttocks, thighs, and pubic triangles, sometimes without faces. These exquisite sculptures have been traditionally dismissed as "Venus figures" or, as Eisler puts it, "ancient analogue[s] for today's *Playboy* magazine."[4] Archaeologist Marija Gimbutas, who more than any other person has brought about an enlightened understanding of these ancient sculptures, stresses that they "are not beauties" and that it is a great error to think of them as Venus figurines. "Their functions were *much* more important than those of a Venus. The functions were life-giving, death-wielding, and regeneration."[5] Thus, for our Paleolithic ancestors, the power of woman, as represented by the Goddess sculptures, was the same power that would thousands of years later belong exclusively to God the Father.

Further insight into the psyche of the ancients is provided by their cave paintings. Traditionally, the primitive yet highly evocative line drawings have been viewed strictly as hunting scenes. Overlooked in this explanation are the many instances of dancing women and the simple representations of trees and vegetation. Though many paintings undoubtedly are hunting scenes, others most likely depict food gathering and important community rituals in which women played vital roles.

Eisler also documents the strong presence of the feminine in

the burial practices of the Paleolithic. "Both the ritualized place-
ment of the vagina-shaped cowrie shells around and on the dead
and the practice of coating these shells and/or the dead with red
ocher pigment (symbolizing the vitalizing power of blood) appear to have been part of the funerary rites intended to bring the
deceased back through rebirth."[6] What we do not find in the burials
are any weapons or other signs of male domination or the glorification of violence. Rather, our ancestors seemed to hold a deep
reverence for the cycle of life and death and a healthy awe of woman's place in that cycle.

As both Eisler and Gimbutas have stressed, these findings by
no means add up to matriarchy (the domination of men by women)
or some utopian existence. "Because of the scarceness of their
remains and the long time span between us and them," writes
Eisler, "we probably never will be entirely certain of the specific
meaning their paintings, figurines, and symbols had for our Paleolithic forebears."[7] Nor can we hope to accurately describe the social
structures of these ancient people.

However, from the existing evidence, we can clearly make as
strong a case for an egalitarian, partnership way of life as has been
made for the traditionally held Man the Hunter and dominator
view. And if it is only our intuition insisting that, "of course our
ancient ancestors lived in peaceful partnership," why shouldn't
we listen?

The Cradles of Civilization

We now know that there was not one cradle of civilization in Sumer about 3,500 years ago. Rather, there were
many cradles of civilization, all of them thousands of years
older.
                              —*Riane Eisler*[8]

When we move forward into the Neolithic era (ca. 10,000 B.C.)
the evidence of a partnership past grows much stronger. Recent
excavations of Çatal Hüyük, an early Neolithic town located in
what is now Turkey, show advancements in culture, technology,
architecture, and agriculture that were previously assumed to

have originated in Sumer some five thousand years later. As James Mellaart, the British archaeologist who managed the excavation of Çatal Hüyük, has written, "Çatal Hüyük is remarkable for its wall-paintings and plaster reliefs, its sculpture in stone and clay as well as for its advanced technology in the crafts of weaving, wood-work, metallurgy and obsidian working. Its numerous sanctuaries testify to an advanced religion, complete with symbolism and mythology; its buildings to the birth of architecture and conscious planning; its economy to advanced practices in agriculture and stockbreeding; and its numerous imports to a flourishing trade in raw materials."[9]

Moreover, as Eisler stresses, Mellaart found "wall paintings, plaster reliefs, stone sculptures, and large quantities of Goddess figurines made of clay, all focusing on the worship of a female deity."[10] Thus, the Goddess-centered art of the Paleolithic contin-ued into the Neolithic. Likewise, the evidence indicates that women were held in high esteem in this early culture. Thus, they must be credited with much of the civilizing advances. As Mellaart puts it, "The position of women was obviously an important one in an agricultural society. . . in which a goddess was the principal deity."[11]

One other important finding from Çatal Hüyük: the town had no fortifications and shows no signs of warfare, despite the fact that its people actively traded with surrounding regions. "There are no individuals among the burials that showed signs of violent death."[12] For over fifteen hundred years, the people of Çatal Hüyük lived and thrived without recourse to or fear from organized violence. If, as I am asserting, domination (male or female) and violent abuse always go hand in hand, this represents strong evidence of a culture in which women and men lived in true partnership.

Another telling example of an early partnership culture has emerged from a continuing examination of the Neolithic civiliza-tion on the island of Crete. Though first discovered and excavated at the turn of the twentieth century, it is only recently that scholars have begun to look at Crete without the prevailing biases of patriarchal thinking. The developing picture is one of an advanced civilization beyond some of our wildest and most optimistic modern dreams.

Cretan civilization existed from around 6000 B.C. until at least 2000 B.C. This four-thousand-year period, incidentally, is longer than the time traditionally thought of as modern, recorded history. And, as with Çatal Hüyük, there are few signs of military technologies or fortifications during this entire civilization. Instead, we find exquisite art, inspired and well-planned architecture, beautiful (and rather sexy) clothing, and a steady evolution of functional tools.

The Cretans were a prosperous people. They began with agriculture, and over time they learned to breed animals, developed a wide range of crafts and small industries, and eventually founded a large mercantile fleet that successfully traded throughout the Mediterranean. As archaeologist Nicolas Platon concludes, after more than fifty years of studying Crete, "The standard of living—even of peasants—seems to have been high. None of the homes found so far have suggested very poor living conditions."[13] Thus, for all their wealth, the Cretans apparently avoided the typical patterns of class stratification and domination.

Nor does the evidence indicate the domination of men over women. Though Crete developed a centralized form of government, it is not entirely clear whether the rulers were male or female, for there is a significant lack of representation (in statues, portraits, and special burials) of kings *or* queens. It does appear that secular power worked in cooperation with religious power, and the religious power was clearly that of the Goddess. "The fear of death," writes Platon, "was almost obliterated by the ubiquitous joy of living. The whole of life was pervaded by an ardent faith in the Goddess nature, the source of all creation and harmony. This led to a love of peace, a horror of tyranny, and a respect for the law."[14]

Moreover, while the complexities and great advancements of Cretan society caused inevitable divisions of labor and social roles, there are no signs of a dominant class or sex. "Even among the ruling classes personal ambition seems to have been an unknown; nowhere do we find the name of an author attached to a work of art nor a record of the deeds of a ruler."[15] Rather, as Eisler puts it in one tantalizing sentence, "In Crete, for the last time in recorded history, a spirit of harmony between women and men as joyful and equal participants in life appears to pervade."[16]

I will discuss the decline of Crete in the next chapter. For now, it is worth stating again that, from all appearances, Crete thrived as a partnership culture for thousands of years. Men with their muscles and testosterone and penises worked and played alongside women with babies and breasts and menstrual periods, and they lived in relative peace and prosperity for thousands of years.

While Crete is certainly the most exciting of Neolithic partnership cultures, Eisler stresses that "the numerous Neolithic excavations that have yielded Goddess figurines and symbols span a wide geographical area."[17] As far east as India, as far west as the British Isles, and throughout the Mediterranean and mainland Europe, countless representations of Goddess worship, including tens of thousands of figurines, have been discovered. While this certainly does not prove that the entire region lived with the grace of Cretans, it does indicate a prevailing attitude toward the cosmos that lent itself to more harmonious relations.

As Marija Gimbutas has shown through a lifetime of research and field work, southeastern Europe from 6500 to 3500 B.C. also held a flourishing partnership civilization. In her major work, *The Gods and Goddesses of Old Europe*, she writes, "The inhabitants of this region developed . . . a complex social organization . . . forming settlements which often amounted to small townships, inevitably involving craft specialization and the creation of religious and governmental institutions. . . . If one defines civilization as the ability of a given people to adjust to its environment and to develop adequate arts, technology, script, and social relations it is evident Old Europe achieved a marked degree of success."[18]

As in Çatal Hüyük and Crete, the people of Old Europe developed complex social, religious, governmental, and economic systems without rigid sexual or class hierarchies. Gimbutas has thoroughly documented that the women of Old Europe held high positions and that an egalitarian relationship between the sexes prevailed. "A division of labor between the sexes is indicated, *but not a superiority of either* [my italics]," she writes, continuing, "I can see there no ranking along a patriarchal masculine-feminine value scale."[19] Moreover, as in Crete and Çatal Hüyük, we find much evidence of active trading, and yet little in the way of military fortifications or weaponry. Thus, again, we find an absence of organized violence within a thriving partnership culture.

Through a Darkened Glass

Going farther back in time, we are all sourced in an ancient collective people who worshiped the Mother Goddess, and we still contain a deep memory of how to create and live on the planet in a peaceful, healthy way.
—*Barbara Hand Clow*[20]

There are limits, of course, to how much we can consider proven from the excavations of Çatal Hüyük, Crete, and Old Europe. Gerda Lerner warns in *The Creation of Patriarchy* that the ubiquitous presence of Goddess sculptures throughout the Neolithic by no means proves universal Goddess worship or the high status of women. She points to a similar instance in the "statues of the Virgin Mary in the Middle Ages. If an archaeologist of the future were to find thousands of such statues in the villages of Europe, she might be seriously misled, if she concluded from such a find ing that a female deity was being worshiped there."[21]

On the other hand, as Lerner goes on to say, in the Middle Ages we also find an abundance of male religious figures. As Gimbutas and others have stated, there are significantly fewer male religious figures from the Paleolithic and Neolithic eras than there are female figures. Thus, when all of the evidence is considered, the conclu-sion of widespread female-centered religious experience and the higher social status of women is hardly unwarranted.

A greater mistake would be to repeat the error of traditional scholars (and some feminists) in assuming that an absence of patriarchy implies matriarchy. Discovering societies in which men did not dominate women by no means forces us to conclude that women must therefore have dominated men. As Eisler writes,

"The archaeologic data we now have indicate that in its general structure prepatriarchal society was, by any contemporary standard, remarkably equalitarian. [Although] in these societies descent appears to have been traced through the mother, and women as priestesses and heads of clans seem to have played leading roles in all aspects of life, there is little indication that the position of men in this social system was in any sense comparable to the subordination and suppression of women characteristic of the male-dominated system that replaced it."[22]

The notion that "if it isn't patriarchy it must be matriarchy" is a product of a patriarchal worldview that assumes domination as a primary and necessary human social structure. If men weren't on top, then women must have been; the possibility of shared power and responsibilities is not even considered. However, as Lerner writes, "there is not a single society known where women-as-a-group have decision-making power *over* men."[23] Since there is little evidence of any actual matriarchies, the tendency has been to ignore, marginalize, or seriously misinterpret the preponderance of evidence for women's early power that does exist. If all we ever look for is patriarchy or matriarchy, that is, if we are only thinking in terms of ranking humans hierarchically, then we will forever fail to see true cooperation and partnership.

Yet another problem we must consider in looking backward toward our partnership past is the terrible ferocity with which patriarchal civilization later attacked and obliterated any signs of Goddess worship or partnership social structures. With the coming of male domination, female power was brutally suppressed and restricted and Goddess-related statues, artwork, writings, shrines, and, in some cases, entire cities, were destroyed for all time.

In the Old Testament, God the Father is merciless toward the pagans, heathens, and worshipers of the Queen of Heaven: "If the inhabitants of a town that once served the Lord your God now serve other gods, you must kill all the inhabitants of that town" (Deut. 13:15). "You shall destroy their altars, break their images, and cut down their groves, for thou shalt worship no other god" (Exodus 34:13). And, "You shall surely destroy all the places where the nations whom you shall dispossess served their gods, upon the high mountains and upon the hills and under every green tree: and you shall overthrow their altars, and break their pillars and burn their groves with fire; and you shall hew down the graven images of their gods, and destroy the names of them out of that place" (Deut. 12:2).

Such commands and admonishments run throughout the Bible, leading to centuries of violence and brutality against Goddess-centered practices as well as to the utter destruction of any offending artifacts. For all the evidence of Goddess religions and prepatriarchal social structures that has been gathered, how much more did God the Father's fanatical legions forever eradicate?

Ironically, the Bible gives us some of the best evidence of just how widely spread and all-pervasive the Goddess culture was. As Merlin Stone writes, "There are continual reports of 'paganism' in every era; it loomed as a constant problem, described throughout the Old Testament. The prophet-priests of Yahweh threatened. They scolded."[24] And, with time, they virtually succeeded in eliminating all signs and remembrances of how we once lived.

Though somewhat unscientific, it would nevertheless be negligent, I think, not to assume that for every Goddess sculpture that survived into the present, a thousand more were hammered into dust by God the Father's minions, that for every Çatal Hüyük discovered, a thousand similar towns were burned to the ground by violently dominating conquerors; that for every surviving sign that women and men once shared power in peaceful partnership, a thousand other signs were forever erased from the archaeological record by the very men who brought partnership to an end.

Though we could certainly err in seeing too much partnership culture in the archaeological record, a greater mistake would be in failing to see enough. Whatever capacity for balanced, cooperative, peaceful living our early ancestors may have had holds an important key to the present and future survival of our race. If we have lived in peaceful partnership before, we can live that way again.

Memories of Paradise

Whether it happened so or not I do not know; but if you think about it you can see that it is true.
            —*Black Elk*[25]

We are learning to tell a new cosmogonic myth, a new myth of creation. And as the fundamental myth of all other myths this promises healing.
            —*Gloria Orenstein*[26]

Archaeology is considered a "hard" science because it deals with fossil remains, preserved artifacts, dwellings, burial sites, and the like. Archaeologists take solid physical evidence—stones and bones—and piece together pictures of the past. Though their own biases and misinterpretations do inevitably intrude, more or less "softening" the science, the basic evidence remains solid. With time, the archaeological record tends toward greater accuracy.

Mythology, on the other hand, is considered by most to be a "soft" science. The main body of mythological record is comprised of legends, stories, and tales, sometimes written but often only oral, that have been passed down from earlier times to the present. While a fossil or pottery shard has a slow-changing solidity to it, ancient myths and stories seem less solid and thus less reliable as accurate readings of our past.

Of course, not all cultures share Western science's concept of truth or dedication to hard facts. Richard Heinberg, exploring the nature of myths in *Memories and Visions of Paradise*, tells of cultures for whom the rules of true and false are rather different. "A narrative may consist entirely of factual elements, and yet be a 'false' story if it has been taken out of context to make a point that is self-serving or merely entertaining. Another story may be entirely fictional, yet remind us of situations we have all encountered and, by drawing us into the action of the narrative, may tell us something about ourselves and the workings of the world that we may not yet have seen. That is a 'true' story."[27]

Seen in this light, myths are powerful allegories—metaphor-laden teaching stories told to connect people with *present* truth. Joseph Campbell, in his lifetime devotion to the meaning of myths,

stressed this inner, psychic dimension of mythology. "The wonder," he wrote, "is that the characteristic efficacy to touch and
inspire deep creative centers dwells in the smallest nursery fairy
tale. . . . For the symbols of mythology are not manufactured; they
cannot be ordered, invented, or permanently suppressed. They
are spontaneous productions of the psyche, and each bears within
it, undamaged, the germ power of its source."[28] The question of
whether a myth actually happened, then, is hardly relevant, since
the power of the myth is so vital in the present moment. As Jean
Houston put it, "Myth is something that never was but is always
happening."[29]

And yet, others have made the case that myths, for all their
allegorical power, do nonetheless have foundations in actual historical fact. As Heinberg writes, "The factual core of the mytholo-
gized narrative unquestionably persists, whether in the biography
of a heroic political leader, in a historic Russian folktale of the
Napoleonic invasion, or in a Greek epic narrative of the Trojan
Wars. History exists in myth as surely as 'myth' persists in history."[30]

In a similar vein, William Irwin Thompson suggests that "a
myth can reflect light from many facets," "that all variants of a myth
must be considered," and that "all the modern schools of thought
are equivalents of variations of myth, and all must be taken into
account."[31] Thompson also reminds us of Niels Bohr's dictum that
"the opposite of a profound truth may well be another profound
truth." The "whole truth" of human origins is ultimately made up
of all of the world's myths, along with the many reasonably
considered and yet-to-be-encountered theories of hard science.

For the most part, those who have attempted to correlate
factual history with myth have been ignored by mainstream scientists. Immanuel Velikovsky, for instance, showed that the persistent worldwide myths telling of floods and cataclysms have their
origins in "actual cosmic debacles witnessed by our distant ancestors."[32] James Churchward argued convincingly, in an echo of
mythologies around the world, that there was once a major continent in the Pacific called Mu that disappeared through a monu-

mental catastrophe. Likewise, a great number of scholars, starting with Plato, have argued for the existence of ancient Atlantis, which suffered a fate similar to Mu.

Historian, biblical scholar, and linguist Zecharia Sitchin has documented a mind-boggling correlation between ancient myths and prehistoric events in *The Earth Chronicles* series and in his latest book, *Genesis Revisited*. Sitchin's primary thesis has been popularized in the term *ancient astronauts*. He believes that Earth was visited long ago by advanced, humanlike beings from another planet. Their interactions with early humans greatly accelerated human genetic and cultural evolution and gave humans access to scientific knowledge—thoroughly explored by Sitchin in five-thousand-year-old Sumerian texts—that is only now being *re*discovered by modern science. Furthermore, Sitchin asserts, this story is all related in the biblical creation mythology found in the book of Genesis.

Each of these theories is supported by impressive amounts of "hard" evidence, including signs of ocean-level changes and sudden mass extinctions, several geological indications of submerged continents, the ubiquitous presence of unexplained artifacts such as the pyramids and Stonehenge (which show technological, mathematical, and astronomical sophistication unwarranted for "early man"), and the volumes of Sumerian texts that Sitchin cites. There is no lack of evidence to support the existence of advanced, prehistoric civilizations.

Of course, if such civilizations did exist, they would not necessarily have been partnership cultures, and they may well have been patriarchies. Still, just considering their possible existence forces us to broaden our assumptions about human origins, which in turn opens our minds to the notion that something other than patriarchy may once have flourished on this Earth. Furthermore, if legends such as those of Mu and Atlantis and the ancient astronauts turn out to be true, then we would do well to pay much closer attention to all of the mythologies of our world. Indeed, I suspect the real difficulty that mainstream scientific thought has in accepting such "pseudoscientific" theories lies not so much with the evidence presented as with the degree to which so many ancient mythologies have long told the same story.

Virtually all cultural mythologies tell of a great global catastrophe, the most common being the flood, as related in Genesis. The tale of a lost original island or continent shows up as Avalon, Antilia, or St. Brendan's Island in various European traditions, as Aztlan to the Aztecs, as Muia to the Hopis, as Mu to the Samoans, as Hava-Iki in much of Polynesia, and as Kahiki-honua-kele ("the land that moved off") to the Hawaiians, to name but a few. Likewise, the theory that superior beings visited the Earth and played a role in early human evolution is supported by many of the world's mythologies. "The Africans' insistence that at first God lived on Earth with the people," writes Heinberg, "and the Australian's memory of the Dreamtime, when the Creator-Heroes walked the land, echo the biblical image of Adam and Eve strolling naked and unashamed in the Garden with God."[33]

It is this widespread similarity between mythologies that Heinberg refers to as "the problem of mythic unity." Though he stresses that there is certainly great diversity to be found among the world's mythologies, he further stresses and goes on to beautifully document that there are also striking parallels to be found. *"Why,"* he asks, *"would ancient peoples in geographically remote places, under unique circumstances, have arrived at such similar beliefs?"*[34] And why, especially, would the core of so many mythologies be the belief that humans once lived in Paradise?

As Heinberg shows, the myth of a distant time when men and women lived together in peace and harmony with all of nature is common to virtually every culture on Earth. Moreover, certain characteristic features of Paradise are also common everywhere: a magical landscape of sacred mountains and trees; wise, beautiful, and luminous beings possessing miraculous powers; perfect communion with plants, animals, and the deity; perfect health and greatly expanded lifespans, if not immortality; and, of course, a complete absence of violence toward fellow humans and nature. "Here—in word pictures that seem inevitably to reappear in story after story, from pole to pole and continent to continent—is the

universal, primordial description of humanity's happy and innocent beginnings."[35]

Does a planetwide, fairly unified, mythological vision of Paradise prove that women and men once lived in partnership? While
Heinberg does not directly address the issues of male and female
status, roles, and responsibilities, the portrait of Paradise that he
draws from myths around the world—especially the lack of violence, the communion with nature, and the presence of male *and*
female deities—does conform with the essentials of partnership
culture. If the Paradise myth is indeed rooted in historical fact, it
represents further evidence of our partnership past.

It may be that the Paradise myth is an exaggerated and embel-
lished remembering of life during the Paleolithic and Neolithic
eras. J.V. Luce, for instance, builds a strong case for Atlantis having
been the island of Thera (part of Minoan Crete), until it suffered a
massive volcanic eruption.[36] It may also be that the Paradise myth
merely reflects an archetypal longing for "better times" shared by
all human beings. We may never know for certain. However,
given the archaeological evidence of a more harmonious existence
during prehistoric times, the Paradise myth clearly strengthens the
argument that humans did indeed once live as true and equal
partners.

Moreover, this myth provides hope for the future and a measure of guidance. "If we were able to live in Paradise once," writes
Heinberg, "we ought to be able to do so again. And if the most
natural and healthy way of life available to human beings is defined by the expression of the essential paradisal qualities of character and the subsequent experience of universal harmony, then
what is natural should in principle also be attainable. In short, we
may be *designed* to live in Paradise."[37]

We may be designed to live in Paradise, to enjoy the bounties
of this Earth, to share freely without resorting to violence, as
partners—man and woman, human and nature. Though recorded history and much of our present experience argue otherwise,
voices of our Paleolithic and Neolithic ancestors, as well as many
mythmakers, tell us that we *can* achieve and sustain peace—

between nations, between races, and between the sexes. We know how to do it because we have done it before.

A Partnership Present

Community is expressed in many ways for the !Kung. . . . People are encouraged to act and believe in ways to increase the common good, though there is respect for individual differences. —*Richard Katz* [38]

A living link to our partnership past can be found in the study of our world's surviving gatherer-hunter cultures. Though any existing primitive cultures have been steadily influenced (or contaminated) by their contacts with "civilization," and though there is clearly a rich diversity of traditions and practices among primitive peoples, the anthropological record indicates certain common features of preagricultural societies: They tend to share rather than compete, they commune closely with nature, they evince highly evolved social and spiritual values, they enjoy greater leisure time than modern men and women, and they do not engage in warfare. This is, to be sure, a general description, and there are many exceptions to these rules. Still, it is fairly safe to conclude from the observation of gatherer-hunters that they favor partnership over domination.

One much-studied and wonderfully fascinating gatherer-hunter culture is the !Kung of the Kalahari Desert in southern Africa.[39] The !Kung have their roots in the Neolithic era and thus practice a lifestyle that has succeeded for thousands of years with very little change. They live a simple, nomadic existence, moving camp five or six times per year. As they must be able to carry all they own, they have few possessions. Moreover, all their possessions are easily made and replaced, so they have no reason to accumulate things.

Most of the !Kung diet is made up of wild vegetable foods gathered by the women. About 25 percent of their total caloric intake is provided by the men through hunting. As one !Kung observer, Richard Lee, has written, "Hunting is a *high-risk, low-*

return subsistence activity, while gathering is a *low-risk, high-return* subsistence activity.[40] On average, the !Kung spend fifteen hours a week on securing food, and another five to ten hours a week on routine activities such as gathering firewood or carrying water. The rest of their time is free for leisure, play, crafts, ritual, and socializing.

The !Kung place great emphasis on sharing as a primary social value and means of interaction. As another !Kung observer, Richard Katz, has written, "Resources of all kinds circulate among members of a village and between villages, so that any one person can draw upon resources far beyond his or her own capacities to obtain."[41] This sharing includes all of the necessities of !Kung life— land, waterholes, meat, and vegetables—and extends to a rich and vital tradition of giving gifts. As one !Kung tells it, "We give to one another always. We give what we have. This is the way we live together."[42]

As one might expect from the above remark, "the Kung are an intensely egalitarian people. There is a marked absence of disparities in wealth among them. Any surplus is quickly equalized by social pressure, because accumulation has distinct disadvantages. But equality is not merely material; it affects all aspects of Kung life."[43] Though individual differences obviously exist, such as one man being the best hunter, or one woman being a beautiful dancer, these differences do not confer social, political, or economic advantage. No one exerts power over any other, and everybody has an equal voice in all decisions.

As many observers have noted, the !Kung's egalitarianism applies especially to the relationship between men and women. Neither sex dominates the other; both are fully involved in all aspects of community life. Though each sex tends toward certain roles, there is no rigid hierarchy invoked, and some women will join in the hunt, for instance, just as men will often do "women's work." Quite simply, the !Kung appreciate the differences between the sexes while affirming that all people are of equal worth. And they easily *enjoy* the differences between the sexes—sexual contact is free, open, unselfconscious, and with a refreshing lack of rules.

Both sexes likewise share in the raising of children. !Kung fathers are as actively present in the lives of their children as !Kung mothers. Most importantly, children are taught to be partners in life. As Katz stresses, "Authoritarian behavior toward children is . . . avoided by parents of both sexes, as are physical aggression or abuse. . . . The general rules for !Kung infant life are indulgence, stimulation, and nonrestriction."[44]

Though the !Kung lead a simple life, it would be a great mistake to conclude that they are "unevolved" as human beings. As Katz has beautifully illustrated in his book, *Boiling Energy*, the !Kung have a highly sophisticated approach to healing that is both effective and spiritually transformational. They have a rich tradition of rituals, expressed through regular singing and dancing, which permeates all aspects of their lives. They speak rather matter-of-factly of such psychic events as telepathy, healing at a distance, predicting the sex of infants, traveling out of body, and conversing with God. As I noted in an earlier work (*Dancing with the Fire*), they have taken the ancient ritual of dancing barefoot on burning embers to miraculous dimensions while providing a clearer explanation for how it is possible than Western science's most astute physicists. Simply stated, whereas the West has concentrated on *industrial* technologies, the !Kung have developed the requisite *human* technologies for living in partnership communities.

Of final interest is the !Kung's approach to conflict resolution. !Kung life is not idyllic—they experience droughts and famines, they know hunger and cold, and they have the usual personality clashes. They rarely resort to violence, however, and see it as a terrible aberration. They do not abuse their children, men do not abuse women, and they do not engage in the organized violence of warfare. They talk things through, resolving conflicts as and within community. They understand well that violence is the bane of any partnership and that partnership is the essence of their lives on this Earth.

Obviously, much of the !Kung's way of living with one another derives from the unique characteristics of their world. Where there is no accumulation of things, there will be neither greed nor theft. Where communities are small-sized, true participatory democracy is more manageable. Where there are no great advantages to be gained from dominating others, cooperation comes easier.

I am by no means suggesting that the !Kung's culture is a valid model for modern men and women. They do, however, prove that partnership is possible and that the fundamental doctrines of patriarchy are false. We are not irrevocably destined to male domination and violence by God, social roles, or sexual biology. When taken with the archaeological and mythological evidence for our partnership past, the experience of the !Kung and similar primitive cultures, helps to open our minds and clear the way to create something different. If we can believe that men and women *have* lived and *do* live as partners, then perhaps we can imagine such a life for ourselves.

Personal Reflections

Do you have any experiences of true partnership in your present life? Who are the people that you easily share power with? Do you have intimate friends of the opposite gender? Do you experience equality with those of other races? Do you feel comfortable with those of other religions? Do you feel superior to those who are poorer or wealthier than you? Do you feel inferior to those who are wealthier or poorer than you?

Do you think children should strictly follow the will of their parents and elders? Can you imagine honoring and respecting a child's reality as equal to your own?

Do you have difficulty sharing power with women? Do you often feel intimidated by beautiful women? Do you easily take orders from a woman? Could you receive spiritual guidance from a woman? Can you imagine working alongside women without experiencing sexual tension or creative conflict?

Do you have difficulty sharing power with men? Do you often feel intimidated by big, strong men? Do you think men are just naturally competitive? Can you imagine working alongside men without experiencing sexual tension or creative conflict?

Can you imagine a world in which cooperation replaces competition as a central organizing principle? Can you imagine women and men cooperating in the raising of children? Can you imagine businesses cooperating to build the best products and provide the best services? Can you imagine the different branches of government cooperating to manage a nation's affairs? Can you imagine different nations cooperating to solve global challenges?

Can you imagine living in a partnership world? Will you imagine?

FOUR
The Great Reversal

The basic doctrines of patriarchy have been attempts to prove the inevitability of patriarchal culture by showing that there can be no other way: God the Father ordains dominant/submissive relationship; our social roles require it; our biological and psychological differences invoke it; historical progress causes it. Human nature is presumed to be designed for patriarchal culture: We have experienced patriarchy from the very beginning, and the evolution of our societies has followed the inexorable logic of domination ever since. Such are the doctrines of patriarchal inevitability.

Yet the strong likelihood of a partnership past, coupled with the evidence of living partnership cultures such as the !Kung, somewhat undermine the doctrines of patriarchal inevitability. The holy word of God the Father is largely of human invention. Differences in social roles and sexual biology and psychology do not of necessity lead to the structures and abuses of domination. Nor do advances of civilization, such as the discovery of agriculture, necessarily cause patriarchal patterns of relationship. These realizations prompt the question: If patriarchy is neither the way life has always been, nor the way life has to be, how then do we account for it?

In attempting an answer, I would first like to clarify the term *patriarchal inevitability.* There are at least two different ways in which patriarchal relationship is said to be inevitable.

First, a supposed inevitability stems from *immutable* facts of life that necessarily condition human reality regardless of human choices. The biological differences between men and women, for instance, have always existed and will for the most part never change. So if we believe that differences in genitalia, sexual response, physical musculature, or hormonal secretions necessarily cause dominant/submissive patterns of relationship, then our world is inevitably patriarchal. The fact that women have babies and men do not will probably never change. So again, if we believe that the social demands of birthing, nurturing, providing for, and protecting a child necessarily cause dominant/submissive patterns of relationship, then our world is inevitably patriarchal. Complaining about patriarchy, from this perspective, is like complaining about one's gender, or one's height at maturity, or the color of one's skin. Once we posit any unchanging fact about humans as a necessary cause of patriarchal relationship, we are saying that patriarchy is now and forever inevitable.

A second level of patriarchal inevitability stems from *mutable* historic events, such as the rise of monotheism or the building of agrarian societies. There are many cultures, for instance, that worship a combination of male and female gods, while easily tolerating the diverse spiritual beliefs and practices of other cultures. It is clearly not inevitable that human beings choose a stern male deity who insists that he is the only God and who demands absolute conversion of all who believe otherwise. A survey of the world's monotheistic religions shows that they have spawned the most aggressively dominating societies on Earth. Though monotheistic religion represents a choice and thus is not inevitable, societies dominated by monotheistic religion tend to become patriarchal.

There are also many viable and healthy human cultures such as the !Kung that have never engaged in farming, so agriculture itself is hardly inevitable. However, amongst societies that have become agrarian, there is a strong tendency to shift toward patriarchal patterns of relationship, with the major exceptions to this being the partnership cultures of the Neolithic era.

There are two levels of inevitability demonstrated here, and the difference between them reflects the creative power of human choice. One level states that immutable biological and social conditions cause our lives to be the way they are. Rocks are hard, water is wet, and humans are inevitably patriarchal. Nobody created patriarchy, nobody caused it to happen, and nobody can significantly alter its course today. Since humans were not creatively involved in causing the world to be patriarchal, they should not concern themselves with trying to cause the world to be any different.

The second level of inevitability states that, once specific events or changes in *some* human societies occurred, these societies inevitably shifted toward patriarchy. The necessity of patriarchy, from this perspective, came *after and as a result of* free human choice. Social evolution proceeded in one direction for an agrarian, monotheistic culture and in an entirely different direction for a gatherer-hunter, pantheistic culture. Each culture faced and made specific choices that determined just how patriarchal or egalitarian they inevitably became. All human cultures face similar choices, and all similarly influence their own social evolution.

Those who adopted a monotheistic faith also altered other key aspects of their society. Restrictions were placed upon women's spiritual leadership and all indications of Goddess-based worship were eliminated. The conditioning of children shifted toward God the Father's demand for compliant girls and aggressive boys. Sexuality was forcibly suppressed and tightly controlled. War was embraced as a holy method for spreading God's word. Eventually, the adoption of monotheism made patriarchal relationship inevitable for all levels of society and, even worse, for all other societies that were marched upon and "saved."

Likewise, every tribe of gatherer-hunters that began the transition toward farming found themselves making a string of choices: Where do we settle down and plant? What do we plant? How do we plant? How do we keep it watered? How do we harvest? How much do we store? How do we process for better edibility? From these choices, new behaviors and technologies developed and the societies began to shift, for the most part, in the direction of patriarchy.

Monotheism and agriculture were only two of a confluence of mutable factors that led human beings into patriarchy. Yet a third, the appearance of organized violence (which we will soon explore in greater depth), added enormous thrust to the necessary development of dominator cultures. Such factors, taken together, have made patriarchy inevitable for our world. And, I should add, they have made the *immutable* factors of sexual biology and social roles seem all the more reasonable as original causes of patriarchy. Early humans made specific choices, from which patriarchy developed. Early humans, then, were creatively involved in the future direction of human social evolution.

This understanding leads to the sobering conclusion that we must be equally involved in the future direction of our own societies: The choices that we make now can and must significantly alter the next stage of human social evolution. Just as our ancestors made choices that led to patriarchy, so must we take responsibility for leading our world beyond patriarchy. We must purposefully evolve toward the necessities of human partnership.

Clearly, if the ways of patriarchy continue to evolve—toward bigger and better bombs, greater technologies of land-rape and pollution, and the persistent focusing of power and money in the hands of the few—then our world is in serious trouble. The dangerous logic of domination must give way to the life-embracing logic of cooperation. Human social evolution must shift, soon, at all levels, toward partnership culture.

The next stage of our evolution can weaken, disfavor, and diminish the ways of domination. The next stage of our evolution can strengthen, empower, and expand the ways of cooperation and living in partnership: man with woman, people with people, and human with nature. We are poised on the brink of evolutionary possibility. Our future evolution will follow specific human choices, and we are challenged to positively alter the whole fabric of human existence. Nothing less than a global, pan-species transformation will do, and we, through the powers of creative human choice, are the doers.

A Turn upon the Wheel

The current crisis is not just a crisis of individuals, governments, or social institutions; it is a transition of planetary dimensions. —*Fritjof Capra*[1]

Many of those calling for such a sweeping transition are using the term *paradigm change*, first suggested by Thomas Kuhn in *The Structure of Scientific Revolutions*. The controlling paradigm of a society, Willis Harmon writes, "refers to *the basic ways of perceiving, thinking, valuing, and doing, associated with a particular view of reality*."[2] When a controlling paradigm changes, that is, when people's perceptions, thoughts, value systems, and activities undergo significant transformation, then cultural reality changes. In essence, what it means and how it feels to be human changes. Most paradigm changes are themselves brought about by the creative choices of human beings; all paradigm changes are times when human nature significantly changes, for better or for worse.

One often-cited example of a major paradigm change was the great transformation caused in sixteenth-century Europe by Copernicus's assertion and proof that the Earth was not the fixed center of the Solar System. In removing Earth, and thus man, from the central place in the universe, Copernicus's ideas ultimately impacted all aspects of his contemporary society. "The Copernican revolution amounted to a successful challenge to the entire system of ancient authority, requiring a complete change in the philosophical conception of the universe. It was heresy on the grand scale . . . and we now look back on it as an unqualifiedly positive evolutionary step."[3] The creative process of a single man powerfully influenced the present cultural reality and the future evolution of his society.

Other major paradigm changes have occurred with the rise of monotheism, the advance of agricultural society, the Cartesian-

Industrial Revolution, and the Nuclear Age. Though one might question whether each of these changes represents a "positive evolutionary step," there is no doubt that in each case cultural reality—what it means and how it feels to be human—has been significantly altered. People made collective choices that determined, or made inevitable, their own future social evolution.

Unfortunately, most of the paradigm changes during the past five thousand years have been of dubious merit since human social evolution has largely been driven by the dangerous logic of domination. Generation after generation, humans have degenerated toward the necessities of patriarchy. It is this nearly inevitable degeneration of human nature that we must ultimately address and reverse if we are ever to live in a partnership world.

Many different traditions around the world refer to the onset of this degeneration of essential human nature as "the Fall." Though not all would agree that the Fall marked the beginning of patriarchy, and though many consider the Fall more a metaphor for a necessary stage in the evolution of human consciousness than a historic event, there is general agreement that a radical shift in human nature occurred in the early stages of civilized culture. A great sorrow, achingly palpable in the surviving literature of the time, seemed to overtake the human race. The Fall, according to Joseph Campbell, was a time when "the one point not previously conceded so much as a place on the [human] agenda, namely the moral problem of suffering, moved to the center of the stage, where it has remained ever since."[4]

Campbell called this time the "Great Reversal," a period marked by an end of the easy innocence of our ancient ancestors and the coming of the many tortured faces of human suffering. "The Great Reversal," writes mythologist Jamake Highwater, "was an epic moment in history, when a negative conception of destiny arose that would eventually be symbolized by that Original Sin which makes pain and punishment an implacable aspect of Western life."[5] Campbell goes further, suggesting the universality of the Fall, or Great Reversal: "In the Buddha's teaching, the image of the turning spoked wheel, which in the earlier period had been symbolic of the world's glory, thus became a sign, on one hand, of the wheeling round of sorrow, and, on the other, release in the sunlike doctrine of illumination. And in the classical world the turning spoked wheel appeared also at this time as an emblem rather of life's defeat and pain than of victory and exhilaration."[6] Richard Heinberg, in his survey of the world's Paradise myths, also stresses the universality of the Fall: "In no tradition does the Golden Age last forever. According to all peoples, Paradise came to a tragic end."[7]

I am proposing that there was indeed a Fall—a Great Reversal, a monumental paradigm change, a historic period during which what it meant and how it felt to be human was profoundly altered. I am further proposing that at the core of this monumental change was a universal shifting to patriarchal relationship, and that this shift followed certain choices made by early human cultures. Though we may, in the grand scheme of things, come to view this great change as a positive evolutionary step, there can be no question that over the past few thousand years it has been a hard fall and tragic reversal from the early promise of partnership culture.

I believe, along with many others, that we are now living through an equally monumental paradigm change, the chief characteristic of which will be the final passing of patriarchy. My whole purpose in writing this book is to lend support to the change and to give some sense of where we might be heading and how to get there. An important step toward understanding this current transformation is exploring in greater depth its mirror opposite, the Great Reversal that took place some four to five thousand years ago: the global shift from partnership culture to patriarchal domination.

The Saddest Story

Life became known as a fiery vortex of delusion, desire, violence and death, a burning waste.
—*Joseph Campbell*[8]

The war between the ancient matricentric and new patricentric mentality was fought out in the world of myth.
—*Jamake Highwater*[9]

For every Paradise, there is a Fall; for every Golden Age, an Age of Sorrow. All of the world's mythologies agree. But are they really telling us of an historic fall into patriarchy?

On one level, the universal myth of the Fall is but a rich psychospiritual drama that has more to do with the evolution of human consciousness than any socio-historical event. Ken Wilbur argues in *Up From Eden* that the Fall represents the descent of the all-encompassing spirit into differentiated flesh, a moment from which humans have been evolving upward ever since. Jungians assert that the Fall is a stage of growth in the collective unconscious of the human species. Buddhism teaches that the Fall is just another turn upon the eternal wheel of life. From such perspectives, myths of Paradise and the Fall are powerful metaphors arising from the depths of the human soul to give meaning and direction to our lives as they forever unfold.

Still, some myths certainly have their roots in history, and some myths of the Fall are surely describing the passing of prehistoric partnership cultures. As with other aspects of the Paradise myth, certain themes consistently appear in the story of the Fall.

Above all, the Fall involved a clear change in human character for the worse. While people had lived close to the gods, and in harmony with nature and each other, they now experienced a sudden debasement, degeneration, and loss of wholeness. Aberrant behaviors arose, with people becoming so cruel and rapacious that ultimately the gods themselves withdrew from the earth, leaving the people to their "suspicion, fear, greed, mistrust, and violence."[10] Truly, a Great Reversal.

The appearance of violence is, I think, quite significant. In many African myths, for instance, the first sign and cause of the Fall is people striking out against animals, killing them for no good reason and thus terribly offending nature and the gods. In most of the world's myths, sudden human violence closely corresponds with, or is the first cause of, the Fall. Though it may well be that violence was just one of the many *effects* of the Fall (as in Genesis, when Cain murders Abel *after* expulsion from the Garden), the connection between violence and the Fall is an important one, as noted in many mythologies. The end of Paradise was marked by the sudden and tragic appearance of human violence.

Richard Heinberg offers that a primary cause of the Fall was a commitment by the first people of some foolish and irreversible act of disobedience for which all of humankind was forever punished. Lilith spoke the name of God, Eve ate the apple, Pandora opened the box, and, there you go: damned for all time. Leaving aside the interesting detail that Lilith, Eve, and Pandora are all women, what strikes me most about the notion of innocent disobedience leading to divine retribution is how thoroughly patriarchal it is. An eternal spanking for one childish prank; massively abusive punishment for a single transgression of the law: such mythological features are more probably reflections of life *under* patriarchy than reliable descriptions of the fall from partnership.

This illustrates a problem that vexes all of our attempts to understand the past. We are always looking backward through the cultural haze of present reality, and even the most solid of physical evidence can be shaded by the personal biases of an archaeologist or historian. This is especially true of efforts to envision the coming or passing of patriarchy. Steeped as we are in the all-encompassing reality of patriarchal domination and the virtually unquestioned "laws" of human aggression and violence, it is difficult to even imagine some other way of living. This is why so many people routinely accept that dominant/submissive relationship is our natural state, and it is why the doctrines of patriarchal inevitability make such unrelenting sense.

Indeed, the myth of innocent disobedience leading to divine retribution is itself but another immutable doctrine of patriarchal inevitability. To assume that God the Father was there from the start, issuing his commands and decrees while almost casually inflicting abuse on uppity women and the like, is to deny any possibility of partnership culture. *If humans were born into a dominator's Garden then there never was any Paradise to fall from.* The myth of disobedience was surely created at some point *after* the Fall. It is just what we would expect to spring from the psyche of a patriarchally abused people—or to be invented by dominators with a mind toward strengthening their grip.

A second common mythological theme that Heinberg cites as a possible cause of the Fall is humanity's acquisition of the knowledge of good and evil. "Then, some were aware that there were distinctions, but not yet aware that there was right and wrong among them. When right and wrong became manifest, the Tao thereby declined."[11] So wrote the Taoist philosopher Chuang Tzu (fifth century B.C.), in close harmony with the Genesis tale of the tree of knowledge. In this theme, the Fall is caused not so much by a foolish mistake as by a natural process of human evolution. Ignorance *was* bliss, while the evolving capacity to reason over good and bad and to decide right and wrong—the intelligence to make distinctions—led invariably to judgment and discrimination, and thence to suffering. In this way, women and men who were living as partners may have actually *progressed* into alienation and separation. Patriarchy, then, is not so much a Fall as a stage along our journey "up from Eden."

Heinberg found that forgetfulness was another common mythological reason for the Fall. "According to Gnostic, Hindu, and Buddhist traditions, it is the act of forgetting one's true identity and purpose, because of distraction with the physical world, that produces the misery of the fallen condition."[12] As with the knowledge of good and evil, this spiritual amnesia is not so much a mistake that humans made as an inescapable condition of incarnation. Some would even say that we intentionally forget our true nature upon entering this world so as to make life interesting—a world without separate and alienated creatures would have no drama, no challenge, and no lessons learned. In any case, once we have forgotten, it is only a short fall into the abuses of patriarchy.

Finally, there are the countless myths of great floods, earthquakes, volcanic eruptions, famines, and other environmental traumas (many of which are confirmed by historic and archaeological records). While Heinberg lists these as *effects* of the Fall, and while many myths tell of such global upheavals as punishment for our ancestor's sins, this is surely more divine retribution for innocent disobedience. Again, it is to be expected that people living in a patriarchal world would look back on a terrible ecological disaster and see it as God the Father's wrath for human indiscretions. It follows that such people could only create myths to reflect this belief.

What we modern people know too well is that changes in the environment can powerfully control the direction of a society, often in the most dehumanizing ways. It is quite possible that the recurring image of the deluge in the world's mythologies is an accurate reporting of the simplest, yet most unavoidable of reasons for our Fall from Paradise: the environment turned harsh and abusive, and we turned with it.

The Battle-Axe People, the Thunder God

> Man cut the umbilical cord to the Great Mother with a sword, and it has been hanging over his head ever since.
> —*William Irwin Thompson*[13]

"At first it was like the proverbial biblical cloud 'no bigger than a man's hand'—the activities of seemingly insignificant nomadic bands roaming the less desirable fringe areas of our globe seeking grass for their herds."[14] So writes Riane Eisler as she begins to answer the question of what brought the partnership cultures to an end.

"Over millennia they were apparently out there in the harsh, unwanted, colder, sparser territories on the edges of the Earth, while the first great agricultural civilizations spread out along the lakes and rivers in the fertile heartlands. To these agricultural peoples, enjoying humanity's early peak of evolution, peace and prosperity must have seemed the blessed eternal state for humankind, the nomads no more than a peripheral novelty."[15] History, we know too well, had other plans. The small bands of nomadic herders became larger bands, and with time began raiding the outskirts of the peaceful Neolithic settlements. Raids grew into full-scale invasions, in wave after wave over several millennia, until, some four thousand years ago, the world historic defeat of part-nership culture was complete.

For the most part, these warrior peoples came from the Eurasian steppes to the north, though one rather significant tribe, the Semites, came out of the southern desert. They are usually referred to as Kurgans (Russian for "burial mound," a distinctive feature of these peoples) or Indo-Europeans, and in specific instances as Aryans, Hittites, Achaeans, or Dorians. *"The one thing they all had in common was a dominator model of social organization*: a social system in which male dominance, male violence, organized warfare, and a generally hierarchic and authoritarian social structure was the norm."[16]

Another vital characteristic of the invader cultures was the primary worship of God the Father. Merlin Stone reports that "it was these northern people who brought with them the concepts of light as good and dark as evil (very possibly the symbolism of their racial attitudes toward the darker people of the southern areas) and of a supreme male deity."[17] As we have already seen, God the Father and his servants showed no mercy in the violent suppression and outright eradication of Goddess worship wherever she was encountered.

What occurred during this period of invasions was a total and irreconcilable clash of cultures, much like the coming of Europeans to the American continents. The invading cultures were fundamentally structured toward domination: they had metal weapons and military tactics, a patriarchal social system, an expansionist philosophy, and an all-commanding monotheology. The Goddess cultures were fundamentally structured toward partnership and simply powerless to prevent this unfortunate tide of history.

The first wave of invasions occurred in Old Europe in the middle of the fifth millennium B.C., and the final destruction of Crete came some three thousand years later. The chronology of this violent history is precisely recorded in the archaeological remains of the known partnership cultures of Crete, Çatal Hüyük, and Old Europe. There is a gradual appearance of fortifications in towns that had previously shown no indications of warfare. Evidence of patriarchal social structures increases throughout the period, even as the numbers of discovered Goddess figurines steadily decline. Burial practices go through a profound change, with many indications that high status was shifting to male warriors and kings. Metal weapons appear, as do art works glorifying violence and the Thunder Gods of war and destruction.

Eisler stresses that a fundamental characteristic of the conquering civilization was that it valued the destructive powers of the blade over the life-generating powers of the chalice. "[The invaders] characteristically acquired wealth not by developing technologies of production, but through ever more effective technologies of destruction."[18] This, of course, has remained true of the dominators throughout history and into our present age: whatever legitimacy a dominant individual or group of individuals pretends to is always backed up by the ability to inflict the greatest abuse. Of the many factors and reasons contributing to the passing of partnership culture into patriarchy, the most compelling of all was the driving force of violence.

The Parable of the Tribes

Imagine a group of tribes living within reach of one another. If all choose the way of peace, then all may live in peace. But what if all but one choose peace . . . ?
—*Andrew Bard Schmookler* [19]

The Parable of the Tribes is both the title of a book and the essence of a remarkably elegant theory of social evolution offered by Andrew Bard Schmookler. Schmookler's concern is with the seeming inevitability of coercive power in human civilizations. He defines power as "the capacity to achieve one's will against the will of another. The exercise of power thus infringes upon the exercise of choice, for to be the object of another's power is to have his choice substituted for one's own."[20] His definition of power matches the definition of domination I have been using.

Schmookler suggests that power became an issue in human relations when the activities of differing groups began to encroach upon one another. He believes that steady increases in human population eventually brought individual societies, or tribes, into contact. Natural conflict arose over mutual needs and desires for land and resources. "As the expanding capacities of human societies created an overlap in the range of their grasp and desire, the intersocietal struggle for power arose."[21] Each society, exercising its freedom of choice, began to infringe upon the free will of other societies. The society that could best "infringe upon" or dominate others tended toward more certain survival.

Schmookler's question, "What if all but one choose peace?" is the crux of the Parable of the Tribes. If, in the pursuit of conflicting desires, one society resorts to violent domination, *then every other society of necessity is driven toward similar behavior.* The only other choices, such as they are, are to be destroyed, to be absorbed into the dominator's culture, or to retreat to new territories. However, *"in every one of these outcomes the ways of power are spread throughout the system."*[22] If a society is determined to survive intact, it must meet the threat of violence by itself becoming aggressively dominating or passively submissive. This is what Schmookler calls "the dangerous logic of power." Once social evolution selects according to aggressive domination, all societies are compelled toward dominant/submissive patterns of relationship. All societies are thus compelled toward patriarchy.

The irony, as Schmookler details, "is that successful defense against a power-maximizing aggressor requires a society to become more like the society that threatens it. . . . The defensive society will have to transform itself into something more like its foe in order to resist the external force."[23] If just one society is driven by the Thunder God and battle-axe mentality, then, with time, all societies will be. Once the dominator's means and methods enter into human relations, all human relations slide into patriarchy. Viewed in this way, domination is a social virus that eventually infects all aspects of society once it has entered the system.

The partnership cultures of the Neolithic era obviously found other ways to deal with conflicting desires between groups and individuals, for their societies showed few signs of the dangerously contaminating logic of power. They must have settled disputes through noncoercive means, respecting the inherent equality of all parties. They surely understood creative power as a force linking people (power-with), rather than a weapon to be marshalled against others (power-over). Within their domination-free territories, they created the healthiest of human civilizations. Unfortunately, the poison of patriarchal abuse, once it was loose in the world, was bound to contaminate all human societies sooner or later.

Still, the questions remain. Why would early humans choose violence? How did coercive aggression and abuse get loose in our world? Schmookler, with many others, sees the choice of violence as an inevitable result of civilization, an assertion that the civilizations of Crete, Çatal Hüyük, and Old Europe would seem to contradict. Indeed, without the examples of those civilizations to temper our views, the Parable of the Tribes becomes just another immutable doctrine of patriarchal inevitability. Though we may accept the spreading of patriarchal patterns of relationship as an inevitable outcome of the meeting between the northern invaders and the Neolithic partnerships, we do not have to accept that the northerners were inevitably dominator cultures. In our search for the Fall, the question remains of how the invaders themselves became dominator-infected.

I believe that all of the theories reviewed so far hold some measure of the truth. Most likely, it was a complex combination of factors, some mutable and some not so mutable, that pushed early humans through the upheavals of the Great Reversal. I am especially intrigued by the role of the environment. Several years of harsh winters and arid summers, plus an earthquake or two, could easily have driven one or more tribes toward mean-spirited and overly aggressive behavior, and a dominator plague would be underway. But that's just another theory.

The beauty of the Parable of the Tribes is that we really do not have to know how the Great Reversal got started, nor must we concern ourselves with assigning blame. If our goal is to responsibly encourage another changing of paradigms—a second Great Reversal—then it is enough to understand the virally-spreading, self-sustaining, dangerous logic of patriarchal abuse. We are all victims *and carriers* of this ancient disease of human culture.

Personal Reflections

> One aggressive and potent actor upon the scene can impose on each of the others the necessity of gaining power to protect itself, or the inevitability of becoming absorbed into the power of another. Thus, because power acts as a contaminant, it is also in such a system a necessity.
> —*Andrew Bard Schmookler*[24]

Look for the workings of the Parable of the Tribes in your own life. Look for the relationships in which you feel forced into patterns of dominant/submissive behavior. Look for the situations in which you are coerced by a greater will. Look for the situations in which you are the greater will coercing another. Look for the times that you feel compelled to follow the dangerous logic of power.

Who are the people that currently hold power over you? Your parents? Your spouse? Your employer? Your therapist? Teachers? Bankers? Doctors? Authorities? The government? The church? How do you usually respond to people who hold power over you? By submitting? By retreating? By becoming more aggressive?

How might you respond differently to such people? What powers-within could you draw upon? Is it possible to assert your power without compelling the dangerous logic of domination? How?

Who are the people that you currently hold power over? Your children? Your spouse? Your employees? Your clients? Students? Those who are weaker? smaller? poorer? less intelligent? Can you see when you are coercing them—forcing them into patterns of submission, retreat, or increasing domination?

What would it mean to share power with such people? What would it look like? What changes can you make in your communications and behavior to engender greater cooperation? How can you use your power to lead the way to partnership?

FIVE

The Dominator Virus

My reference to the "social virus of domination" may be perceived as just a metaphor, as in "power contaminates social systems in the same way that viruses infect biological systems." However, I conceive that the "dominator virus" functions much like a biological virus and that our ability to free ourselves of its debilitating effects rests on understanding it as such.

"Viruses are the simplest of all reproducing creatures," writes Guy Murchie. "In a sense a virus is a gene with a coat on, out wandering about the world, for its core is made of either deoxyribonucleic acid (DNA) or its subsidiary ribonucleic acid (RNA), carrying hereditary information and wrapped in protein."[1] A virus is a spiral of densely packed information about living processes enfolded within the most rudimentary of material forms. However, a virus cannot reproduce by itself: it requires a living host cell. Left to itself, a virus resembles and acts much like an ultramicroscopic rock or crystal that may sit inertly for hundreds of years.

"Yet, unlike a rock, it may 'wake up' at any moment. All it needs is the warmth and moisture of some vulnerable cell that it can swiftly enter and infect, in the same motion reproducing itself hundreds of times within the hour."[2] A virus can even lie dormant within a host cell, sleeping for many years before suddenly coming alive with venomous force. When it does wake up, it forces the host cell to manufacture "protein coats" for its own unique information, thus engaging in reproduction. In the end, the virus often gets to dominate its environment while the host cell is maimed or destroyed for its unwitting assistance.

In 1918, a single influenza virus spread throughout the world, killing twenty million people. Though we have learned much about the flu virus since then, every winter brings a new outbreak of the flu, and we are no closer to curing the flu "bug" or common cold than we were seventy-five years ago. This points to a striking characteristic of the virus: its ability to continuously and rapidly adapt to a changing world. (We usually use the word *mutate* when describing the evolution of creatures we fear; I prefer not to blame the virus for its lifestyle.) We will forever have difficulty finding "final solutions" to viruses because they have an innate capacity to learn from new information in their world and to evolve accordingly.

A virus is pure DNA—the same DNA that is the foundation of all organic life. A virus is genetic information packaged in the merest material form necessary to allow for viable movement from one organism to another—a "gene with a coat on, out wandering about the world." While the virus's "coat" is made of simple proteins, what exactly is the gene made of?

Strict materialists will answer, "Strands of DNA and RNA, which are in turn made up of the nucleic acids adenine, thymine, cytosine, guanine, and uracil." Like Cartesian physicists, such scientists seem confident that we can describe a basic indivisible building block of life, something solid and objectively real. DNA and RNA seem solid enough, and the steady deciphering of the universal genetic code, leading to steady advances in our ability to biomechanically alter genes for specific purposes, offers much validation. The fact of genetic engineering alone suggests that genes are solid little structures that can be intentionally manipulated by intelligent humans.

Yet we also know that genes can change, or evolve, without the help of human engineers. When we consider that our minds and bodies are connected, interwoven, and wholly subsumed with living human consciousness, these microscopic packets of information take on even more fluidity and mutability. As Deepak Chopra writes, "You may not think that you can 'talk' to your DNA (another prejudice that comes from seeing DNA as only a material blueprint), but in fact you do continually. The fleeting chemicals that race through you at the touch of thought, the receptors hanging out on the cell wall waiting for their messages, and every other speck of life are manufactured by DNA. . . . Thinking happens at the level of DNA, because without the brain cell sending out a neuropeptide or other messenger, there can be no thought."[3]

Once more, we are reminded that there *is no* actual separation between body, mind, and spirit. Therefore, our emotional, mental, sexual, and spiritual energies must be interactive with our most elemental cellular processes. "I have little doubt," writes Murchie, that "genes know what they are doing, for they are memory incarnate, letters of living purpose, the script of life in a material universe. Stretching my imagination a little, I can think of them as grains of mind or even psychic feathers or scales, as veritable units of thought 'made flesh.'"[4] If we stretch our imaginations wide enough to include the creative powers of human consciousness, then the idea that genes are mutable is truly a source of positive encouragement.

The virus, then, can also be seen as a fluid, mutable bundle (or field) of information that necessarily interacts with and is affected by whatever host body it inhabits. Moreover, when a virus inhabits and is affected by a human body, it is certainly also affected by the specific qualities of vitality and consciousness of that human.

Thus, we play host to a variety of viruses throughout our lives, and yet most remain dormant, never reproducing and thus threatening our health. Why does a flu virus suddenly "wake up" in your body, but not in the body of your equally flu-inhabited spouse? Why, for that matter, did it wake up in your body one day after sitting inertly for many months? And why, in a question of pandemic urgency, does the virus that causes AIDS (HIV) remain dormant in one body while exploding into illness in another?

Strictly biomechanical answers to these questions have pointed to excessive stress and breakdowns in the immune system. Holistic answers include the biomechanical ones but go further, asserting that excess stress and immune dysfunction both are rooted in psychoemotional causation. The physical state that finally gives in to a virus, allowing it to come awake, is understood to be the result of mostly unconscious mental, emotional, and sexual-energetic personal patterns. I may harbor the flu virus (and many others) for my entire life; I will *get* the flu only if I have rendered myself vulnerable through specific patterns of behavior, thought, feeling, and energy exchange. And when I do get sick, it is an opportunity to learn—to update my bodily wisdom on the current nature of the world—and to become that much stronger in the process.

HIV is, I believe, especially responsive to the consciousness of its host and may thus be the quintessential teacher of our times, for it is a "retrovirus." Unlike most viruses, HIV is not content to wait outside a cell wall until circumstances permit its entry and reproduction. Instead, it goes right in and blends itself into the host's DNA. It takes off its "coat" and, as pure DNA, intertwines itself with the host's DNA—which makes it frustratingly invisible, highly mutable, and extremely difficult to deal with.

As long as we look for the "building blocks" of HIV, I have no doubt that we will fight the same sort of permanent losing war against AIDS that we have been fighting for so many years against cancer and the common cold. If instead we look for the unique field of information that is HIV and pay close attention to its relationship with the larger fields of consciousness of its human host, then we will make genuine progress and learn much about human beings in the process. HIV is information about our world and the current state of human affairs; when we stop trying to kill the messenger and begin instead to really listen to and learn from it, we will initiate a powerful transformation in human relationship.

Another modern virus deserves a brief mention here. Much like HIV, a typical computer virus is a bundle of specific information that under certain circumstances can totally incapacitate its host, in this case a computer. A computer virus is created within the electrical field of its creator's computer. It may then be encoded onto a floppy disk—a temporary coat for the field of information—or it may be transmitted directly through energetic computer connections (modems and telephone lines) without ever putting on a physical coat. When such a virus invades an unaware and unprotected computer system, it inserts itself, retrovirus-like, into the computer's controlling information. Then it waits until the right moment to wake up and do its thing. Like any biological virus, a computer virus is pure information with the minimal form necessary to viably move from one host to another. Ultimately, every bout with an especially nasty virus makes the computer world that much wiser.

Given the above, is it accurate to speak of the "dominator virus"? I think so. When two people meet and one inflicts domina-tor-type abuse upon the other, a whole matrix of information about the nature of the world and human relationship is "transmitted" through the abuse. The man who forces himself sexually upon a woman is psychoemotionally contaminating her with ideas of shame, sin, inadequacy, helplessness, and weakness. Wealthy people who use their financial power to manipulate and control less-advantaged people are passing on the most rudimentary of "truths" about the "real" world. Parents who physically or ver-bally abuse their children are spreading the most viral of poisons from old bodies to young bodies, teaching, "This is the nature of human relationship."

A person suffering any form of human-inflicted abuse is as a matter of course conditioned to dominant/submissive relation-ship: a specific bundle or field of information about the world enters into and intertwines with the person's beliefs, opinions, attitudes, philosophies, dreams, expectations, and patterns of be-havior. Such poisonous information ultimately seeps into the person's essential nature, thus affecting and infecting all her or his future relationships. Domination is always abusive, always infec-tious, and almost always virally self-perpetuating.

The dominator virus obviously does not move about the world in the protein coat of HIV or an influenza virus. Rather, it is passed on through specific interactions among people. Like a computer virus carried along the electrical connections between computers, the dominator virus moves along the vital connections between humans: family relations, physical contacts (especially violence), sexual intercourse, verbal communications, strong emotional interactions, financial dealings, shared work, and professional relationships such as doctor/patient, teacher/student, and therapist/client all are potential coats for a specific, dominating bundle of information. If the underlying pattern in a relationship dictates that one person exert power over the other, and if a vital exchange occurs to coat and carry such a pattern, then the dominator virus is passed along.

Like a retrovirus, the dominator virus does not need its coat once it has invaded and corrupted the human organism. Its information about reality and human relationship, once transmitted, is encoded in the vital heart of each cell—it becomes virtual human nature. The micropatriarchies of traditional families and the larger patriarchies of organizations and governments, through their continual transmission of the dangerous logic of power-over, naturally serve to reinforce the virus's internal grip. The doctrines of patriarchal inevitability seem as indisputable as any scientific fact because domination has been carved into the cellular processes of most all human bodies and into the primary commandments of most all human relationships.

We can no more avoid the dominator virus than we can a common flu virus. Nor, however, must we manifest the aberrant sickness of dominant/submissive relationship any more than we must get the flu. The dominator virus, manifesting as "grains of mind," is entirely confined within and controlled by the greater consciousness in which it resides. We can consciously choose, always, the direction and continuing pattern of relationships in our lives. We can be consciously interactive, always, with our most fundamental structures of body and mind. And we can always (however slowly) be consciously shifting our personal and political worlds from patriarchy toward genuine partnership.

The key word here is *consciously*. If we are to free our bodies and societies of viral domination, we will need to greatly expand human consciousness about the connections of body, mind, and spirit; about childhood conditioning; about common and collective sexual abuse; and about dominant/submissive patterns of relationship. Most urgently, overcoming the dominator virus demands that we bring increasing awareness to infectious attitudes and behaviors within our family systems.

The Common Infection

> If we want to diminish violence, not just punish it, we have to take seriously the overwhelming evidence that those whose minds and bodies are invaded and treated with violence in childhood are the most likely to continue wounding others, themselves, or both.
>
> —*Gloria Steinem*[5]

The dominator virus is primarily spread through the family; long-infected parents, however loving, naturally pass their poisons on to their children. The best of "coats" for the virus are familial relationships: physical and sexual contacts, verbal communications, and strong emotional interactions. If the older members of a family are unaware of the nature of their own psychoemotional disease, they can only infect their children. Such family contamination is so normal and so unconscious that it can continue unquestioned for thousands of years despite its fundamental abusiveness.

In effect, every family reenacts the Parable of the Tribes. The parable is not limited to describing the behavior between groups: it pertains to all manner of human relationships. When any two members of a family have conflicting desires, and the conflicts are resolved through coercive, power-maximizing dynamics—such as the father exerting power over the mother, or a parent exerting power over a child—then the whole family is exposed to the dominator virus. The dominating poison of one person in the family spreads throughout the system, forcing all the others to think, perceive, feel, and act in much the same way.

Nowhere is this process more apparent and more urgent to

address than in our treatment of infants and children. *Babies are born free of the dominator virus.* They are beings of love incarnate and, treated as such, will only grow into greater love for themselves and others. Children, potentially, are innocent of all violent drives and abusive behaviors; they are designed for pleasure, play, and the mutual respect of human partnership. Every new child brings the promise of Paradise back into the world and will fulfill that promise if given sufficient love, compassion, and support.

Unfortunately, almost every new child is conditioned instead with the poisons of dominator reality by those who are themselves infected. The collective abuses of patriarchal relationship are passed on—like a common infection—as the otherwise innocent child is fundamentally debased toward the necessities of domination and abuse.

Alice Miller has painstakingly documented the child's infection with the dominator virus and the resulting effects for society at large. She shows that what most people consider normal child-rearing is more often an insidiously poisonous pedagogy that terribly damages children and, for that matter, all members of the family. Moreover, she makes clear that, if we remain unconscious to the patriarchal contaminations within our families, we invariably create likewise contaminated societies.

Some of Miller's most provocative work examined the childhoods of the famous and infamous and then showed the connections between the poisonous pedagogy they received as children and the adults they later became. For instance, though it hardly absolves him of his actions, it is quite instructive to know that Adolph Hitler was beaten by his father throughout his childhood, that he witnessed on many occasions the violent abuse of his mother, and that he was treated literally like a dog. In his own words, from *Mein Kampf*: "At the age of six the pitiable little boy suspects the existence of things which can fill even an adult with nothing but horror. . . . All the other things that the little fellow hears at home do not tend to increase his respect for his dear fellow men."[6]

Similarly, the Romanian dictator Nicolae Ceausescu grew up

in dire poverty and was, with his nine brothers and sisters, regularly beaten by his alcoholic father. He took to torturing animals as a child and was in jail by the time he was a teenager. Again, this does not absolve him of his horrible crimes against his people, but it certainly does help us understand him, or at least sense the internal pains and horrors that drove him to inflict such pain upon others. Patriarchally abused, he grew into a violently abusive patriarch; dominator-infected, he became a deadly plague upon his society.

The dominator virus is most powerfully transmitted to children through physical and sexual abuse. The victims of such abuse can become society's most malignant individuals as they mature. When accurate biographies are available (and biographers have not ignored or overlooked poisonous pedagogy), the connection between childhood abuse and adult abusive behavior is readily apparent. Virtually all serial killers, as well as all murderers currently on death row in the United States, were victims of early abuse. Most battered wives were earlier in life physically abused by their fathers or mothers, as were most prostitutes. Those who evince the worse characteristics of patriarchal culture were invariably infected with the dominator virus through the worst of abuses at an early age.

Some will argue that while the dominator virus may be for real, and while poisonous pedagogy is clearly commonplace, few children grow into Adolph Hitlers or serial murderers. While most people may be born into dominant/submissive family patterns, few become violently abusive adults. We cannot blame our parenting, society, *or* the dominator virus, the argument goes: it is the individual who is ultimately responsible for how she or he turns out. If one person is capable of living through an abusive childhood without becoming abusive to others, then all should be able to. The sins and crimes of an individual are the failures of that individual; it is compounding failure to blame one's parents or society.

I have several responses to this argument. First, understanding that I am dominator-infected by my parental conditioning is *not* the same as blaming my parents for my present behavior. I am still a free agent, responsible for my own actions. But knowing the unique thrust of my childhood conditioning can help me to even greater freedom, for an unexamined childhood is being lived now, whether worthy or not. Moreover, I realize that my parents were conditioned by their parents too, who had parents also, who had parents also . . . It is not a question of laying blame, but of consciously naming, as a first step toward ending generations of patriarchally poisonous childrearing.

Second, while it is true that all abused children do not grow up to be Hitlers, the evidence strongly suggests that all Hitlers were terribly abused as children. Rather than ignoring the effects of poisonous pedagogy because some manage to overcome it, we should be working to end it altogether. Why beat, humiliate, humble, shame, dominate, or abuse *any* child, unless it is necessary to do so? *It is never necessary to do so.* Only time and experience will tell if history can create a Hitler, a serial killer, a slave, or a whore without the help of toxic parenting and patriarchal social conditioning. For all our perpetual yearning for solutions to the problems of this world, it would be monumental foolishness not to try something as simple as greeting the present generation of children with love, respect, honesty, and gentle protection.

Third, the fact that most children do not grow up to be violently abusive does not mean that they are uninfected by the patriarchal abuses of their childhood. Murder, rape and torture are only the far extremes of a broad spectrum of pathological behaviors that have their roots in poisonous pedagogy and the dominator virus. From the more personal problems of substance abuse, addictions, eating disorders, workaholism, low self-esteem, sexual aberrations, excessive phobias, suicidal tendencies, and nightmares to the greater problems of racism, sexism, bigotry, political and religious totalitarianism, and predatory capitalism, the psychoemotional poisons of childhood render us all damaged and tragically limited adults who can only create damaged and tragically limited societies.

Finally, the experiences of those who have survived the harshest of childhood abuse without becoming horribly pathological adults provide important insights into overcoming the dominator virus. According to Miller: "If mistreated children are not to become criminals or mentally ill, it is essential that at least once in their life they come in contact with a person who knows without any doubt that the environment, not the helpless, battered child, is at fault."[7] What every child needs is to be treated as an equal by at least one other person—a true ally, an adult who listens, hears, and respects the child's experience while offering honest and noncoercive support. Until we meet children as *differently equal partners* in life, we are only teaching them patriarchy, with its inevitable abuses.

But, of course and alas, we are fairly compelled to teach them patriarchy, as we ourselves were taught. From birth through childhood, the forces of human culture seem demonically driven to undermine and destroy a child's innate tendencies toward cooperation and partnership. The adults unconsciously inflict viral domination upon the child's primary condition of innocence and simple, bodily pleasure. The child is taught, "This is a hostile and abusive world; survival demands that you become hostile and abusive."

This teaching often begins with the well-intended abuses of techno-birthing (a hard slap on the buttocks of a terrified newborn is sexual abuse.) It continues through the various poisons of foolish pedagogues, the pleasure-is-sin-so-just-say-no morality of God the Father's followers, the unconscious avoidance of all things sexual where children are concerned, and the more malicious crimes of incest and rape.

This conditioning of children away from their original innocence—this spreading of the dominator virus—is a nearly universal fact of life. We tell ourselves that we are preparing our children for the "real" world with its inevitable pains and hardships. We worry that we are overindulging or pampering them if we allow them too much happiness or control of their affairs. We work to rein in their childish impulses and to provide them with "grown-up" disciplines and values. We eagerly coax them toward reading and writing and doing their sums while tragically undervaluing the more essential teachings of hugs and kisses and spontaneous, physical play. We try so hard to do everything "for their own good" even when so much of it clearly does not feel good.

We are especially harsh and abusive toward a child's innate sexuality. Our own sexual confusions and abusive patterns are projected into every act of diaper changing, bathing, feeding, dressing, and toilet training and can leave an indelible trail of shame within the child's body. The idea that masturbation is sinful, when forced upon a growing child whose fingers *must* explore, creates an insidious self-hatred. Likewise, the failure to positively prepare a boy for wet dreams or a girl for menstruation can turn these basic human events into utter tragedies. Above all, adults dutifully, if mostly unconsciously, inculcate their children with the sexual beliefs and expectations of their culture. This is unfortunate, since virtually all human cultures agree that pleasure must be controlled, that sexual energy must be repressed, and that any sexual contact between two people must be discouraged first and then tightly regulated.

We are thus led away from the innocent pleasures and intimate relationships of peaceful cooperation. Instead, we are conditioned to bodily displeasure, sexual sins and suppressions, vital disconnections, and the basic experience of human separation. We may be born to cellular joy and living partnership, but we are taught instead to distrust the body and live in a world of overriding patriarchal abuse.

This is the Great Reversal forced upon every new generation of girls and boys. This is the worst damage that can ever be done to human beings. The child who is conditioned to viral domination and patriarchal abuse takes on patterns of body and relationship that continuously dictate a patriarchal and abusive world. Once a child damns and suppresses the vibratory thrill and pulse of ever-innocent, sexual aliveness, the child is deeply wounded, perhaps never to fully recover. That we can take such damage in children for granted merely indicates how deeply wounded *we* are.

This is the passing on of the dominator virus. The long and depressing story of human violence is peopled with those who were conditioned as children to hate their bodies, to distrust pleasure, to disconnect from others, to suppress and deny their sexual energies, and to either aggressively dominate or passively submit to others as an unconscious strategy in life. There is nothing natural about such people nor the common abuses they inflict. We are not inevitably patriarchal. We are not inevitably abusive. Patriarchal abuse is neither our natural nor inevitable state; it is something we must be infected with, invariably, by those to whom we are most vulnerable.

In later chapters, I will explore in greater depth what it means to be an equal partner to a child, a spouse, an employee, a stranger, or a member of the opposite sex. For now, it is enough to acknowledge that any transition to a partnership world is heavily burdened by the dominator-infected patterns of our own childhoods. What we received as children largely affects our giving and receiving as adults. As Miller puts it, "Child-rearing is basically directed not toward the child's welfare but toward satisfying the parent's needs for power and revenge."[8] It follows that most human relationships are directed toward satisfying the individual's dominant/submissive needs that stem from family patterns.

Thus, any real transformation of our world must involve a significant change in how we raise our children. We must resolve the Parable of the Tribes as it plays out in the family; we must reverse, once and for all, the dangerous logic of viral domination. Until we manifest true partnership with our most intimate family members—until we heal the wounds of childhood and no longer carry and spread the dominator virus to others—we cannot expect our world to really change. The personal is political. Unless we become conscious of and move beyond the common poisons of our family systems, we will hardly notice, much less overcome, the collective poisons of our societies.

Domination and Denial

I tremble for my country when I reflect that God is just.
—*Thomas Jefferson*[9]

Thomas Jefferson owned slaves. So did George Washington, John Adams, James Madison, James Monroe, and a majority of the founders of America, so commonly accepted was the practice. Still, it is most bothersome to think of Jefferson as a slave owner. The man who so inspired our documents of freedom and who wrote that "all men are created equal" also owned other human beings to be commanded as his personal property.

Jefferson is known to have treated his slaves well compared to other slave owners. He worried over their living conditions, taught some to read and write, and freed many, though not all, of his slaves before he died. Moreover, he actively supported the abolitionist cause, he bravely worked toward emancipation for the state of Virginia, and he spoke and wrote often against the abominations of slavery and the slave trade.

Yet the fact remains that throughout his lifetime he engaged in the buying and selling of human beings to support and sustain the plantation lifestyle of Monticello and the old South. In so doing, he freely participated in a system that kidnapped able-bodied men, women, boys, and girls from African villages; that killed any who resisted or stood in the way; that forced a long ocean voyage under inhumane and often lethal conditions; and that fostered the frequent use of shackles, whips, rape, and murder.

I raise this issue not to denigrate Thomas Jefferson, a man I greatly admire, but to ask, *How is it possible*, this capacity for otherwise good, intelligent, and well-intentioned men (and women) to behave so poorly toward other human beings? As Jefferson biographer Fawn Brodie has stressed, "Jefferson was too sensitive not to see the contradiction in his own life between theory and action."[10] Then how did he do it? How did he courageously devote his life to the cause of freedom while simultaneously profiting from the inherent abuses of slavery?

In Jefferson's defense, it must be said that two hundred years ago the patriarchal enslavement of others (wives, children, and strangers) was not only well accepted, but had been a common and barely questioned practice since the days of Sumer and Babylon. Every major civilization for five thousand years of human history had countenanced the abusive subordinations of slavery. It was supported philosophically by such thinkers as Plato and Aristotle. It was seen as good Christian treatment for women and other inferior people. It was considered a natural practice, like raising sheep and cattle. Most importantly, it made sound economic sense, for the prosperous throughout history were those who owned the most slaves.

In light of this historical context, Jefferson and his compatriots can hardly be blamed for founding yet another dominator culture. The genocidal mistreatment of Native Americans, the enslavement of Africans, the rape of the environment, and the second-class status of women have all been conventional and mostly unexamined continuations of patriarchal civilization. If anything, the founding fathers are to be congratulated for planting democratic seeds and traditions that would eventually lead to greater equality for all people and that may one day carry us beyond all the wounds and abusive patterns of patriarchy.

Still, it is hard to reconcile the positive legacies of such great men with the sometimes questionable details of their personal lives. When we point to the glaring contradictions in Thomas Jefferson's life and ask, "How is it possible?" we are asking a question of paramount importance, for we are pointing directly at the unseen and insidious workings of the dominator virus.

Jefferson's ambivalence regarding slavery epitomizes patriarchal contamination and its inevitable debasement of human nature. Somehow, we must get inside Jefferson's head and discover how he did it: how he spoke so movingly of freedom while still enslaving others. Somehow, we must get inside the varied minds of men and women down through the centuries as they have justified and accepted the daily insults of patriarchal culture. Where has the brilliant mind and vital spirit of humanity been through all these centuries of patriarchal infection and abuse?

How has such a powerful force as the dominator virus gone undetected, unchallenged, and unresolved for thousands of years?

Personal Denial

But childhood is a place where each of us already has been. To deny one's own origins there, or to compensate for or seek revenge on another for what was done to oneself—this is not only to continue the vicious circle and to degrade other human beings, but to deny and degrade ourselves.
—*Robin Morgan* [11]

Each member shares the mythology of the family trance. Each unconsciously agrees to share a certain focus and a certain denial. The denial constitutes the family system's "vital lies."
—*John Bradshaw* [12]

If Thomas Jefferson were to walk into a modern twelve-step meeting and tell his story—"My name is Tom; I am a leader of the greatest social experiment in the history of mankind, but I am also a lifelong owner of slaves"—every head in the room would soon be shaking side to side and thinking the same thing: "Denial. Major-league denial, Tom."

"Denial" is an unconscious psychoemotional mechanism that functions to protect the status quo in our lives by obscuring the truth. It is a form of ego-protection, a matrix of energetic, mental, and emotional forces that operates well below the surface of conscious awareness to shield and defend the often fragile and ever-evolving sense of self. An individual, family, organization, or nation is said to be "in denial" when it unconsciously suppresses certain truths, memories, or insights that would reveal the need for serious change if they were brought to conscious perception and reflection. Denial is how it is possible to sustain continuing behavior or relationship that is in flagrant violation of our most heart-felt human sensibilities.

Thus, we may be in denial about our spouse's alcoholism: we may fail to notice behavior that is obvious to everyone else because fully experiencing the truth might lead to a divorce. We may be in denial about abusive sexual patterns: we somehow manage to ignore or even embrace the most blatant patterns of male domination and female submissiveness because fully experiencing the truth would mean shaking the foundations of our lifestyle and relationships. Or (especially) we may be in denial about early childhood: we cannot remember extremely traumatic or formative events because fully experiencing the truth could upset our family structures. In all such cases, the psychoemotional mechanism of denial is functioning below conscious awareness to suppress key thoughts, feelings, images, and memories and thereby spare us the more challenging work of facing truth and encouraging change.

Denial is not the same as deliberate lying. When we deliberately lie, we consciously protect ourselves and accept the costs of our dishonesty as necessary. When we are in denial, we unconsciously protect the status quo in our lives and remain largely unaware of the costs to ourselves and others. For instance, an alcoholic may engage in much deliberate lying (hiding bottles, sneaking drinks, and so on) to protect a lifestyle that he or she considers necessary. At the same time, the alcoholic *and* family members may all be mired in unconscious patterns of denial as each suppresses certain truths—old wounds, communication breakdowns, failing relationships, financial pressures—that would threaten the existing family stability if brought to conscious awareness.

The difference between lying and denying is primarily one of awareness. Liars know they are lying and tend to recognize the costs of their dishonesty. Denial is far more insidious and dangerous, because it is unconscious and its consequences generally go unseen and unowned.

Since denial serves to protect the status quo, and since the status quo in human affairs has for so long been dominator-infected relationship, the human capacity for denial has been a crucial determinant in the establishment and continuing existence of patriarchal culture. (Denial also protects the status quo in partnership-based relationships. Relationships tend toward poisonous dysfunction, however, when any truth is denied for too long.) If people were incapable of denial—if we were acutely conscious of the whole truth at every moment in our lives—then the ugliness, shame, foul odor, and unending abuse of patriarchal relationship would force us into either mass suicide or constant revolutionary strife. As it is, the mechanism of denial has allowed the human race to sink into a psychic swamp of collective amnesia bordering on outright insanity—a perfect state of consciousness for the inhumane ways and means of patriarchy.

Denial helps to answer the question that has persisted throughout this book: "How did men and women together create, and how do men and women together continue to sustain, the dominant/submissive relationships of patriarchy?" However the dominator virus was first introduced into human relationship, and however inevitably it was spread from tribe to tribe, all of the men and women it touched engaged in some measure of denial as the simple human truth of partnership was attacked, degraded, and finally lost. Every act of patriarchal abuse, from the dawn of recorded history to the present moment, has simultaneously invoked the mechanisms of denial within both the abuser *and* the abused. Everyone involved in a patriarchal system must deny the true nature of reality if they want to go on living with the status quo and effectively survive in a dominator-infected world.

This is not to say that dominators are absolved of their abuses, nor can we blame the dominated for their silence and submission. Rather, all members of a patriarchal system necessarily and unconsciously engage in denial as a fundamental fact of life. When abusive patterns of domination and submission touch and infect an individual's reality, she or he *must* suppress as much of the pain as possible, along with any inner sense that there could be a better, kinder, more honest, and more loving way of life. When the dominator virus has been passed on, all notions of genuine partnership are strenuously, though unconsciously, denied.

I cannot overly stress the unconscious nature of denial. Denial has its roots in earliest childhood (and earliest civilization) and, for this reason, is difficult for any but the most determined to admit to, much less recognize and begin to change. As Alice Miller writes, "It is the tragedy of well-raised people that they are unaware as adults of what was done to them and what they do themselves if they were not allowed to be aware as children."[13] Conditioned to unawareness and denial as children, we grow into essentially unaware adults lacking the very feelings, perceptions, and acumen necessary to understand the depth and enormity of our dilemma.

Denial begins as a childhood survival mechanism. Faced with conflicting and untenable feelings and situations—"I want to live/ I am born to violence and separation"; "I love my father/my father abuses me"; "I love my mother/my mother is an embarrassing alcoholic"; "I feel wonderful pleasure in my body/my body is mistreated and abandoned"—the child screens from conscious perception and reflection those truths that are the most threatening. All the love and nurturance present in the family is acknowledged while any dysfunctional behavior is suppressed from conscious awareness. The child holds to the best that the family system offers (the status quo) and denies the abuses, contradictions, lies, and eventually, sadly, her or his own easy innocence and innate capacity for loving and pleasurable partnership.

The child must do this to survive. It is difficult enough being in a small, dependent body; to live with the constant awareness that one is unloved and at risk from one's caregivers, or that the family is on the verge of breaking apart, or that the experience of bodily pleasure is being abused and degraded, is an unbearable burden. Nobody can reasonably live and securely grow among such harrowing disparities and uncertainties. So the child denies as much of the truth as possible while focusing upon, and sometimes inventing, more loving and stable truths. The child fashions a worldview with beliefs, attitudes, opinions, desires, emotions, dreams, and memories to fit the world that he or she has landed in; whatever does not fit is denied.

If we accept that children are both hyperconscious and psychoemotionally creative, then, given the abusive conditioning they receive (in even the best of families), their capacity for denial can be seen as a mercy and a saving grace. How else could they survive their initiations into violence? How else could they survive the lack of genuine bonding and the fall from innocence that passes for a "normal childhood?" How else could they go on living, separated from the elementary partnership with the Mother—with life, with the world—that every child is born to? Denial is a shield, a balm, and a way of making sense of a terribly mixed-up world. Denial is a movement of the child's vast and creative intelligence, ironically so, since denial must ultimately also inhibit intelligence.

It is safe to say that all children engage in some measure of denial as a function of growing up, though obviously the more patriarchally abusive the family system is, the more the need for denial and protection. To the extent that families are dysfunctional and thus threatened as stable environments, children deny the abusive dysfunction as much as is psychoemotionally possible. They do this to survive, to carry on, and to make the best of what life gives them. While this is an effective short-term strategy for dealing with harsh realities and represents the best that children can do (though they may offer *their* children better options), denial in the long term greatly diminishes them as human beings and somewhat complicates the task of transforming patriarchy.

From the beginning, denial is an awful waste of a person's vital energies. The difference between a child feeling a warm, tingling pleasure throughout his or her body and a child suppressing all pleasurable feelings (as well as the reasons for doing so) is a quantifiable depletion of sexual and creative energies. The difference between a child alive with eager, eye-sparkling intelligence and a child trying hard not to see or hear the truth is a qualitative degradation of innate potential.

It takes vital energy to suppress the truth, and the more painful the reasons for doing so, the more effort it requires. It also takes continuing energy to sustain such denial and keep the truth far from conscious awareness. Though the causes of denial may be immediately compelling, the child pays for denial with essential life force for the rest of his or her life. To the extent that we are sustaining the denials of childhood, we are literally crippled from within; the truth denied by the child becomes the sickening lie of the adult.

Yet another cost of denial is that it makes us ignorant. "Denial is a form of withdrawal," writes Starhawk, and "when we withdraw we shut out information."[14] The child who is unconsciously suppressing certain truths is also repressing a significant amount of native intelligence. The child cannot withdraw from specific family dysfunctions without withdrawing in some measure from the rest of the world. Nor can the child diminish awareness of certain abuses without also becoming less aware of life in general.

Furthermore, the blinders that we erect in childhood to screen out family abuses and dysfunctions do not go away; rather, they persist through time, rendering us unable to fully comprehend our world. The more urgently we deny reality as children, the more we are prevented from seeing as adults. The web of denial, once specific to a given situation, becomes a general shield from all truth. Our short-term protection of unconsciousness becomes a long-term *lack* of consciousness. We become ignorant.

We become too ignorant to notice the gross contradiction of owning slaves while preaching equality; too ignorant to recognize the injurious interventions of techno-birthing; too ignorant to see that we are reactively abusing our children as we ourselves were abused; too ignorant to realize that sexual repression is the death of human beings; too ignorant to comprehend the utter insanity of killing in God's name; too ignorant to insist that women and men must be equal partners in this life; and, most often, too ignorant to perceive and understand the self-inflicted nature and continuing costs of denial. Having unconsciously withdrawn from the truth during childhood, we may never reach our full intellectual capacities.

It has become something of a cliché to say that we humans are using but a small portion of our brains. Certainly there are many indicators that we are capable of far more than what passes for the human norm. Much of our latent potential is tied up as sexual energy, emotional charge, and mental force in this dynamic of dominator-driven denial. Moreover, the tenacious strength with which the doctrines of patriarchal inevitability hold our world derives from the common and collective denial of countless generations of girls and boys and women and men. It is our self-imposed submission to denial that gives the dominator virus a viable medium in which to thrive.

Political Denial

> In our age of slaughter, madness threatens every think-
> ing person. To dwell on the absurdity of a culture that
> congratulates itself on its "progress" while carrying out
> geocide is to risk hearing your mind go spronnnng while
> spending the rest of your days gnawing the bark off trees.
> —*Brian Swimme*[15]

> Facts are stupid things.   —*Ronald Reagan*[16]

The personal denial of Everychild naturally becomes the political (governing) denial of every patriarchal religion, organization,
corporation, or government. All patriarchal systems are ruled by
mechanisms of political denial that originate in and perfectly reflect the denials of ordinary childhood. Just as whatever capacity
we have to reach our full individual potential demands that we first
recognize and overcome our deep-seated denials, so does the task
of transforming planetary patriarchy demand that we recognize
and eliminate the ubiquitous denials of our political systems.

System-wide political denial arises, like childhood denial, as
a necessary mechanism for the protection of the status quo. Status
quo for a child is found in her or his developing ego and the stability of the family. Status quo for a political system is found in the
positions, perks, and powers of the ruling elite and in the stability of the system's operational ways and means, including access
to the very necessities that give the system its purpose for being.

Status quo for an organized religion resides in its priesthood,
its creeds and doctrines, and its promise of certain salvation for
its followers. Status quo for a corporation resides in its high-
level management, its financial and legal structures, and its ability to consistently turn a profit for its shareholders. Status quo for
a government resides in its most powerful politicians, its laws
and enforcements, and its continuing delivery of such necessities

as food, shelter, employment, education, and health care to its populace.

The people who make up a political system tend to deny any information or experience that does not effectively serve or protect the status quo. (Denial could also be a difficult factor within partnership cultures, should the status quo of such cultures become inflexible and unchanging.) Since "the people" are already accomplished deniers in their personal lives, it is relatively easy for them to deny the contradictions, lies, and abuses in their political lives. There is, in fact, little difference between the denial within a dysfunctional family and the denial within a dysfunctional political system—it is merely a question of the child growing up into an "adult-sized" version of the suppression of awareness. And just as the child's denial of family dysfunctions serves to support those very dysfunctions, so the adult's denial of political dysfunctions serves to keep the system in place, whatever its failings.

Moreover, any patriarchal system develops mechanisms of political denial that are above and beyond the personal and habitual denials of its individual members. The system's governing documents and laws, its key institutions, and its operational ways and means all tend toward rigid support of the status quo, however dishonest or abusive. Thus, they are fundamentally denial-based. Not only is the system comprised of dominator-infected human beings, but its structural parameters actively and forcefully spread the infection.

A simple choice of words in a governing document—such as "All *men* are created equal"—can hold a system-wide dysfunction in place for generations. Many of the written laws of civilized culture are personal denials literally translated into political forces, such as the law that forbids contraception or the law that permits members of the citizenry to bear arms for the primary purpose of shooting one another. The basic institutions of any system, such as the male-only priesthood, or the electoral practices that favor the wealthy, or the utter lack of personal accountability within corporations, can serve as unyielding structural denials for the worst of abuses. And the basic operational ways and means of a system, such as the accounting practices that ignore costs to the environment, or the myriad forms of culturally-sanctioned racial and sexual discrimination, support an all-pervading atmosphere of unconscious denial and virally contaminated relationship.

Just as children must engage in some measure of denial to survive, the political denial of a patriarchal system is absolutely necessary for the continuing survival *of the system*—even if it means massive loss of life for its people. And just as a child's denial only succeeds at dire cost to the child's overall levels of creative energy and intelligence, so systemwide political denial only succeeds through the enormous waste of human and environmental resources and the incessant suppression of free thinking and spontaneous creativity.

This is easily recognized in modern totalitarian systems in which total denial is the law. The fascist and communist states of the twentieth century had to commit vast internal resources to their mechanisms of suppression: the S.S. and concentration camps, the K.G.B. and gulags. The need to keep a populace under constant police scrutiny is as energy depleting to a society as a child's continuous suppression of past events; it eventually wears the system (or body) down from within, thus planting the seeds for its own destruction. Totalitarian states ultimately fall apart in strict accordance with the second law of thermodynamics: they are entropic (energy-wasting) rather than regenerative systems. They are entropic largely because they waste energy by vigorously enforcing the denial of anything that might threaten the rigidly defined status quo.

Totalitarian states also fall apart because they suppress the continuous flow and exchange of information that is vital to any regenerative system. This was especially apparent in the breakup of the Soviet Union: after generations of actively suppressing the free creativity of its populace, controlling all information flow within the country, and preventing all exchange of information with those on the outside, the erstwhile superpower collapsed in a condition of sorry and embarrassing ignorance. In the end, the West did not win the Cold War; the resource-drained and intellectually stunted Soviet Union simply lost the will and capacity to keep on fighting.

While totalitarian states present stark and obvious examples of systemwide political denial, all patriarchal systems are dominator infected, denial based, and invariably self-destructing. America—a nation founded upon the brutal oppression of indigenous cultures and African peoples, as well as the routine suppression of women—has never fully resolved its abusive past and has added layer upon layer of world-class denial with each passing generation.

Though not quite a police state, America has more people incarcerated per capita than any other developed country; has more violence on the streets of its own capital than many battle zones; seems to thrive on fighting prohibitionary wars against alcohol, Reds, hippie protestors, and now drugs, despite the ever futile and ruinous results; demands capital punishment of its poorer citizens with religious zeal; and, especially, takes great pride in being policeman to the world, eager to jump into armed conflict at the slightest provocation.

This represents a tragic waste of the nation's energy and resources, but what is even more tragic is that it is practically impossible to have an intelligent conversation about any of this, so thick is the repressive fog of American denial. As Brian Swimme suggests, to be a modern American is to live at constant risk of the mind going *spronnnng*.

For all the power of its democratic institutions, its free press, and its First Amendment rights to free expression, America is freely evolving into a dull and stultifying stupor. Signs of denial-based national ignorance abound: from the steady decline of an educational system that fails in comparison with that of other Western countries to the sound-bite mental floss and fluff that passes for an electoral process; from the growing dominance of corporate-controlled television as the primary path to knowledge to the nearly inescapable and virtually irresistible "consumin' human" reality of modern advertising; from the sorry inattention to the basic needs of pregnant women (carriers of vital human intellect) to the brain-maiming violations of techno-birthing. From sea to shining sea, America is suffering through the grosser pathologies of a dominator plague, but we are too denial bound to fully comprehend the danger or take necessary steps toward genuine change.

Indeed, it is perfect that America has been and continues to be a world leader, for America powerfully illustrates the underlying contradictions of patriarchy and the insidiously supportive mechanisms of personal and political denial. America is a standing demonstration of the basic principle that *denial perpetuates denial*: once a system engages in the suppression of truth, it becomes increasingly enmeshed in self-imposed and ultimately self-destructive delusions. America has lived in denial from its very beginning and will likewise die if it does not soon rouse itself into radical wakefulness.

America presently has all the signs of being one big dominator-infected, denial-bound, utterly dysfunctional family: growing debt, poor health, failing intelligence, dishonest relationships, censored communications, crumbling infrastructure, constant intoxication, and a national proclivity toward violence as a solution to problems that is culminating in a wargasmic pride at being able to obliterate bothersome little nations. Yet it is also in America that the twelve-step movement was founded, that women's liberation was so resolutely thrust upon the world, that childhood abuse has been so seriously confronted, and that the essential work of overcoming denial and moving beyond the dominator virus must finally occur. I sense (parochially, perhaps) that it is in America that humanity will either see its way through the ancient haze of planetary domination and denial to personal peace and political partnership or perish from the rampant excesses of modern patriarchy.

It is in our struggle with denial that the lines between the personal and political become almost invisible. Childhood denial engenders men and women perfectly suited for the inhumanities of patriarchal systems; in turn, systemwide political denial allows for legal, institutional, and operational structures that actively suppress every man, woman, and child's energy, creativity, and intelligence. There is a vicious cycle to the perpetuation of denial in our world: crippled human beings create crippled systems that cripple human beings. The truth, we have been told, will set us free. But how shall we see, hear, and even touch the truth?

Personal Reflections

The truth will set you free but first it may make you miserable.
—*Antero Alli* [17]

Look for the status quo in your present life. Identify the belief systems, memories, personal behaviors, patterns of relationship, and societal structures that give you the greatest sense of security. Look for the elements of your life that you are most attached to keeping just the way that they are. Feel for the possible changes in your world that you fear the most.

Now look for any serious contradictions between your "status-quo world" and your most heartfelt human sensibilities. Do you have any strongly held beliefs that run counter to the possibility of peaceful, egalitarian culture, such as the belief that people are naturally inclined toward violence, or the belief that there will always be poor people in our world, or the belief that "it's every man for himself?" Are you willing to believe differently?

Do you habitually engage in obviously self-destructive behaviors? How do you justify these behaviors to yourself? Do they seem inevitable? Can you imagine yourself living free of such addictions? Can you face your fear of change? Will you?

Do you have difficulty remembering events from early childhood? Do you question the relevance of "going back there" and disturbing the past? Would you be willing, even eager, to see the truth of your personal history, though it might threaten the stability of your current family system? Could you let your family change?

Are you avoiding giving specific feedback to a close friend for fear of damaging the relationship? Can you imagine telling the

*truth in all your relationships? Do you remain silent about
certain procedures or policies at work for fear of losing your job?
Can you imagine living the truth at work?*

*Do you ignore certain inequities in society for fear of endan-
gering your own social status? Can you imagine working
actively to bring greater equality to all levels of society? Do you
deny the harshest abuses of your nation for fear of seeming
radical or unpatriotic? Can you imagine a whole nation shifting,
at its very core, toward partnership culture? Are you ready for
the change?*

SIX
The Light of Awareness

> Affairs are now soul size. The en-
> terprise is exploration into God.
> Where are you making for? It takes so many thousand
> years to wake, but will you wake for pity's sake?
> —*Christopher Fry* [1]

In November of 1985, after suffering for more than a year with a set of increasingly debilitating physical symptoms, Niro Markoff Asistent tested positive for HIV and was diagnosed with AIDS-related complex (ARC). Three months later, the results of a second blood test brought dire confirmation: she should expect to die of AIDS within the next eighteen months.

Today, Asistent is alive and well, and her experience is movingly recounted in her book *Why I Survive AIDS*. Not only has she survived far beyond the prediction of her original prognosis, but, even more significantly, *she is now testing HIV negative*. This, according to prevailing notions regarding HIV, is impossible. Yet Asistent is alive and telling the tale, with medical records to chart her journey into AIDS and out again. The medical world, inexplicably, has ignored her experience: "I cooperated fully with my doctors, who drew quite a few pints of blood from me, but unfortunately I never heard from them again to know what they did with it. I guess I was naive to have believed that the medical establishment would be open to and willing to explore alternative possibilities."[2] For those who will listen, however, she is a living, breathing expert on dealing with the most dominating of viruses.

Asistent does not offer a simple, how-to prescription for all those living with AIDS. Her story is highly personal, and her healing grew out of her unique history and circumstances. Still, one clear message leaps from every page of her extraordinary book: "This condition was my 'wake-up call.' I could have chosen either to respond to the message or to roll over and go back to sleep. . . . Every crisis, whether it be illness, the consequences of addiction, or the loss of a loved one, offers us an opportunity to wake up."[3] Though she accepts the biochemical dimensions of viral disease, she views them as secondary to the psychoemotion-al reality of the infected person. She offers the bold promise that becoming *consciously aware* of one's psychoemotional reality—waking up—is the key to ecstatic living and "healing into death."

During her healing process, Asistent developed what she called her Daily Awareness Routine. A combination of medita-tion, diet, exercise, and long walks along the ocean shoreline, the routine became her moment-by-moment commitment to total awareness of all aspects of her life. She opened to the suppressed energies and conditioning of her childhood, the dominant/sub-missive patterns in her current relationships, and her deepest fears and furious rage at facing death from AIDS. "I had begun to lift the veil of denial, open my eyes, and honestly view my life. I had taken my first step on my path of healing."[4] Ultimately, she did not fight the virus in her body; instead, she used the illness as a call to radical wakefulness and an opportunity for the emer-gence of genuine health.

Niro Asistent considers her current HIV-negative status as a clear sign that miracles do happen in our world. I would go a bit further and suggest that she consciously regenerated her cellu-lar processes. Though HIV had insinuated its deadly instructions for immune dysfunction into her DNA, she—with the light of conscious awareness—composed a song of living joy to take its place. Maybe she chased the virus out entirely, or maybe she transformed it into less deadly information, even as it transformed her. "When we finally surrender fully to the truth," she writes, "then we begin to live our life fully, from conscious choice, instead of in our unconscious state of sleepwalking."[5] When we become aware of, and then move beyond, our lifelong patterns of denial, miracles *do* happen and the most incurable of human diseases may be transcended.

If we can transcend AIDS, then we can also transcend the millennial-old disease of patriarchal domination. Like Niro Asistent, I cannot offer a how-to cure for all personal and political domination. Yet I will join her in saying that, however domination-afflicted we are, however shameful and ugly "human nature" may seem to be, a first and critical step toward genuine healing is for us to rouse into radical wakefulness and shine the light of conscious human awareness onto every facet of our world. The truth *does* set us free: our innate, incorruptible, and ever-human capacity to become wholly aware in each moment of our lives is the embodiment of truth.

Our primary struggle is not so much against patriarchal domination and abuse, for such a struggle would almost certainly strengthen dominant/submissive patterns. Rather, we must turn our focus to the heavy costs of personal and political denial that keep patriarchy's most despicable lies hidden from the transformational light of human consciousness. Patriarchy is a creature of the dark. Patriarchy is only inevitable to the extent that women and men choose to live in shadowy unconsciousness. Patriarchy will fade from human affairs as women and men choose to make "daily awareness" both routine and all-encompassing.

At the political level, this means—above all—keeping a significant portion of the media free from the controlling biases of governmental and corporate dominators. It means spreading inexpensive video cameras throughout the world to document the abusive excesses of patriarchy. It means bringing so much media attention to each new war that the next one becomes that much harder to justify. It means a global network of computer-linked social activists. It means thousands and thousands of totally independent, desktop-published newsletters. It means bringing television cameras into key political hearings and processes so that *we all can see*. We are blessed to be living in a time when the technology exists to make systemwide political denial virtually impossible.

However, a video camera or editorial page can only bring authentic enlightenment to those who are personally ready to see. Men and women steeped in personal denial will have great difficulties perceiving the most blatant of political abuses. Thus, even as we work to cleanse the world of political denial, we must simultaneously work to cleanse ourselves. We must openly face and see through our most denial-bound patterns of intimate relationship and allow genuine partnership to reemerge.

"Affairs are now soul size" indeed. "*The enterprise is exploration into God.*" The enterprise is exploration into the cellular pulse of our embodiment, the vital heart of our being human, and the widest reaches of our free awareness. Our challenge is to come into radical wakefulness, to spread living light to and through all our relations. It is, in the end, nothing more or less than a simple choice. But will we wake?

Grains of Mind

Our orthodox models in medicine have come to the same fate as the models of the first scientific revolution: they are sadly inappropriate to studies of the living.
—*Larry Dossey, M.D.*[6]

Each body, burning like a flame as two and a half million red cells come into being each second, is far less solid than we think. The earth is tinder for spirit. All of it is ready to burst into new flame.   —*Michael Murphy*[7]

During the fourteenth century, bubonic plague struck with devastating results, wiping out half of the population of Europe and much of Asia. Called the Black Death, it was caused by an infectious bacterium spread by flea-infested rats.

I can remember as a child watching a movie about the Black Death and being struck by one scene in particular: A big man, all dressed in black, was driving a cart from house to house, picking up the dead bodies and carrying them off to be buried. I thought, "Why isn't *he* dying?" Here was an incredibly bad bug, killing one out of every two people, and this man was going into infected households, handling dead, infected bodies, and somehow still managing to stay active and strong.

Since the fourteenth century, we have learned a lot about bubonic plague. We know all about the bug that causes it: what it looks like, how it lives, how it travels, how it affects the human body, and how to kill it, which we have been quite successful at doing. On the other hand, we know almost nothing about the man driving the cart and how and why he survived.

In fundamental ways, Western medical science over the past few hundred years has been geared to studying the half of Europe that died and ignoring the half that survived. We enthusiastically dissect the dead and show little interest in the living. Doctors say, "The survivors just have greater resistance; they have natural immunity." But what does that mean? Is it God's will? Are they born with it? Are they just lucky?

"God's will" was the most accepted answer at the time of the plague—people lived or died according to the commands of God the Father who, it was assumed, had his reasons. Such is life in the dominator's garden: eat the wrong piece of fruit and you run the risk of horrid death and eternal damnation. Leaving aside the eternal conundrum of all religious people—Why does God so often take the good while sparing the venal and vile?—if God the Father's displeasure is the source of our problems, then our world is inevitably patriarchal. Though we can conceive of a genuine partnership relationship with God in which "God's will" takes on a whole different meaning, to believe that it is God the Dominator's mysterious will that one person die while another lives is to become forever submissive and creatively impaired.

It surely is far more sensible and liberating to say that the man on the cart survived because he was born with some actual immunity that many of his neighbors did not have. Everything we are now learning about genetics and DNA supports this viewpoint: the survivors of the plague were no doubt genetically disposed toward greater immunity. Wound into their DNA was a strand or two that answered the plague's challenge. Moreover, humanity's bout with the plague, damaging as it was in the short term, in the long term taught all human DNA the basic data of the survivor's immunity. Thus does humanity evolve.

Still, saying that the man on the cart was born with a genetic immunity that saved him, while his dying neighbor was not, leaves us squarely between God's will and dumb luck (and brings to mind Einstein's assertion that God does not play dice with the universe). Though it is true that each of us is born with our own genetic makeup and that one person is disposed from birth toward strengths, weaknesses, and unique traits that another is not, it seems increasingly unlikely that our physical constitution is rigidly fixed, unchanging, and limited to prenatal inheritance. Rather, given the elemental fluidity of all material forms, the vital connectedness between any two body cells, and the creative powers of the greater mind in which our genetic "grains of mind" reside, natural immunity, along with other genetic traits, surely continues to develop throughout life. Human nature, including the body, is essentially mutable and continuously interactive with all movements of emotion, mind, spirit, and relationship.

Of course, genetic engineering is now a rapidly advancing science, so the notion that genes are mutable through chemical and mechanical means is not in dispute. Genes can be purposefully changed, and fundamental living characteristics, such as immunity to illness, can be changed as a result. However, techno-genetics seems to me as ill conceived and disastrously fated as techno-birthing.

Once again we are attempting to displace nature with machinery. Once again we are blundering into a natural and organic process that we have never wholly understood and yet are convinced we can improve. (And, of course, we will turn a profit in the process.) Once again it is all unnecessary: just as the cells of the female human body are programmed for healthy pregnancy and delivery by millions of years of evolutionary learning, so every human being is imbued with the requisites of cellular regeneration. Rather than growing into a culture in which women can feel supreme confidence in their biocreative powers, we have erected the violent apparatus of techno-birthing; rather than embracing an innate capacity for conscious cellular regeneration, we are erecting an equally violent apparatus of techno-genetics.

Though we will surely learn much about human DNA from the complex tools and procedures of techno-genetics, we would learn far more from a thorough study of conscious "evolutionary mutants." These are the typically happy and healthy humans who feel at ease in quiet spaces, find pleasure in the flesh, and live to push the outer boundaries of human possibility. There are many such people populating our planet at this time, and we would do well to listen to their stories. If we are ever to transcend our viral patterns of domination, it is "we the living" who must surely lead the way.

It is the grossest of negligence for the medical establishment to continue to publicly pronounce AIDS as "incurable" and to decline to study Niro Asistent and others like her. It is the grossest of negligence for there to be so little recognition given to the creative and destructive powers of mental and emotional states after so many billions of dollars have been poured into our failed war against cancer. It is the grossest of negligence for modern science to steer its enormous resources away from in-depth studies of such "low-tech" healing approaches as acupuncture, ayurveda, homeopathy, naturopathy, chiropractic, midwifery, herbalism, vegetarianism, water birthing, and infant massage, as well as such boundary-pushing activities as firewalking, Taoist meditation, shamanism, and the use of psychoactive plants.

We are squandering untold resources and energies on big-ticket techno-cures that avoid all references to the consciousness of ailing persons (and the consciousness of medical personnel). That which cannot be precisely quantified is ignored. Meanwhile, medical costs continue to escalate, more and more people find themselves without access to basic medical care, and (ah, denial) it has become impossible to even consider simple, fundamental health care as beginning in the consciousness of each human be-

ing. Our difficulty is in establishing a medical system that embraces
the creative spirit of the individual within a culture that vigorously
denies and actively assaults that spirit at every turn. Our challenge
is to free ourselves of the senseless suppressions of our culture and
to recover our innate healing abilities, including our capacity for
conscious cellular regeneration.

We are on the verge of a brave, new, humanizing obligation:
conscious participation in the cellular evolution of the race. We
are being called to active awareness of the grains of mind that give
us form and function. We must learn to change our minds for
the betterment of life. Deepak Chopra writes of "the ability of
one mode of consciousness (the mind) to spontaneously correct
the mistakes in another mode of consciousness (the body)."[8] Fred
Alan Wolf sees future advances involving human consciousness
"not only of organs and cells but even molecules, electrons, and,
perhaps, the ultimate—photons of light."[9] And Michael Murphy
dreams of altering DNA through "cellular and molecular
psychosurgery," creating a body strong enough to "hold the
'supramental light.'"[10]

Consider where we must start. Recent statistics predict that
one million pregnant women in America will be physically abused
by their husbands in the coming year, and the focus of most at-
tacks will be the abdomen.[11] One in every three Americans will
be the victim of overt sexual abuse as a child.[12] And, "one out of
eight Hollywood movies depicts a rape theme. By the age of 18,
the average youth has watched 250,000 acts of violence and
40,000 attempted murders on TV."[13] Though we may quarrel with
some of these numbers, given the suppressive power of personal
and political denial, the truth could surely be even worse. The ra-
pid proliferation of twelve-step recovery groups during the past
decade—as sexual abuse and incest have come into widespread
awareness—cautions, at the very least, that to be conceived,
born, and raised in modern America is to enter into a festering
cauldron of senseless pain and twisted relationship.

All children exposed to abuse within the womb and the
home are infected, at the deepest levels of self, with the dominator

virus. Electrochemical strands of violence, shame, rage, apathy, separateness, hate, self-doubt, and low self-esteem are woven into children's primary cellular processes. Ultramicroscopic fields of information—"the world is a violent place," "you're always hurt by the one you love," "pleasure brings pain," "sex is sin," "buying things makes it all better"—darkly contaminate children's grains of mind. As they grow, it will seem unquestionably true to them that they are solitary consumers in a hostile and abusive world, and they will inevitably pass on and reinforce such "truth" in others. When the nation turns its collective eyes to the heavens and cries, "How can we be so violent?" the answer, sadly, is, "How can we not, given the depth, force, and continuing insanity of our conditioning?"

This is where the main work of conscious cellular regeneration must occur. Though we must obviously stop inflicting fresh abuse on the current and coming generations of children, we must simultaneously work on our own cellular "mal-mutations." Indeed, given the viral nature of domination, we can only do as well with our children as we first do with ourselves. Each of us must take the time and make the effort to cleanse our*cell*ves of patriarchal conditioning. We must purposefully mutate toward the necessities of partnership and create bodies strong enough to hold, at last, the supramental light.

Just as Asistent transcended the AIDS virus through her commitment to daily awareness, so may we transcend the dominator virus through our commitment to radical wakefulness. This begins with wanting to see through denial at every level of our lives and continues with urgently desiring to open to and express the whole truth. The dominator virus cannot live in the honest light of human awareness. Painful though it often is, the truth sets us freely moving toward a genuinely new world order.

I am always reminded of Alice Miller's basic prescription for abused children: "That at least once in their life they come into contact with a person who knows without any doubt that the environment, not the helpless, battered child, is at fault." Though we all suffer through the covert and overt abuses of childhood, some of us are listened to, heard, respected, and affirmed. Some of us are blessed with the open, compassionate, feeling awareness of another person and are treated as human equals. Simple, humane awareness given to a child's often painful reality makes the difference between "I am alone in a hostile world" and "I am safe, with loving caregivers." There is a cellular difference between unconscious degradation of a child's spirit and heartfelt praise, cleansing, and benediction.

Similarly, all of the extraordinary healing power of the twelve-step group process comes from the open, compassionate, feeling awareness of other human beings. When people find the courage to stand in a circle of their peers and tell the truth as they know it, and when their listeners offer respect, kindness, and gentle affirmation, then these people change. Addictive behaviors cease, destructive emotional patterns are healed, and family systems undergo great transformation. The core energetic information and fields of an individual are consciously altered. It is the light of awareness—"I am listening to who you are, to what you've been through, to how you hurt, and to who you wish to become"—that generates the healing and positive growth at such times. This unwavering commitment to simple awareness, combined with the spirit of egalitarianism, has made the twelve-step movement a strong force for personal and social change.

Finally, our greatest opportunity for conscious cellular regeneration is sexual intercourse. Anytime two humans arouse the potent energies of sex, they are drawn into a sea of alchemical possibility. The Earth moves, for better or worse. They are stirring the deepest levels of themselves and they are changed by the whole story of the moment: Are they in love? Are they meeting as partners? Are they seeking balance? Are they thrilled to be bodies? Are they feeling the peace of power-with? Or are they engendering domination and submission? Are they inflicting pain? Are they encouraging violence? Are they degrading the body? Are they feeling the conflict of power-over?

Every act of sexual intercourse brings either the cellular curse of sexual domination or the cellular blessing of sexual peace. Every moment of sexual peace offers transcendence to both lovers: They are lifted beyond the ancient and inevitable patterns of human domination and given a touch, a taste, and a precious vision of human partnership. This is the reprogramming of human beings in the creative heart of each cell and in the spiral dance of every gene; that it can also be such a wonderful pleasure is a certain indication that it is a sound and evolutionary practice.

What if a child is conceived through such practice? The primordial meeting of egg and sperm brings a merging and mixing of DNA at its most fluid and mutable. Is there any doubt that a child conceived in love and mutual respect is influenced differently from a child of rape? The moment of human conception affords the most powerful of all opportunities to alter personal and political realities: The child's essential DNA may be consciously blessed with the loving energies of partnership, an act that may lead to a grown human being who *knows* that genuine partnership is possible. That the vast majority of human conceptions are less than fully conscious, and too often without love, is yet another strand of patriarchal inevitability woven into human nature.

The idea of "conscious conception" leads to a final thought: What if humans evolve to the point where contraception is a conscious, internal practice for women and men, and conception is thus possible only with the willing consent of both partners? There is already anecdotal evidence of women who have learned to consciously prevent conception, and men can control conception through simple conservation of the orgasm. Is it too farfetched to think of women and men understanding from an early age their powers of mutual conception and conscientiously developing such powers?

A common capacity for conscious "birth allowance" would fundamentally shift all relationships between women and men. What if women (rather than laws) really did control their bodies? What if men could only become fathers with the conscious consent of willing partners? What if forced sex never brought a new child into the world? Wouldn't it be grand to leave behind the lose-lose question of "choice" versus "life"? Wouldn't it be delicious to let go of all artificial techno-controls of sexual fertility and potency? Could there be any more effective way to positively alter the cellular grains of mind that give us form and function? Shouldn't we try?

Practicing Partnership

The breezes at dawn have secrets to tell you.
    Don't go back to sleep!
You must ask for what you really want.
    Don't go back to sleep!
People are going back and forth across the doorsill
    where the two worlds touch;
The door is round and open.
    Don't go back to sleep! —*Rumi*

A good friend recently graduated from a Model Mugging course, a self-defense and empowerment training for modern, mostly urban American women. The "model mugger" is a man dressed from head to toe in a suit of heavy padding so that every portion of his body is covered and protected. His job is to aggressively assault the women in the class, who are taught to fight back, to strategically kick and punch, and to overcome their would-be attacker.

Many of the women drawn to Model Mugging classes are survivors of earlier rapes and assaults who are learning to develop their personal power so that, perhaps for the first time in their lives, they can feel both strong and safe. Others are just realists attempting to protect themselves from the unrelenting threats of modern misogyny. All come away from the classes with both a practical training in dealing with abusive men and enhanced personal feelings of self-esteem and pride in being female.

At the final session of my friend's class, the teachers videotaped each of the women defeating the model mugger so that each could take away a record of the process for reminders and review. My friend urged me to sit and watch her tape. She left me alone as, one by one, some twenty women confronted and overcame their worst fears and greatest nightmares. For those who had lived through a previous assault, the model mugger duplicated the circumstances—attacking in the same way and using the same hateful language. It was obvious that for those women, especially, this was much more than a course in self-defense; the reenactment reached into the very core of their beings, touching terror, shame, grief, and rage while simultaneously opening the way to a whole new self.

The women had been taught a simple practice to perform immediately after the mugger was defeated and down on the ground. They would stomp one foot hard, just beside his body, and scream, "No!" Watching the tape, I could feel a palpable wave of emotional energy flowing from the screen. It grew stronger as each woman found her power and asserted her will, quite tangibly exploding with each new shout of "No!" For myself, with every burst of woman's rage, my eyes welled up with the tears of a heavy and ancient sadness. By the time the tape was finished, I felt that I had paid witness to a gaping, painful wound of dominator culture. Yet, somehow, I also sensed that this process was a potent step toward women and men experiencing partnership again.

I can hear some worries, from men and women both: For all the necessity of a Model Mugging course, isn't it just teaching women to emulate the worst traits of men? Isn't it but another sorry outcome of the Parable of the Tribes? It is helpful, certainly, for individual women, but doesn't it create further degeneration of our species as woman aspires to man's capacity for violence? Shouldn't we just focus our efforts on stopping men from mugging?

I know that some of my own sadness came from such thoughts. It is the same sadness I feel, for instance, when women demand the right to serve in armed combat. Still, learning to defend oneself is not the same as becoming aggressively violent, and I doubt that any Model Mugging graduates are out stalking the streets looking for their next male victim. The point of the class is not to teach women to be as abusive as some men can be; the point is to bring focused awareness and emotional force to age-old patterns of female submissiveness and to work a psychophysical transformation. The woman who knows that she cannot be forced into sex and that her "No!" is the final word is fundamentally altered, at her most basic levels of self, from the woman who feels herself forever at the mercy of a man's aggressive power.

As a man, I found that just watching a video of women graphically asserting their equality had a profound effect on me. Though it may be presumptuous of me to say so, I think that I "get" the nature of women's reality somewhat better now. I definitely feel greater respect for women's rage. In the past, I might have responded to angry reports of various male abuses with traces of doubt, denial, defensiveness, and even some boys-will-be-boys jocularity. (The reports were from "shrill" and "hysterical" feminists, of course—two words chosen to defuse women's rage.) Now I always feel the sadness first, followed by a deep appreciation for every woman who finds the courage to stomp her foot and scream, "No more!" Really, I think I get it. And please, my sisters, keep going.

I suspect that, in any conscious meeting of long-suppressed male sadness and long-suppressed female rage, a deep transformation can be fostered and nurtured. If both man and woman are open to change, both can come away more whole and more healthy as human beings. I feel such transformations working at the core of humanity, touching and moving the grains of mind that give us form and function, resolving toxic patterns from past conditioning and positively altering the creative essence of being woman or being man. I further believe that it is a primary obligation of our age for all men and women to seek out experiences that will encourage the fresh thinking, passionate feeling, and powerful movement of our fast-evolving selves.

Clearly, none of this will happen without conscientious and sustained effort on all of our parts. We are so powerfully defined and determined by the weight of human history, by the sociopolitical structures of our day, and by the dominator virus moving within our bodies and relationships that the mere notion of treating one another with full respect and sincere cooperation can seem like a radical's agenda, if not an idiot's fantasy. Patriarchal thought, feeling, and behavior run so deeply in our lives as to seem fundamental to human nature; we cannot expect to simply turn away and be done with them.

The simple truths of partnership have always made sense to most people—witness the eternal appeal of what Aldous Huxley called *the perennial philosophy*. However, the problem has always been putting such clear and simple truths into daily practice. The problem, as the saying goes, is "walking our talk." Sitting alone or with our closest friends, the ancient entreaties to "love your neighbor as yourself," to "turn the other cheek," to "see God in all things," and to "live in one world of peace and plenty" can be powerfully inspiring, perfectly reasonable, and easy enough to follow. Partnership, at such times, can seem like the real essence of human nature.

But then we must step back into the real world of unhappy spouses and demanding children; of nasty and intractable neighbors who refuse all attempts at communication; of racial, ethnic, and religious bigots; of petty tyrants bent on increasing power through aggression and violence; of industrialists willing to desecrate anything in pursuit of profit; of the many dehumanizing demands of modern economic survival. Almost inevitably, we find ourselves compelled once again along patriarchal currents of domination and submission. The problem is not so much in knowing the truth but in putting the truth into actual practice.

Years ago, during my Bob Dylan-wannabe days, I was doing some recording in a sound studio. After an especially frustrating session, the sound engineer told me that he was going to put a large sign over the front door of the studio that said, "Practice, practice, practice!" This was his wisdom, gleaned from years of helping musicians tangibly express their inner dreams. Our greatest creations derive from conscientious, sustained, regular practice.

Our situation now, as hopeful co-creators of personal and planetary transformation, is quite the same. Though we may easily hear the rhythms and harmonies of simple, human partnership, our attempts to tangibly and practically express these dreams are fraught with difficulties, delays, and utter failures. No one can really be blamed for skeptically or cynically dismissing all of this partnership talk as so much New Age nonsense. Our lives are filled with evidence to support this cynicism: events, relationships, and problems that forcefully discourage and degrade any efforts toward partnership.

Still, to say that living in partnership is entirely hopeless is to turn the world over to the dominators and abdicate our true nature and responsibilities. *We've got to try.* We must understand that creating a partnership world of mutual respect and heartfelt co-operation among all peoples demands that we persevere in our dreaming. We must learn from the dominators while not being infected by them, and, through the worst of frustrations, we must continue to practice, practice, practice.

Niro Asistent, with her Daily Awareness Routine, discovered the transformational power of regular practice. As she herself says, what healed her was not so much what she did as the commitment she made to a moment-to-moment and day-after-day healing practice. She worked at it, persevering even when the dominating strength of AIDS wore her down. Likewise, I do not think the act-ual specifics of Model Mugger training—punch like this and kick like that—are as important as the fact that women are gathering on a sustained, regular basis to practice physical equality with aggres-sive men. In both cases, human beings have found the courage to face would-be unbeatable foes and have not expected to just suddenly win (as much as they may have deserved to). Rather, they have committed themselves to working at it and then made "working at it" a central element of their daily existences.

A scenario in which human beings vigorously pursue and effectively embody the cooperative ways and means of partnership is just as improbable as one in which a person fully overcomes AIDS or one in which women viscerally feel themselves the equals of physically larger and stronger men. Yet, if we make practicing partnership the central element of our daily existences, there is good reason to believe we will succeed.

Practicing partnership begins with an unwavering personal commitment to the sustained exploration of new patterns of relationship and behavior. This must be done moment-to-moment and day-after-day—even when it hurts, even when it frustrates, and even when those with whom we are attempting new relationships are rigidly uncooperative and denial-bound. We must, as a primary condition of being alive, take responsibility for examining all our patterns of personal and political relationship. When relating the old way is obviously patriarchal, we must try something different.

I am offering no sure set of partnership behaviors or formulas; nor am I suggesting that we should always know and follow some personally and politically "correct" course of action. Rather, we must be committed to becoming fully conscious of the true nature of our diverse relationships while growing beyond all doctrines of patriarchal inevitability. We must see through the heavy haze of personal and political denial and actually get what's happening between ourselves and others. We must enthusiastically explore and practice new patterns and structures of relationship. We are, after all, attempting nothing less than a planetwide paradigm shift—the greatest of all reversals. We can and must work at it, work at it, and work at it.

Moreover, just as we are all differently equal, so must we all find our ways, differently and uniquely, to partnership relationships. Any single answer, or set of new commandments, or one and only "partnership way" could easily become but another pattern of domination. The simultaneously liberating/threatening and exciting/frightening truth of our times is that there are few models for partnership behavior and relationship; there are even fewer teachers who practice power-with others without exerting power-over them. It is time for each of us to come awake to our power-within—the inner voice, the inner guide, the inner creative force—and discover the even greater power of feeling connected to others and working together.

No one can tell you how to do this, though it will always be obvious when you are not doing it. You know all too well the thoughts, feelings, and behaviors of patriarchy. Look to your life and relationships now, this moment, and sense the ways you are coercing, forcing, manipulating, or dominating others. Sense the ways you are giving up your power, bowing under, or submitting in any situation. Feel for the pointless abuses in your current relationships and find the courage and resolve to try something different.

Keep going. Practice. Don't go back to sleep.

Beyond War

The means are to the ends as the seed is to the tree; we must *be* the change we wish to see in the world.
—*Gandhi*

We shall require a substantially new manner of thinking if we are to survive.
—*Albert Einstein*

With the phasing out of the Cold War and the real or imagined need to sustain a massive military budget, there has been much talk in America of "the peace dividend": the money that could now be redirected toward long-ignored social needs. Various social activists have patiently stressed how even a small portion of military expenditures, when redirected for peaceful purposes, could have an enormously beneficial effect.

Thus, for the price of a single nuclear-powered submarine, we could immunize every child in the world against six deadly diseases that currently account for one million deaths per year; for the price of ten B2 bombers, we could provide basic prenatal care to every pregnant woman in America; and "spending $1 billion on guided missile production creates about 9,000 jobs . . . while spending the same amount on educational services would yield 63,000 jobs."[14] Without a doubt, if we made providing for the basic needs of children, women, and men as vitally urgent as we once made the defeat of Nazism and communism, then all the energy, money, intelligence, and resources to do the job and do it well would be available. "Waging peace" would be cheaper, easier, and more enjoyable, and it would pay much greater dividends than waging war.

This is simple, straightforward arithmetic that underscores

the eternal truth of war being a terrible waste of human and natural resources. Yet turning "swords into plowshares" is hardly a new idea, and we are not the first people to soberly do our sums before sadly pondering what society could be if it invested as avidly in the essentials of social welfare as it does in the engines of global warfare. Nor, I worry, are we the first to hear optimistic voices talking about lasting peace and a new world order. War, as pacifists throughout history have discovered, has a tenacious and insidious inevitability to it once it gets loose in the world.

War is tenacious because, as the Parable of the Tribes warns, when a violent aggressor approaches a nation's borders (or, in the case of America, its global interests), that nation must itself become violently aggressive if it wants to survive. War is insidious because, once a nation commits its human and natural resources to the exigencies of organized violence, it is unable to fully provide food, housing, education, and medical care to its people; this in turn produces the social conditions of a mean, aggressive, violent nation.

If we are to genuinely move beyond the dominator virus, and thus beyond war, we must grasp the extent to which war has been a primary progenitor of human evolution. War has forced men, women, and their societies to tragically adapt to the demands of organized violence. The linchpin lie of war—that our enemies are less than us and that their suffering does not count for as much as ours—is retained, long after the battles have ended. It becomes an inevitable law governing the behavior of individuals and the direction of society. The ways and means of war—insensitivity, ruthlessness, and competition unto death—become the governing principles of a society and the celebrated attributes of its prominent individuals.

It is no surprise that such a war-driven society considers reasonable tasks, like providing care for pregnant women and children, to be terrible drains on its resources. "Let them compete for their needs with the rest of us," says the corporate executive. "It will make them strong, give them character," says the rugged individualist. "We just don't have the money for such things," says the military power broker. "They're all a bunch of welfare cheats," says the conservative politician.

This is human social evolution gone horribly awry. When no longer competing against an external enemy, the people compete against one another for access to the basic provisions of life, liberty, and the pursuit of happiness. When no longer projecting "different and unequal" onto the enemy, the people project it onto one another. The linchpin lie of war becomes the linchpin lie of all social relations and future evolution. The dangerous logic of competition, with its inevitable trail of suffering and abuse, becomes the nation's proudest anthem. Cooperation, well, that's for children, fools, and hopeless romantics.

Our process now, I pray, is carrying us beyond the dangerous logic of war and its inevitable misdirection of human social evolution. We must transcend the repeating loop of human violence. We must find a solution to the world's villains other than becoming more villainous ourselves. Perhaps we had no other choice with the varied Hitlers of human history: that was then, this is now, and we must embark upon a whole new path of human social evolution, a path that will carry us beyond the ancient social viruses of competition, violence, and war.

A critical first step upon this new path is making a commitment to the whole truth in all international relations. This may seem like a wild fantasy. However, with the growing electroinformational web of telephones, faxes, computer networks, satellite links, and television and radio waves that increasingly connects all parts of our world, global comprehension of the whole truth in any international affair is becoming both possible and probable for the first time in human history.

Ever since America dropped its atom bombs on Japan—two penultimate acts of war that coincided with the dawn of the information age—we have been inching our way toward a "global comprehension of the whole truth." The mushroom-cloud photograph of massive Japanese death has been reproduced and spread throughout the world to each new generation of children (as have been the equally horrific photographs of the Nazi holocaust).

For the first time in human history, everybody has seen the savage and indecent act. Everybody has paid witness to the dominator's mentality and behavior, and everybody paid witness to the horrible aftermath. It is no accident that Hiroshima marked the end of the last "good war": the whole world has paid stark witness to the ugly truth of war and—there is hope for us—we have had growing difficulty with warring ever since.

Stewart Brand once commented that the first picture of planet Earth, taken from outer space, caused a tangible shift in people toward more holistic thinking. I believe a similar process began with the visual reporting of the atomic devastation of Japan and the unthinkable war crimes of Nazi Germany. This process has continued in the ensuing years with the steady improvements in media, communication, and information systems. Humans are developing a universally-spread "light of awareness" that is gradually eroding the power of mass denial and thus undermining all justifications for organized violence.

The linchpin lie will not stand up under common and collective international scrutiny; only closed-off, separate, and insular nations can sustain the foolishness of "different and unequal." Though patriots everywhere will protest, we are coming to the end of closed-off, separate, and insular nations. We are all different peoples, of course, because vitality demands diversity. But we are intrinsically linked in the most essential ways—through economics, resource distribution, environmental systems, and global communications—and we shall always be perfectly equal in any accounting of basic human rights. Through an international recognition of this linchpin *truth*, spread by the growing light of global awareness, all the ways of war are coming to be seen as unworthy, unhealthy, and unjustifiable.

Though the process is obviously moving too slowly for all those caught up in the continuing carnage of human affairs, it is moving nonetheless. As we encompass our world with a nearly instantaneous informational net (which we *must* keep reasonably free from corporate and governmental control), the age-old lies of patriarchy become ever more difficult to sustain. The electro-vibrational pulse of communication systems racing at ever-increasing speeds about the globe is the tangible manifestation of an entire world rousing into radical wakefulness. *There will be no more good wars because war can no longer happen in the dark shadows of human deceit and denial.*

The Gulf War in the winter of 1991 unfolded as a test-case for this growing global comprehension of the whole truth (though calling it a "war" rather than a "slaughter" was pure denial). It was no small irony that the specter of Hitler was raised during the American buildup to the slaughter. The idea was to make Saddam Hussein's Iraq look every bit as nasty and despicable as Hitler's Germany. This would provide the inspiration and justification for another good war.

Long before the bombs started falling, however, it was already common knowledge (to those who were not too denial-bound to see beyond the corporate press) that Iraq was the whole world's creation. It became especially apparent that the Western allies who were preparing to eradicate Iraq, with such oh-so-righteous indignation, had themselves built its army and munitions, provided its financing, and somewhat encouraged the Iraqis in their aggressive ways. In the end, it was impossible for any but the most denial-dumb to ignore the simple fact that this was yet another tragedy brought on by weak and dishonest dealings on the part of all involved. Through the light of the trans-status-quo media (the discorporate media?), which spread all about the globe, people everywhere could see that this slaughter, like all others, was neither inevitable nor justifiable.

Despite the fear-pandering obfuscations of their leaders, people are coming to know that the organized violence of war is approaching obsolescence. Such knowledge is slowly weaving its way into the genetic code of human beings, even as modern communication systems enable the almost instantaneous connectedness of whole nations. Slowly, we are coming to a healthy resolution of the Parable of the Tribes: when an aggressive nation moves against its neighbor, the whole world instantly knows, and, because all nations are intrinsically linked, the aggressor's powers of domination can be cut off. No nation stands purely alone any longer. No nation can pursue power over another without international support, and such invidious "support" can no longer be kept secret.

We are now in the midst of a truly Great Reversal. The parable can turn and work in the opposite direction: if enough nations choose peace, then all nations must choose peace. If enough nations commit to the open ways and honest means of partnership, then all nations will be partners. Cooperation is every bit as contagious as competition, power-with every bit as compelling as power-over, and partnership every bit as viral as domination. Monumental changes are already underway in our world as the "partnership virus" spreads through personal, political, and international relations. The realization that we are all differently equal—the organizing truth of partnership—is positively altering the creative course of all human affairs. Indeed, "human nature" itself is changing—for those awake enough to feel and allow for deep transformation.

Personal Reflections

This condition was my "wake-up call." I could have chosen either to respond to the message or to roll over and go back to sleep. Every crisis, whether it be illness, the consequences of addiction, or the loss of a loved one, offers us an opportunity to wake up.

—*Niro Asistent*

Think back over the past year or so: Have you gotten any urgent wake-up calls? Have you felt battered by events beyond your control? Have you been seriously ill? Did a key relationship change suddenly and without warning? Has your body been complaining, perhaps quietly, but on a regular basis? Has your livelihood been threatened? Have you been accident prone? Have you done anything that you immediately regretted but that had irrevocable consequences?

These events are vital warnings—indications that you must wake up to necessary changes in your world. How do you usually respond to such warnings? Are you at least considering making significant changes in your lifestyle? Changes in your family? Changes at work? Changes in your diet? Are you grateful for your wake-up calls, and are you moving freely through the changes? Or do you resent and resist them? Would you rather go back to sleep?

If you thought you had only eighteen months to live, what would you do differently? Would you want to sleep through your final days? Would you settle for your status-quo world? Or would you choose to pursue life with a greater intensity and deeper commitment, purposefully rousing yourself into radical wakefulness? What would it take to make such a choice freely, right now—to come awake without the harsh blare of unwanted circumstance?

Imagine that you have just received an urgent wake-up call and that the future of the world depends upon your hearing it and responding to it. What would it be? What aspect of your life would most likely come into sharp focus and present the need for deep and lasting transformation? Do you really want to know? Are you truly willing to see?

Could you respond by developing a Daily Awareness Routine—a simple set of practices incorporated into your day-to-day life? What would your ideal Daily Awareness Routine look like? What are the specific elements or disciplines of your ideal Daily Awareness Routine that you already know? What is keeping you from practicing them now?

SEVEN
Sexual Peace

The Clarence Thomas confirmation hearings for the U.S. Supreme Court inadvertently opened a bleak and seamy view into the heart of patriarchal culture. The sight of the solitary Anita Hill, stoically bearing the often vicious scrutiny of a panel of old, white, wealthy men, will forever be etched in the American consciousness as a flawless portrait of dominator reality. By the time the hearings had played out, Americans had learned volumes about the abuse of power and had paid collective witness to the strengths and self-oppressing habits of the status quo, as well as to the slimier nature of sexual politics in action.

Largely overlooked, however, was the most important lesson: that we will never fully resolve the sort of sexual conflict demonstrated by Thomas and Hill through our courts and legal systems. While increasingly just laws are critical steps toward more egalitarian societies, men and women cannot hope to litigate their way out of the patriarchal tensions of the past several thousand years. The dominator virus will not be legislated out of existence.

This is not to say that the various legal gains of the women's and civil rights movements should go unappreciated. It is certainly better to have the vote than not, to have access to better education and employment than not, and to be protected, however little, from harassment than not. But only a fool (or a self-serving dominator) would claim that women and racial minorities are now as powerful as the dominator elite in our political systems, or that they are treated equally within our schools and businesses, or that they experience genuine freedom from the foul climate of sexual and racial harassment. It is one thing to change a law; it is another thing entirely to change deep-seated human habit.

Moreover, as veteran feminists, civil rights workers, and environmentalists can attest, the dominators have never really given up their power, despite their occasional legal setbacks. Like the proverbial wounded bear, there is nothing as dangerous as a patriarchal system under attack. (My apology to all bears.) For every legal gain in the struggle against patriarchy, there has been a backlash of even greater proportions: the passing of *Roe v. Wade* brought "Operation Rescue" and a staunchly conservative Supreme Court; the passing of the Civil Rights Act brought backsliding quarrels over "quota bills" and the dangers of multi-culturalism; the passing of the Endangered Species Act brought twelve years of rabid anti-environmentalism. The most sincere and well-reasoned attempts to weaken patriarchal domination have typically given rise to new strategies and weapons on the part of the dominators.

The collapse of communism throughout the Soviet Union and eastern Europe is another case in point. Despite its other faults, most of the communist world managed a fair equality between the sexes and various ethnic groups, if only because quasi-egalitarianism was enforced as law. As each communist government has been overturned and the people have become "free," ethnic and religious hostilities have exploded, while women's numbers in government have quickly declined. Without the constraints of the totalitarian state, certain patriarchal tendencies that had been held in check have become unobstructed, and ancient patterns of domination and oppression have backlashed into new expression.

We cannot and should not cease our revolutions against oppressive masters nor our steady struggle against oppressive laws. Ultimately, however, any such struggle that fails to fundamentally alter patriarchal reality only feeds it. As Andrew Bard Schmookler puts it in *The Parable of the Tribes*, "Not to resist is to be transformed at the hands of the mighty. To resist requires that one transform oneself into their likeness. Either way, free human choice is prevented."[1]

We cannot let the dominators have their way, and yet we cannot fight them with their own methods. (Actually, our intuition whispers, we should not fight them at all.) This is most apparent with respect to violent assaults and overthrows—for the dominator virus thrives in violent relationships—but it is every bit as true with respect to most legal and democratic methods. The laws that govern any patriarchal system are critical determinants of that system, as are the prescribed methods for changing the laws. Thus, our most conscientious legal work from within the system, if only directed toward piecemeal correction of the system, rarely results in genuine, meaningful change. It is exceedingly difficult, if not impossible, to do direct battle with patriarchal reality without simultaneously giving substance to the dominator virus within one's own realm of existence.

Certainly, social activism against the excesses of patriarchal culture is both necessary and noble. But it is mostly a holding action, like the buttressing of a shoreline against vast ocean tides. Our ultimate challenge is to fundamentally change the ocean (patriarchy) itself, which means working with the dominator virus as it moves within our own bodies and immediate relationships.

Only through transforming patriarchal reality as it is embodied and sustained in our personal lives can we bring about a genuine transformation of political reality. The solutions to the political lie wholly enfolded within the personal. As Morris Berman writes, "The life of the body, and the emotions, and the subjective experience of how mind and body interact, constitute the real events of our lives, and condition, if not cause, everything that happens 'historically.' The challenge for history . . . is to start seeing the larger dramas in these somatic and 'subatomic' terms, and to come up with a methodology that convincingly relates the visible to the invisible."[2]

Our challenge, living here on the edge of changing paradigms, is to look within our own bodies for both cause and cure of the

patriarchal evils of our world. All human bodies are contaminated with the virulent poison of domination, and all human bodies
are living remedies in the making. If we turn our attention to our
bodies, and bring greater awareness to the physioemotional well-
springs of our lives, we will discover that our most powerful and
potentially most enjoyable path toward real personal and political
transformation is sexual. When we recover the primary sexual
experience of partnership, we will finally loosen and resolve the
age-old grip of domination.

The Human Electric

> Of what is the body made? It is made of emptiness and
> rhythm. At the ultimate heart of the body, at the heart of
> the world, there is no solidity. Once again, there is only
> the dance.   —*George Leonard*[3]

Any methodology that examines the subatomic dramas of the
human body and "convincingly relate[s] the visible to the invisible"
must address energy as it moves within and beyond the human
body. This is a difficult subject for many in the West, especially for
those conditioned to the modern medical model. The prevailing
tendency of this model, developed over the past few hundred
years, is to think of the body in strictly mechanical terms and to
ignore, discount, and at times actively suppress any data pertain-
ing to subtler dimensions of the human experience. This leads to a
stubborn refusal to even consider mental, emotional, and spiritual causes of human illness and healing. Moreover, as humans are
born and educated into purely physical notions of the body, they
lose the ability to even perceive these more subtle realities.

This is a natural outcome for any culture that splits the spiritual
from the physical: if we believe that the body is separate from and
beneath the realm of spirit, we will likely fail to experience the
tingling pulse of embodied spirit that should come so easily to humans. The inability of scientists and researchers to personally feel
the merging of spirit and flesh as a simple fact of life has led to an
extremely limited medical model. This is not to say that it has not
been a successful model in many ways. However, it has funda-

mental shortcomings that, if they could be fully addressed and resolved, would make Western medicine infinitely more effective. More than anything else, the Western model lacks a comprehensive understanding of energy as it moves through and radiates beyond the human organism.

This is ironic since Western science has so effectively (if not safely) described and controlled various energies *external* to humans. The march of industrial progress and relevant human history over the past few centuries has involved the steady mastering of such energies: the discovery of fire, the harnessing of steam power, the building of coal furnaces, the development of the internal combustion engine, the advent of the petroleum era, the splitting of the atom. Humanity has been propelled forward and increasingly defined by its ability to gather, store, and efficiently release energy for specific purposes. Power as a human being, and as a nation, has come to mean access to and control of external energies. Dominance, in the modern world, goes to those who own and govern power plants, oil fields, and high-energy munitions and technologies, and to those who are able to wield such fires and forces to their own advantage.

Yet, for all of its vaunted success with the workings of external energies, Western science has been slow to understand the movement of the internal energies of "the human electric" in the timeless drama of human relationship. A variety of instruments for measuring human energies, such as electrocardiograms (EKGs), electroencephalograms (EEGs), CAT scanners, and magnetic resonance imagers are now standard equipment in medical research and practice. There has been much progress in delineating various energy phenomena within and surrounding the body: the minute electrical storms that rage in the nucleus of every living cell as food sugars are converted into caloric force; the ways that our senses of sight, sound, smell, taste, and touch all rest upon the perception of energetic vibrations; the changing electrical potentials at the site of any injury that are a possible key to all healing; the contraction or elongation of muscle cells from the stimulation of electrical impulses; the waves of electricity that drive the heart; the sea of overlapping electrical fields in which the brain swims; and the complex web of streaming electrons and positively charged ions that composes the nervous system and brings order to the various bodily systems. As physicist Fred Alan Wolf writes, "Every living cell uses electricity in some manner or another. We now know that electricity controls the operation of nerves, muscles, and organs; that essentially, all of the body's functions are electrical in some way."[4]

Modern medicine also uses a growing array of energy-based treatments. The discovery and development of x-rays validated the interaction of electromagnetic fields with living bodies and the fact that these fields can positively or negatively affect the health of living cells. X-rays have long been used for both diagnosis and treatment, even as their potential for physical harm has gradually become apparent. Western energy medicine also uses the electrostimulation of spinal cords to block pain, of acupuncture points to produce pain-reducing endorphins, of broken bones to speed healing, and of cancer cells to shrink tumors. Other developments include such energy-based systems as laser-optic surgery, ultrasound diagnostics, and radiation therapy.

There is no question that such progress is slowly shifting modern medicine toward a more energy-based understanding of illness and treatment. As Dr. Richard Gerber writes in *Vibrational Medicine*, an in-depth exploration of the human electric, "Applications of electromagnetic energy to treat human illness may begin to open up the scientific minds of the medical establishment to the possibilities of healing with energy. . . . Many of the so-called 'fringe areas' of medicine are, in fact, applying slightly different principles of 'energy medicine.'"[5] We are clearly progressing toward a future medicine of light, sound, and electromagnetism that will make our current surgical tools and pharmaceuticals seem crude by comparison.

Still, there is a strong tendency in the West to view various human energy phenomena as merely the mechanical effects of physical nature and to strictly avoid any references to mind, emotion, consciousness, or personal nature. Though science has given us an exquisite view into the mostly invisible world of human electrical currents and radiant fields, it is a view that largely disregards the individual person and his or her unique psychoemotional environment. We are told that when a biceps muscle contracts it lets out a burst of ionized calcium ions, that digestion is the oxidizing of glucose to produce caloric energy, and that we "breathe to change 36 molecules of ADP [adenosine diphosphate] into 36 molecules of ATP [adenosine triphosphate]."[6] But where is the person in all this? Are we to believe that the movements of energy within a human organism are mechanical absolutes that occur apart from and regardless of the unique thoughts and feelings of that organism? And if we allow an individual's thoughts and feelings into the human energy equation, what does that do to our precise molecular descriptions?

These concepts stretch into forbidden zones for the classically trained scientist: A fundamental precept of Western scientific inquiry states that the world, including the body, should be studied objectively, without reference to the subjective reality of an individual. While this principle has been sound for most areas of science, it critically limits any study of the human electric. The energy moving within a human being is interactive with and affected by the moment to moment mental and emotional states of the individual, by the quality of his or her relationships, and by a broad range of influences in the environment. We cannot separate the electron dance of a flexing muscle from the psychoemotional reality of the person flexing the muscle. Our most objective descriptions of human energy phenomena will always be significantly limited by the degree to which we attempt to leave the individual's subjective experience out of the picture. Any complete science of the human electric necessarily depends upon the inner movements of human consciousness.

Ayurvedic medicine, for instance, has been practiced throughout India, Tibet, and Nepal for thousands of years and continues to be a viable medical system and description of the whole human organism. As doctor and author Deepak Chopra demonstrates in his wise and incisive writings, the underlying principles of Ayurveda are steadily being confirmed by the varied modern insights of quantum physics, ecology, genetics, and psychoneuroimmunology.

Basic to Ayurveda is an understanding of *prana*: human energy that is gathered and translated in specific energy vortexes (*chakras*) and that can be individually affected by such disciplines as *yoga* and *pranayama*. The physical body, including its healthy function and any illnesses, is considered to be a manifestation of prana, which, in turn, is seen as arising from mind, or universal consciousness. Thus, writes Chopra, "When you look at Ayurveda's anatomical charts, you don't see the familiar organs pictured in *Gray's Anatomy*, but a diagram of where the mind is flowing as it creates the body."[7] Ayurvedic physicians and yogis view the human electric in systemic terms, with causation running from mind through energy to the manifesting body. The notion that the movement of prana could be studied with respect to its physical effect and without reference to mind or emotion is totally backward to Ayurveda: the electrical or pranic reality of the individual is understood to be continuously conditioned by his or her psychoemotional consciousness.

The Chinese call the energies of the human electric *chi*. The practices of acupuncture and Chinese medicine, as well as the disciplines of *chi kung* meditation and most of the martial arts, rest upon the basic experience of chi as a vital force moving within and beyond the human body. Like prana to the practitioners of Ayurveda, chi to the Chinese is not a mere abstraction or mental construct, nor is it viewed solely as a secondary effect of physical processes.

An acupuncturist diagnoses the physical systems and organs of the body by examining the flow of chi through subtle pathways, called meridians. She or he then places needles into specific points along the meridians to affect specific organs and physical systems. Chi kung practitioners and martial artists learn to consciously manipulate their vital energies for increased personal power; they experience chi as a tangible presence that can be intentionally gathered, stored, circulated, and expressed. Again, causation is seen as running from individual consciousness through energy or chi to the body. Again, an individual's ability to feel the movement of chi and to systematically control such movement is considered fundamental to his or her health and happiness.

The Ayurvedic and Chinese human energy systems are thousands of years old, represent the collective and subjective experience of millions of practitioners, and continue to the present day as effective mind-body disciplines. Similar systems are common throughout the world, though none are as widely practiced. The !Kung call human energy *num* and view it as a spiritual force omnipresent in their world that can be channeled by strong healers for the good of the community. Hawaiian *kahunas* call the energy *mana* and learn to accumulate it in great quantities to purposefully express through the laying on of hands and healing at a distance. In parts of Africa, the energy is called *voodoo*: a powerful voodoo practitioner can direct a force of energy that is capable of killing another person.[8]

There are also many viable human energy systems in the West, including homeopathy, bioenergetics, Therapeutic Touch, Reiki, polarity therapy, reflexology, kinesiology, biofeedback, and chiropractic. Each of these systems, in its own way, assumes an individual's ability to consciously manipulate the human electric for specific purposes. The crux of all such systems—East and West, ancient and modern—is that humans are subsumed with a vital energy that flows within and radiates beyond the body, operates according to discernible principles, and is synergistically interactive with mind, emotion, body, breath, and external relationships.

The challenge for Western science is to continue with its meticulous descriptions of human energy phenomena and its development of energy-medicine technologies while simultaneously opening to the creative forces of individual consciousness. It is not enough to describe the electrical firing of a neural synapse if we do not also describe the psychoemotional environment surrounding it. Nor is it enough to use electromagnetic tools for healing the body if we do not also engage and educate the creative human energies that *cause* the body. Ultimately, we need scientists who are as comfortable sitting with their eyes closed and meditating on the movements of energy within the body electric as they are sitting before electron microscopes and EEGs. Both forms of scientific inquiry will serve us better when they are joined together.

Toward an Anatomy of the Invisible

The unseen connection between the physical body and the subtle forces of spirit holds the key to understanding the inner relationship between matter and energy.
                        —*Richard Gerber, M.D.*[9]

We are now aware that our states of consciousness have a strong influence on the energy efficiency of our cells. Our consciousness can actually trigger the precursors and hormones needed to stimulate our cell receptors to quickly accept and utilize nutritional modifiers.
                        —*Christopher Hills*[10]

Our task of convincingly relating the visible to the invisible involves connecting large-scale historic movements with the psychoemotional reality of individual humans, connecting the political with the personal, and connecting bodily experiences with spiritual insights. This task clearly demands a more thorough understanding of the human electric. More to the point, it demands that we, the living, breathing human beings who make such profound connections, actually recognize and feel the vibratory reality of energy as it moves through our own bodies and lives.

The temptation is to just think about all of this—to spend time pondering the nature of patriarchal abuse and theorizing possible causes and cures while unconsciously ignoring the psychophysical patterns of domination and submission that each of us personally embody. If we truly care to change the world, we must start by transforming patriarchal reality as it is energetically determined within our own personal experience.

The dominator virus is an energy demon: It enters the human organism through mental and/or emotional causation, is carried forward as fixed patterns of subtle energy, and informs the manifesting body and its response to relationships. The political task of transforming patriarchal culture requires nothing less than touching, feeling, and finally resolving the patterns of patriarchal abuse that are held and sustained within each individual person.

While this may seem at first to be an overwhelming challenge, in fact it is easier to consciously change our own patterns of energy and relationship than to fundamentally change the macro-patterns of society. Toward this end, we must expand our understanding of energy and the functions of the human electric. We must learn to consciously and intentionally alter personal energy patterns for our own good and the greater good of society.

Scientists working with quantum energies in laboratory experiments and human energy explorers from many different traditions and disciplines are familiar with four basic qualities of energy that can guide us in the work of personal transformation. These four qualities, discussed in the next four sections, are surely not the whole picture of the human electric, nor the final word on human energy systems. However, they are enough to help us effectively alter our individual energy patterns so that we may eliminate the dominator virus and transform our relationships, families, and societies.

Energy Becomes Matter

> O amazement of things—even the least particle!
> O spirituality of things!   —*Walt Whitman*[11]

Albert Einstein showed the world that energy and matter are interconvertible. His formula $E=mc^2$ states that all matter in the universe is comprised of "frozen" energy, or mass, that is in the process, however slowly, of converting back into energy, and that energy can reciprocally turn into matter.

The first practical applications of Einstein's insights involved releasing the enormous quantities of energy held in certain forms of matter. This was a logical step for humans: We have been releasing the energy from material forms since the time of the first wood fires. We progressed through the development of candles and oil lamps, and the invention of gunpowder, to all of the energy marvels of the industrial and nuclear ages. We now understand that when a log is thrown on a fire or a lump of coal is thrown into a furnace and things become warmer, brighter, or capable of doing more work, the material substance disappears as its mass is converted into energy: as mc^2 becomes E.

It is our continuing good fortune that we have not used this mass-into-energy knowledge to incinerate our planet. We can only hope that we will one day have as much facility, but much greater humility, as we reverse the equation and convert energy into matter. In order to do so, we will need to comprehend the special nature of energy in living systems.

The behavior of energy in nonorganic systems is described in the first and second laws of thermodynamics. The First Law of Thermodynamics states that energy is neither created nor destroyed: "The total energy involved in a process is always conserved. It may change its form in the most complicated way, but none of it is lost."[12] The Second Law of Thermodynamics describes an overall trend toward decreasing order in a system of energy: "While the total energy involved in a process is always constant, the amount of useful energy is diminishing, dissipating into heat, friction, and so on."[13] When, for instance, we cook food, some of the energy produced by our stove is absorbed first by the food and then again by our bodies when we eat. This portion of the energy is orderly and usefully conserved. Most of the stove's energy, however, radiates from the cooking pot as heat and then dissipates—it is no longer organized in any useful way.

Taken together, these two laws predict that the whole universe is slowly running down, or increasing in entropy, as an infinity of mechanical processes all steadily lose energy to disorganized heat and dissipation. At the macro level of burning stars and solar systems, the prediction of increasing entropy makes sense (although the universe has a fair amount of time remaining before it expires through "heat death"). At the micro level of living cells, biological systems, and the blue-green anomaly called Earth, however, decreasing entropy is more often the rule: "Living systems display the property of negative entropy, or a tendency toward decreasing disorder of the system."[14] Living systems grow. Therefore, for the whole system that is our planet, life is irrepressibly growing, rather than dissipating.

Consider a dead human body. As it decomposes, much of its energy is conserved by the tiny organisms that feast upon it, while some of its energy is lost through the heat of decomposition. Overall, there is a net gain in entropy, in accordance with the Second Law of Thermodynamics.

A living human body, however, transcends this law through its ability to reconfigure energy into useful mass. Much of the energy that is presumed to be dissipated and forever lost through mechanical processes is actually recaptured by organic processes and put to use again. This is the evolutionary breakthrough of living systems: entropy is reversed as energy becomes mass. Energy, as it moves through living systems, is always giving rise to new order, greater complexity, and fresh material form. The energy of living systems is an infinitely creative force as it infinitely becomes matter. This is the pure essence of being alive.

Moreover, human beings show a unique capacity for conscious manipulation of this living energy. Our every thought sets off a cascade of electrochemical reactions throughout the body (and beyond). As Chopra writes: "At the very instant that you think, 'I am happy,' a chemical messenger translates your emotion, *which has no solid existence whatever in the material world* [my emphasis], into a bit of matter so perfectly attuned to your desire that literally every cell in your body learns of your happiness and joins in. The fact that you can instantly talk to 50 trillion cells in their own language is just as inexplicable as the moment when nature created the first photon out of empty space."[15]

We think, energy moves, and the body becomes: this is the creative essence of being human. Energy sits in the middle of this creative equation—energy becomes the material body even as mind directs energy. As individuals, we tend at any moment toward either entropy or life: toward dissipating into death and disorder or toward growing, evolving, transforming, and transcending. Our qualities of mind—our thoughts, beliefs, dreams, visions, and intentions—ultimately direct the life energy that, in turn, creates our world.

Energy is Connection

For every atom belonging to me as good belongs to you.
—*Walt Whitman*[16]

Of the many mind-bending findings and suppositions of modern physics, my favorite is Bell's theorem. To grossly simplify, in 1964, physicist John S. Bell mathematically demonstrated that even if two particles in a two-particle system were separated by light-years of distance, a change in the spin of one particle would simultaneously affect its twin. There is no apparent connection between the two particles, so this is not only a preposterous finding with respect to Newtonian mechanics, but it is equally preposterous to quantum mechanics, which says that nothing can move faster than the speed of light and thus no signal could pass instantaneously between the particles.

Nonetheless, Bell's theorem has been tested many times and is now considered a valid, if perplexing, description of reality. In some way, the two seemingly separated particles are in fact connected. In some way—the larger implications cannot be avoided—*all of the seemingly separate things in this world are in fact connected.* "Ultimately," writes physicist David Bohm, "the entire universe (with all its 'particles,' including those constituting human beings, their laboratories, observing instruments, etc.) has to be understood as a single undivided whole, in which analysis into separate and independently existent parts has no fundamental status."[17]

Energy is the medium through which all things are connected. Energy is a great omnipresent sea, filling all of the universe. In some places it manifests as specific matter, just as a small portion of a northern sea might manifest as an ice floe. The notion that the ice is somehow separate from the sea out of which it grew and in which it moves is simply false, as is the more reasonable notion that one ice floe is separate from another. The notion that manifest reality is somehow separate from the energy out of which it grows and in which it moves is equally false, as is the more reasonable notion that *this* piece of manifest reality is separate from *that*. Or that I am separate from you.

Information, therefore, can move instantaneously from one "end" of the energy sea to the other end, or from one "piece" of manifest reality to another because, in fact, there is only one omnipresent energy sea. Energy enables universal omniscience: all things are connected to and interactive with one another. Energy is the medium of all connection, and information known by any one thing is, via energy, at least potentially known by any other thing.

Through the one energy that is manifesting as human beings, flowers, tigers, planets, and stars, the changing spin of a single electron anywhere is immediately communicated to electrons everywhere. Through the one energy extending from my body and yours, we are intimately connected and we forever share information, whatever the physical distances or emotional gulfs between us. Through the circulating energies and radiant fields that comprise my being, I am fundamentally connected as body, mind, and spirit—despite the sense of separate parts I sometimes experience—and a change in any one aspect of myself is instantly reflected in every other aspect.

Bell's theorem, applied to the human electric, provides a basis for holistic transformation. Any change in mind affects the body; a simple change in breathing affects the mind; every emotional change affects the breath; all cellular changes affect the emotions. Every spinning electron of a human organism is interconnected. A change in the merest piece brings change to the whole. Moreover, all of our personal changes, at all levels of self, radiate outward to affect our families and cultures. However we choose to consciously move ourselves, we are always moving energy. Thus, we are truly moving our whole selves, and our whole world as well.

Energy as Hologram

I do not doubt but the majesty and beauty of the world
are latent in any iota of the world.
—*Walt Whitman*[18]

Further insight into how energy enables simultaneous effects over great distances, and how information moves faster than the speed of light, and how apparently separate parts are in fact connected wholes can be gleaned from the study of holograms. A hologram is a special photographic plate on which are recorded interfering or overlapping wave patterns of light. When additional light is precisely shined on the plate, it generates a three-dimensional figure. This, in itself, is a rather remarkable phenomenon.

The real fascination, however, lies in the fact that all information is evenly distributed throughout the holographic plate. On an ordinary photograph of, say, a standing human being, information about the head lies solely in the upper portion of the photo while information about the feet lies solely in the lower portion. With a hologram, by contrast, all of the information is evenly spread throughout the entire plate.

Thus, if we cut off a small piece of a holographic plate, that piece, when properly illumined, will still generate the whole three-dimensional figure recorded in the full hologram, though it will be a less distinct version of it. If we cut that little piece in half, and in half again, all of the information for the recorded figure will still be contained within the remaining piece of holographic plate. The tiniest speck of a holographic plate contains all the data and creative potential of the whole.

Like Bell's theorem, holograms are major affronts to ordinary thinking. Unlike Bell's theorem, holograms have been demonstrated and used practically for several decades. During that time, the special nature of holographic reality has been suggested by many as a viable paradigm for universal and human realities.

Physicist David Bohm points out that the basic structure of holograms—interfering wave fronts—is found throughout the universe in the form of energy flows and fields. Waves of sound, light, and heat; gravitational, radiational and electromagnetic fields; and, indeed, all forms of movement create what Bohm has called the "holomovement": a universe permeated with overlapping waves of energy that, holographically, enfold the total whole within every part. As George Leonard writes: "Since every particle in the universe warmer than absolute zero is constantly producing fields of waves, and every organized combination of particles is also broadcasting its own unique fields, the number of intersecting sets of waves approaches infinity. Theoretically, some sort of superholograph could be made at any spot in the universe containing information about the whole universe from that vantage point."[19]

Neurophysiologist Karl Pribram has shown that memory, rather than being stored in specific regions of brain tissue, is actually spread holographically throughout the brain (and possibly throughout the whole body). Others have claimed that cells are microscopic holograms, since every cell contains all of the information necessary to create an entire body. Richard Leviton has suggested that many of the world's energy medicines, including Ayurveda, acupuncture, foot reflexology, Rolfing, and iridology, are based on information that is encoded in wave interference patterns throughout the body: "Overlapping, multilayered body maps are not at all contradictory or mutually exclusive but represent the holographic versatility to store immense amounts of information in nearly the same space."

"The final implication," Leviton adds, "is that the human body, composed of a myriad of smaller holographic projections, is itself an encoded frequency pattern, a cosmic hologram awaiting our illumination."[20] When we shine just the right light—the special light of open awareness—through the holographic plates that comprise our bodies, all of creation may be perceived and understood.

The possibility of creative and intentional human consciousness leads to a further and most exciting implication of holographic reality. If all of the information for the whole universe is contained in the smallest part of the universe, then what happens when a human being changes that part? If our individual, human fields of energy reflect the whole universe, what happens when we purposefully alter our personal energy patterns? The answer is that our every action reverberates outward to touch everyone and everything. We can change the world, including its most historically ingrained patterns, by starting with our individual bodies and minds.

Energy is Omnipresent

O to realize space!
The plenteous of all, that there are no bounds,
To emerge and be of the sky, of the sun and moon and
    flying clouds, as one with them.
                          —*Walt Whitman* [21]

The fact that all matter in the universe is comprised of energy—interconnected and holo-related—tells us that there is no thing, place, or event, nor any relationship between things, places, or events, that does not rest upon energetic phenomena. Energy is everywhere and everything, and everywhen in between. And for all our sincere and reasonable studies of energy, its inescapable omnipresence may forever complicate and frustrate our attempts to describe, define, or even think about it.

The reason for this is best explained by the analogy of a fish in water. How can a fish study water when it is continuously surrounded by and immersed in it? How do we study something for which we have no independent frame of reference? The electron microscope is not only physically comprised of energy, it is powered by energy and is used by a creature who is likewise comprised of and empowered by energy. All of our instruments for measuring energy are only useful to the extent that our brains and senses are energy alive. What can we objectively say about energy when it could not be said nor even thought of without energy?

Paradoxically, we are limited in our ability to know about energy by its very omnipresence. The situation could be compared to looking through a telescope and trying to see the telescope's lens—we may be able to infer much about the lens by the vision that it enables and, if the lens is dirty, we may be able to infer even more about it, but we will never actually see it. The lens is omnipresent in our field of vision and thus impossible to objectively see. Similarly, energy is omnipresent in every aspect of our beings and thus impossible to objectively know.

This does not mean that we should stop thinking about,

studying, and attempting to better understand and use energy in all its myriad forms. It does mean that our data may tend to be somewhat slippery, that our reasoning may often run in circles, and that a certain degree of mystery may always abide.

As we work to transform patriarchal culture, it is critical that we understand the energetic reality of the dominator virus. The human organism, human relationship, and everything else in the universe rests upon interactive waves of energy. All of life is connected through energy and all of life may be affected through energy with the creative light of human consciousness. Though for thousands of years humans have created and enforced energetic patterns of domination, submission, violence, and abuse, there is evidence that we can create and enjoy patterns of cooperation and partnership if we choose.

Presently, we are mostly choosing to be living and breathing patriarchally contaminated patterns of embodied energy. Ending the cycle of violence and abuse in our world means contacting the dominator virus as a vibratory reality within our own beings and choosing anew. There is no better way to do so than through the unique attribute of human sexuality.

The Promise of Joy

Thus, far from being identical to "sin," sexual communion is a human right, a humanizing obligation, and a living instrument of our ultimate and pleasurable sacrifice or translation beyond human psycho-physical structures and human limits of knowledge.

—*Da Free John* [22]

Cultures that do not rigidly divide the body from the spirit invariably tend toward a healthy and pleasurable experience of sexuality. I have already mentioned the !Kung with their sexual experience that is free, open, unselfconscious and with a refreshing lack of rules. Many other indigenous cultures must have expressed a similar sexual nature until the black-robed missionaries came to teach them about the horrors of bodily pleasure. Likewise, the "pagan" cultures of the pre-patriarchal West have been derided as "virgin cults" and "temple prostitute" cultures. However, their people clearly enjoyed sex more than their Judeo-Christian attackers ever could, and they developed spiritual practices that included the joys of sex rather than the denial of sexual experiences as originally sinful and "of the devil."

Synchronistically, the cultures that have avoided splitting the physical from the spiritual have tended toward the clearest understanding of the human electric. Since sexual energy is a primary aspect of the human electric, such cultures have naturally developed the clearest facility with the sexual experience.

The ancient Chinese, for instance, fully integrated sexual practices with the spiritual traditions of Taoism. Taoist masters pursue a perfect balance of all polarities: the universal energies of yin and yang, darkness and light, cold and hot, inward and outward, human and nature, Earth and heaven, of female and male. This balance represents the one supreme path—the Way, or Tao. Taoism is a practical philosophy of partnership: the path toward a harmonious merging of all opposites. With such a philosophical foundation and purpose, Taoism quite naturally embraces sex— the union of opposites—for its high spiritual potential and has developed sexual practices to release and enhance this potential.

The Taoist approach to sexuality is derived from its understanding of universal and human energies. Taoism considers each human to be born with an abundant, though finite, quantity of principal energy, or chi, that governs the body's processes, regulates its organs, is the key to its health, and, through misuse, is the source of all its sickness. Intuitively grasping the first and second laws of thermodynamics, the ancient Taoists taught that while chi can neither be created nor destroyed, humans regularly lose chi through a range of dissipative practices, the most serious being unenlightened sexual activity.

The Taoists consider sexual energy to be a somewhat denser energy than chi that is produced specifically in the sexual organs of men and women. Taoism teaches that a major purpose of sexual energy (after puberty) is procreation, and toward this end the energy manifests as female eggs and male sperm. Both eggs and sperm can be viewed, from such an energy perspective, as extraordinarily potent bundles, or manifest fields, of the human life force.

According to Taoism, when sexual activity produces a child, the energies involved have been wondrously conserved and channeled toward the generation of new life. When, however, a woman discharges the creative energy of her eggs during normal (unenlightened) menstruation or a man discharges the creative energy of his sperm during normal (unenlightened) ejaculation, then those energies are lost. A lifetime of such losses, according to Taoism, brings the human equivalent of universal heat death— premature aging and degenerative illness.

Taoist sexual practice strives to reverse aging and degeneration by conserving and transforming sexual energy. For women, this practice involves a meditative discipline through which the creative energy stored in the eggs is consciously retained (prior to menstruation) and redirected within the body, mind, and spirit for transformational puposes. For men, this practice involves a meditative discipline through which the creative energy stored in the sperm is consciously retained (prior to ejaculation) and redirected within the body, mind, and spirit for transformational purposes. For male or female sexual partners, it involves purposefully arousing the creative energies of sexual play and then consciously directing those energies toward spiritual growth.

As modern Taoist masters Mantak and Maneewan Chia write: "Each time we are sexually active we generate a lot of life-force energy. When we have a normal orgasm, the life-force pours out of us into the universe. If we can learn to redirect the orgasmic energy inward and upward instead of outward, the energy will reach the even greater orgasmic experience known as total body orgasm . . . an experience never felt as a result of normal sex."[23] Thus, not only does Taoism offer a more energy-wise and spiritually adept approach to sex, it promises uncommon pleasure in the process.

India also has a long tradition of spiritually inspired sex. In the Hindu creation tale, Shiva and Shakti, god and goddess, merge their diverse energies through ecstatic union and create the universe. From this mythology has grown the practice of Tantra, a scientific approach to spiritual enlightenment that fully embraces the human sexual experience. As Tantric teacher Margo Anand writes: "The joyful dance between Shiva and Shakti is reflected in all living beings and manifests itself as pleasure, beauty, and happiness. This, in Tantra, is the nature of the divine, the root of all that exists."[24]

Tantric practice closely resembles Taoist sexual practice. It involves the same understanding and experience of human energy (prana) and the belief that men and women are better served through conserving prana than through dissipating it in normal sexual orgasm. There is also a clear understanding in Tantra that merely suppressing sexual desire is not enough, and is in fact injurious to the individual. The discipline must involve a conscious transformation of sexual energy for higher purposes. Tantra provides such a discipline, which uses the powerful polarities that arise in any sexual experience to regenerate and enlighten the sexual-spiritual players.

Thus Tantra, much like Taoist sex, is rooted in a fundamental belief in partnership: The world grows out of a joyful merging of opposites, and humans, through sexual play, can genuinely embody such universal wholeness. Indeed, men and women must come to terms with the vital energies moving through and between all bodies—it is a primary demand of our being embodied. In both the Taoist and Tantric approaches to sex, human sexual energy is felt, liberated, celebrated, and channeled for the equal good of both partners and for the greater good of all living creatures. Every time two humans merge as intimate, harmonious, and vitally-creative partners, our whole world shifts toward greater safety, health, and living joy.

The American adept Da Free John draws from both the Taoist and Tantric traditions in his teaching of spiritual sexuality, or "sexual communion." He writes, "Sexual communion is the process of sexual participation in the [vital energies of life] through free and full feeling, unobstructed breathing, control of the genital spasm, and relaxation-release of the whole and entire bodily being into the Force of Life. . . . The process of sexual communion expresses primary physical, emotional, and mental responsibility via the breath and via the utter sacrificial gesture of love, or feeling-attention, to one's lover. By these means, the lower body cycles of generative and degenerative exploitation of the sexual process are transformed into regenerative or whole bodily and uniquely human sexual process."[25]

Sexual communion, then, begins as a personal, psychophysical process requiring the learned disciplines of bodily awareness, aroused relaxation, conscious breathing, and, especially, control and redirection of the normal genital orgasm. It expands to include the other person—the lover—and the shared experience of total body orgasm. Above all, sexual communion calls upon the lovers to surrender, as partners, into the larger, universal currents of living energy.

The normal sexual experience, with its emphasis on achieving genital orgasm, rarely delivers the lovers to an experience of such ecstatic, universal wholeness. To the contrary, most (nonlesbian) lovers feel oddly separate after a man ejaculates: the genital explosion ends the dance of connectedness. With the exception of those times when new life is conceived, all such sex tends toward entropy. Though there is often an immediate and almost divine blush of joy and satisfaction, it stems mostly from the release of chronic tensions. While this brings short-term pleasure and some degree of therapeutic benefit, it is ultimately a dissipative process with long-term enervating effects for the individual bodies and for the relationship as a whole.

This may explain the religious impulse toward restricting sex to purely procreative purposes. There is a germ of wisdom in such thinking. However, as the long and steamy saga of human history has amply demonstrated, you cannot repress human sexual energy. "Just say no" has never and will never work. Instead, religious and societal sexual repression so muddles the human sexual response, and so damages the human electric, that we are left with almost species-wide sexual frustration and dysfunction that has manifested in a wide range of addictive patterns of behavior. This, unfortunately, only adds to the mistaken impulse to repress or prevent sex.

While the just-say-noers have never been able to actually stop sex from happening, they have managed to profoundly confuse our world. For the past five thousand years, a version of human sexuality has been defined, delineated, regulated, and mass promoted by god-fearing men and women who have purposefully contracted from the experience and possibility of free-flowing bodily pleasure. Taking our sexual lead from such people is like trying to fix a computer with a chainsaw: we will never grow into healthy sexual creatures from the starting place of "sex is sin."

Sexual energy needs conscious, purposeful, loving, and enjoyable redirection rather than ill-informed and self-destructive repression. "Otherwise," as Da Free John writes, "that energy will accumulate or define itself in our finite shape and demand eliminative release."[26] The common human failure to learn and practice the ways of sexual communion has led to a race of energetically pent-up beings given to impulsive and generally dysfunctional discharges. Moreover, sexual repression and dysfunction provide the ideal medium for dominant/submissive patterns of relationship. There is no greater antidote for the dominator virus than whole-hearted sexual communion.

The books by Chia, Anand, and Da Free John that I have cited each give more comprehensive instructions on the practice of sexual communion than I can offer here. However, there are several aspects of sexual communion that I wish to stress.

The first is that our desire for and movement toward greater sexual communion neither denies nor invalidates our present sexual experience. We should not think that only a specific practice of sexual communion is right and that therefore any deviations are sinful and wrong. (The last thing anyone needs is another reason to feel guilty about sex.) If we accept that human sexuality is consciously mutable and that we ourselves are free sexual beings, then sexual communion is a growing edge of awareness in every sexual encounter. Can we touch each other with even greater respect? Can we move together as partners, at times leading and at times following, and become one body of love and pleasure? Can we achieve the spontaneity of children's play, so that we are carried away from our sexual patterns, habits, and addictions? Can we responsibly utilize the vast creative potential in every breath of sexual arousal?

Second, the powerfully fulfilling experience of sexual communion is an inherent possibility for all human beings. Sexual communion is not the sole property of sexual Olympians or yogic adepts. It is as central to the human design as a breath, a gentle touch, a kiss, a suddenly urgent coming together, or a wondrous conception of new life. It does, however, require the conscious participation of the individuals involved. It requires men and women who are willing to grow beyond the impulsive dictates of mere animal sexuality to responsibly pursue the special fruits of enlightened, conscious sexuality. Indeed, sexual communion is a "humanizing obligation." It is a critical step that all people must take if they are to contribute to the successful transformation of this world.

Third, sexual communion is, on all levels, an experience of genuine partnership. It begins with each individual merging his or her own body, mind, breath, and spirit and then becomes an empowering union of two once separate lovers. Moreover, sexual communion demands partnership: It can only work for those who come together in the spirit of true equality and with a commitment to love beyond any patterns of domination and submission. For those who question the ability of women and men, or women and women, or men and men to ever live as real partners, sexual communion is both answer and path.

Fourth, sexual communion must be approached, practiced and understood as a human energy experience. We must go beyond the common biological and psychoemotional functions of genital orgasm to discover (recover) a more sublime and ultimately more vital sexual reality. As we learn the ways of sexual communion, we become experientially conversant with the energy dimensions of the human electric and are thus opened to vast new realms of creative possibility.

Finally, sexual communion is an invitation into the deep and abiding cellular joy that is our birthright. Humans are born into bodies that are designed to feel good as a primary mode of being. Of the many crimes of dominator reality, few are as destructive to the human spirit as the violent negation of simple bodily pleasure. Through the physical and emotional abuses of poisonous pedagogy, the bodily denials of religious doctrine, and the insipid insanities of antisexual morality, we have been shamed. We have given in to the hatred of the body that is so commonly accepted throughout human society. Sexual communion is the intentional recovering of our innate and ever-healthy love of the body and, yes, our love of all bodies. Sexual communion is the purposeful unlearning of the abusive conditioning of patriarchal culture and its legacy of body hate and chronic sexual conflict.

Sexual conflict—"I hate this body and I project the hate I feel onto others"—is the energetic core of patriarchy and the root cause of all of the current abuses of dominator reality. Sexual conflict is the dominator virus: when we are rendered incapable of feeling a true energetic connection with another, then any chance for a partnership relationship is crippled, if not entirely lost, and we tend instead toward the patriarchal patterns of domination and submission.

The resolution of deeply ingrained tensions of sexual conflict takes us inevitably to sexual peace. This experience of sexual peace—"I love this body and easily extend the love I feel to you"— is not something we learn. Rather, it is our natural state when we let go of the foolish and abusive conditioning of patriarchal culture. We, who have fallen from the primary condition of pure, cellular joy, can make our way back to Paradise again. Moreover, we can—and we surely will—support our children in forever embracing their simple bodily pleasures and their inborn capacities for unconditionally loving sexual peace with others.

Personal Reflections

Imagine that you are standing along an ocean shoreline, facing the still water on a cloudless night. A bright and beautiful full moon is rising just above the horizon. You notice that there is a beam of light extending from the moon across the water to your feet. On both sides of the beam of light, the water's surface is pitch black and impenetrable, but within the slice of night illumined by the beam you can see clearly all the way to the horizon.

As you walk along the beach, the beam of light moves with you, step by step, continuing to illumine the water before you whenever you stop to look at it. You ponder that this is the light energy of the sun, traveling millions of miles, reflecting off the moon, and streaming in a clear beacon directly to you, wherever you are. You appreciate this, and realize that you are always perfectly connected to the one source of all energy and life on Earth.

Further down the beach, you see a woman, standing like yourself, looking out into the water. You see no beam of light streaming from the moon to her feet. Instead, the water before her seems dark, as if there is no moon at all. And yet you know that she is seeing her own beam of light—that from her perspective the water before her is brightly illumined. Moreover, you know that if she were to look in your direction, she would fail to see the beam of light before you.

You realize that somehow you are both equally connected to the same source of light even though you are different people standing in different places. You are aware that we are all forever connected to the one source of living light, and thus to one another, though we too often fail to realize our connectedness. Somehow, you know that we are all holo-related—that we are diverse threads of a single living web, even though we do not always perceive the evidence of our relatedness.

Now, a large group of people join you. They stand shoulder to shoulder, from one end of the beach to the other, and look out into the water. Though you can still see only one beam of light streaming directly to you, you know that every other person is likewise seeing their own light. For just a moment, you allow yourself to stand as they are standing, to see as they are seeing, to be a partner in their visions . . . and the night sky fills with a great burst of living, all-connecting light.

EIGHT
Living Partnership

I was babysitting with a three-year-old friend, a bright little wonder named Lily. We were side by side on the sofa, I had my arm around her, and we were happily reading our way through a stack of her favorite books. I was noticing how genuinely good I felt, and I wanted to squeeze her even closer. I could also sense her own enjoyment as she tried to snuggle in tighter to me. It was all quite delightful and much like the pleasure I feel when curling up to my wife of many years.

Suddenly, I felt the first stirrings of sexual arousal. I was immediately and simultaneously alarmed, frightened, confused, and ashamed. I heard myself thinking, "Ah, this is where every father, brother, uncle, or babysitter blows it." Moreover, I sensed that whatever I did in the next few seconds would probably affect Lily, for better or worse, for the rest of her life.

I was acutely aware of how easily I could do wrong—of how "naturally" I could transmit age-old patterns of sexual domination, and of how surely she would suffer abuse. To exploit my connection with her in any way for my own secret pleasure would be to sexually abuse her—even if I was "only" touching her, and especially if I went further. I was meeting her at a most psycho-emotionally creative time of her life: Though she might never consciously remember or understand what I did to her, at her deepest levels of emotional energy and cellular intelligence she would never forget that she had been unfairly used. That information would become a critical part of her self-definition, a scar within her bodily experience, and a shadow upon all her future relationships with men.

The right thing to do, according to my cultural conditioning, was to abruptly disconnect from Lily, suppress all sexual feelings in my own body, and be quite careful never to allow such a dangerous and forbidden moment to occur between us again. Then, I would probably never hug Lily quite the same way, never bounce her on my lap, and never again sit close to her feeling "genuinely good." Rather, I would tend to not feel in her presence, not touch her, not freely play with her, and, ultimately, not really love her in a way that included our bodies and their pleasures. This, sadly, was the right thing to do.

What would this right choice do for Lily? One moment, she would be delightfully alive, feeling good all over, intimately connected to a loving friend and having a wonderful time; the next moment, she would be disconnected, alone, and abandoned, and her loving friendship would never feel quite the same. One moment, she would experience a warm, delicious pleasure; the next moment, cold, sudden distance and unexplained separation.

On some level, she would surely sense that something bad had just happened, if only because the situation felt so bad. Probably, she would blame herself—children usually do. She would think she had done something wrong to make her friend go away, and possibly that she was being punished for some reason. And, tragically, *she would tend to blame the warm, wonderful feeling in her body that immediately preceded the hurt of separation.* She would face a lifelong struggle with feelings of bodily pleasure, never quite trusting them and never quite escaping the sense that pleasure was somehow bad and a certain prelude to pain and punishment.

To me, each choice felt terribly sad and deeply wounding. Either way it seemed as if Lily would receive negative, denial-bound messages about her body and its feelings, and either way it seemed as if our relationship would be doomed to suffer—all because we had dared to feel such simple love for each other.

So what was I to do? Intuitively, I began to breathe more deeply, not suppressing my sexual feelings but enjoying them, and feeling grateful to have this person in my life who could evoke such feelings. Then—and this was the key—I consciously moved the sexual energy away from my genitals and up to my heart. In essence, I allowed myself to feel love with Lily in the way that was most appropriate to our relationship: from and through the center of our two hearts. My process was to first experience awareness, then choice, and then the simplest form of sexual communion: free and full feeling, unobstructed breathing, and relaxation of my whole body toward a state of deepening peace.

After a few moments of breathing quietly and directing the good feelings through my heart, the sense of danger passed. Though I was no longer genitally aroused, I did feel a gentle, tingling pleasure through much of my body and was filled with expanding energies of peace and unconditional love. As my eyes filled with tears, I hugged Lily tighter, and she hugged back.

Lily and I are still lovers. Our little affair does raise some questions, however. The first and most important is, Where do we draw the line? Whether we are speaking of relationships between adults and children, or between professionals and their clients, or between intimate friends, this will always be a vital question. If we reject the notion that any sexual energy passing within such relationships is too dangerous to allow, then just how much is safe and healthy? Where exactly do people cross over from sexual peace into sexual abuse? Can we say that a certain amount of pleasurable connection is good for all concerned but that a certain amount more is abusive? Can we draw a clear and unambiguous line between two people feeling love and the desire to come closer, a line that says, "It's OK to have this much love, but you must suppress the rest"?

Of course, many people will answer that it is not a line we need but a wall—a fixed and unyielding barrier that separates all but the legally married from ever sharing any feelings of bodily pleasure. To those who would create such a wall, the nursing mother who feels a warm, tender arousal is wrong, as are the close friends of many years who are slowly becoming too close, as are all adolescents who find themselves dancing to the world's most ancient song. The wall has a simple message on it: If you are feeling sexual arousal for any but your legal-of-the-opposite-sex spouse, just say no.

We may as well just say no to all spontaneous feelings of pleasure. And while we're at it, let's just say no to breathing, thinking, and eating. We may as well just say no to our bodies when they dare to feel creative passion—when they respond to life with the healthy joy that is our birthright. Just saying no to sexual pleasure as it freely moves within us in the presence of others is a truly perverted act of self-mutilation. All suppression of human sexuality is slow, unconscious suicide and a sure step to unending cultural friction and strife.

The personal suppression of sexual energy is every bit as damaging to human relationship—to any hope for genuine partnership—as are the overt sexual abuses of violent rape, date rape, spouse battering, harassment, and pornography. Sexual just-say-no suppression renders us prone to the most viral abuses of dominator culture and enmeshes us in a constant struggle with basic bodily pleasures.

Rather than saying no to sex, we need to find a healthy, balanced way of saying yes. Again, if we accept that it is possible—and not at all sinful—for healthy feelings of bodily pleasure to freely flow within our relationships, then where do we draw the line?

At the time of my experience with Lily, I sensed that if our physical contact remained innocent while I "merely" indulged in certain selfish fantasies, I would clearly be guilty of violation and abuse. Sexual relationship encompasses not only the physical plane but the psychoemotional fields of energy that connect any two or more people. Therefore, every sexual thought and fantasy *matters,* or makes material. Lusting abusively in one's heart can be as damaging as any overt abuse. There *is* a line between simple human pleasure and the genesis of abuse, and it is the responsibility of the larger, stronger, older, wealthier, or wiser person in any relationship to see it and respect it. It is the responsibility of the (potentially) dominant person in any relationship to transcend his or her own abusive conditioning and to engender healthy partnership instead.

Every moment, and especially every moment we are with another person, is an opportunity to feel sexually alive. Though we may have been conditioned as children to rigidly control all such feelings, or to distrust, fear, deplore, and even degrade such feelings, we can, as adults, choose otherwise. We can feel the pulsing energy of sexual pleasure, enjoy it, and consciously move it in a responsible and transformational way. When we intentionally move this energy through our relaxed bodies, especially through our hearts, we will find that sex is not a grave and sinful danger nor an overwhelming force forever causing us to act foolishly. Healing our sexuality involves saying yes to the living current of our sexual energy and at the same time recognizing our ability and responsibility to feel and express it as we choose.

We must realize that sex is not the animalistic, and thus shamefully uncontrollable, force that so many of us suppose it to be. Sex is, in fact, a humanizing obligation and liberating force on the path to genuine health and spiritual enlightenment. Sex is the vital pulse and connective tissue of any thriving partnership culture.

Sexual play can open great creative possibilities for any two people who dare to feel the truth of their connectedness—creative possibilities that can be explored and unfolded in a wide variety of ways, of which physical intercourse is only one. Being sexually responsible means loving all such moments of sexual aliveness while consciously choosing to recognize and honor the line between creative sharing and destructive abuse. Being sexually responsible means leading the way toward healthy partnership any time we find ourselves the more powerful person in a relationship. And being sexually responsible means becoming responsible for and responsive to the emerging patterns of personal and planetary peace.

Gentle Birth and Sexual Children

But, people will say, you're making love to the child!
Yes, almost. To make love is to return to paradise, is to
plunge again into the world before birth, before the great
separation.
                              —*Frederick Leboyer*[1]

The inevitable elemental yearning to come close, to
fondle, to join is vitiated from the start. In many families,
the "dangerous" areas of a child's body are never touched,
never mentioned. It is as if they do not exist.
                              —*George Leonard*[2]

If we are committed to reversing the abuses of patriarchal
culture, there is no wiser place to focus our efforts than the process
of birth. If we want to purposefully redirect the future evolution of
human society, the simplest of all steps is to assure that the current generation of newborns has a gentle, safe, nurturing, and
celebratory introduction to the planet. Our goal must be to actively demonstrate to every new child that ours is a world of
cooperation between men and women, of deep respect for the
innocent pleasures of the body, and of abiding faith in the basic
goodness and innate intelligence of the human organism.

Yet, our responsibilities toward a mother and fetus do not
begin at the onset of labor. Providing a wise and gentle birth also
means providing sufficient food, shelter, medical care, education,
and other social supports for each pregnant woman. We cannot separate the dominator-driven sufferings of an expectant
mother from the poisonous conditioning her baby simultaneously receives. To be gently born into this world, a child must be borne
in the womb far more gently than is the standard lot of too many
children. To the extent that society ignores the basic needs of
women, and especially the poor and dispossessed, it guarantees
that a portion of each new generation of children will be inherently
damaged and virally inclined toward self- and socially-destructive
behaviors.

Obviously, committing as a society to providing for the basic
needs of all individuals poses daunting difficulties in our modern

world. Only as we move beyond war as the central organizing principle of human societies will we be graced with the will and wherewithal of truly humane culture. However, we are moving beyond war, and we will soon find that providing for the basic needs of all citizens is easier and less expensive than mobilizing to fight world wars and sustain enormous military expenditures. Of course we can make this change.

We are in the midst of a global turning point: We are choosing the beliefs, goals, and social priorities that will create the next stage of human social evolution. We are being called to choose the version of human nature that makes the most sense for these changing times: Are we animalistic sinners in endless competition with one another? Or are we innocents born for the rich rewards of cooperation and living partnership?

If we choose the latter version of human nature, then we will inevitably transform the process of birth. We will do all we can to make the transition from womb to the world as gentle, peaceful, safe, and joyful as possible. We will work to guarantee that the primary conditioning each new child receives is benign, supportive, and inspired with love. We will strive to make each birth an unforgettable example of human relationship at its best.

Practically speaking, we could start by establishing a network of elegantly designed birthing centers—environments specifically constructed for the unique needs of the birthing infant, mother, and family. Midwifery should be given equal status to obstetrics in such centers, demonstrating society's resolve to encourage natural births whenever possible. These centers should not be built inside hospitals, since hospitals are places for the sick and diseased, and pregnant women are neither. Instead, they should be located close to hospitals for quick access should a birth become a life-threatening emergency (which is rare, when wise and generous prenatal care has been provided).

Let me say that for all of my railing against the excesses of techno-birthing, I am grateful that such technologies exist and for the lives that are often saved with high-tech obstetrics. We should keep all of these technologies, but work to refine our applications.

The more complex and expensive obstetrical tools and procedures could be used as emergency backup systems and only engaged as a last resort. The simpler tools such as fetal monitors, labor inducers, anesthetics, and forceps could be unobtrusively designed into birthing centers so that they are readily available when necessary.

However, the goal of every birth—shared by mother, father, and midwife or obstetrician—must be to deliver the infant with a minimum of high-tech intervention. Well-intentioned as such intervention may be, it is alien to the mother and child. It does not fit their bodies' cellular programming for birth—programming that has been developing for hundreds of thousands of years—and thus too easily undermines this most natural of processes. We must make every attempt to support the inherent designs of the pregnant female and birthing infant. When we do so, birth will inevitably require more patience than intervention, more support from loving partners than medical heroics, and more co-creative powers-within of mother and child than external forces of complex technologies.

This is the simplest of steps toward a less abusive culture: give children a gentle, peaceful, safe, and celebratory beginning. All of the knowledge and tools necessary to provide such births already exist, and the financial demands of building gentle birthing centers is minuscule given the enormous dividends we will reap.

Still, it must be said that while techno-birthing is a relatively new and civilized phenomenon, human abuse is both ancient and everywhere. Though the dominator virus is most easily and efficiently spread at birth, all of childhood is fertile ground for abusive conditioning. If we are to create a living partnership world, we would do well to provide gentle and humane births for all new children, surely, but we also need to extend such treatment throughout infancy and childhood.

In *Magical Child*, Joseph Chilton Pearce compares the birth and infancy of Ugandan babies with that of typical techno-birthed American babies. Throughout pregnancy and delivery, the Ugandan mother feels in control of a natural and mostly benign bodily process. After delivery, she resumes her ordinary routines within the hour, in contrast to the often debilitating experience of a civilized woman, for whom birth has become a medical emergency. There is an immediate and uninterrupted bonding between the Ugandan mother and her child, in contrast to the many broken bonds and shattered connections of techno-birthing and modern parenting. Ugandan infants smile soon after birth, rarely cry, and are extremely happy and precocious infants. Yet, as Pearce asks, "Why aren't they all Einsteins? How come they live in those grass shacks and often starve?"[3] Blessed with perfectly peaceful births, why do Ugandans create anything less than a perfect society?

The answer is that in Uganda the abusive split between the child and his or her world comes later. "According to the strict, unbreakable custom or taboo of that culture, the mother specifically, carefully, completely, and without forewarning, totally abandons her child when it is about four years old. . . . The psychological shock of abandonment is overwhelming to the child . . . and many children do not survive the shock at all."[4] Ugandans have reasons for this custom that are every bit as compelling as the American custom of high-tech obstetrics and, ultimately, every bit as destructive to the emerging spirit of the child. The Ugandan child is abusively dominated for the supposed good of society; the sublime partnership between mother and child is resolutely destroyed, and Ugandan culture is crippled in the process.

While the specific customs change from culture to culture, the sanctioned abuse of children for the supposed good of society is nearly universal. Whether the abuse comes at birth or later through any number of taboo systems, initiation rites, and poisonous pedagogies, the abuse invariably occurs. And for all these diverse approaches to and rationales for abusing children, at the heart of them all is an inability on the part of caregivers to accept or deal with children's inherent sexuality.

The notion that children are in any way sexual beings can be difficult to accept, especially for those who have lost touch with the human electric. From a purely socio-biological perspective, an infant's undeveloped body and brain, preverbal intelligence, utter dependency, and seeming lack of meaningful emotions cause it to appear to be an entirely different species, somewhat lower than the human adult on the evolutionary ladder of life. "Just tend to the infant's body," people say. "Keep it alive and healthy until the wonder of mature human consciousness develops."

In fact, infants are infinitely vibrant, vital, and thriving creatures of great and expansive creative powers. Though their flesh is soft, supple, flexible, and amazingly young, their spirit is enormous, bold, and wise, with eons of evolutionary experience. Though an infant's body is totally dependent on others for its continuing survival, the relationship each newborn brings to her or his caregivers is—at least potentially—whole, mutually loving, and of differently equal benefit to all concerned. Though the infant's intelligence is without words and often beyond adult comprehension, the prodigious learning and leaps of understanding that are her or his normal daily fare are indisputable evidence of essential human consciousness in its glory.

From the human energy perspective, infants and growing children are not only whole human beings, worthy of the most conscientious, compassionate, and caring of treatment, they are relatively unsullied, undivided, and unrepressed systems of vital life force. Indeed, energetically speaking, it is we adults who form a sort of subspecies to our children; it is we who have so suppressed, denied, and patriarchally contaminated our energy patterns of body and relationship that we consider the inherent abuses and insanities of dominator reality both normal and inevitable.

If we let go of the notion of human consciousness as something contained within the boundaries of the body, and think instead of consciousness as radiant fields and flowing currents of energy extending from one body to another, holo-relating one life to all others, then our perception of infants (as well as children and adults) is significantly altered. The same small infant body becomes an eager burst of quivering life force expanding outward to fill entire rooms, touching, tasting, sensing, and energetically embracing every other living presence. The same young being, helpless and dependent in so many ways, becomes an immense and unfettered intelligence, learning from every interaction and event, and piecing together a philosophy of life, a personal psychology, and the essential patterns of meaningful relationship.

Moreover, when we anticipate, support, and nurture the whole human infant, we discover—to our delight, surprise, dismay, or alarm—a thoroughly sexual being. The infant is innocently wide open and receptive to whatever others may offer, giving freely from self to others while openly and hungrily taking others in. The infant's body is one whole erogenous zone, giving and receiving a continuous stream of energy with others. And, until she or he receives the negative conditioning of dominator abuse, almost all of the infant's bodily experiences feel good, in much the same way that adult sexual experiences feel good.

Here again we come up against the crippled biases of patriarchal reality. Because we as adults are so far from the pleasures of sexual peace, we fail to recognize the simple delights of small human bodies, and we inevitably misunderstand the sensual and pleasurable partner-play of children's reality. We tend to think of sexual energy and its pleasures in strictly adult terms, allowing no place or healthy purpose for this energy in immature bodies. But, in fact, all children are born to wondrous and all-embracing bodily joy. Or, even if we do see and perhaps envy children's deep sensuality, we may consider it just another aspect of their innocent prehumanness—one more thing to grow out of with the passing of time.

Some people will say that I am utterly confusing sensuality with sexuality and that a child's capacity for bodily pleasure is not at all the same as being sexual. To some extent, this reflects a cultural horror at the thought of even putting the words "child" and "sex" together. And, it is true that if we think of sex purely in terms of genital intercourse and procreation we might reasonably consider children to be asexual until puberty.

However, according to the Taoist understanding of human sexuality, male and female infants naturally produce the specific energies of their respective sexual organs, as do all human bodies throughout their lives. For the first decade or so, the sexual energy goes toward the phenomenal growth and seemingly infinite vitality of childhood. At puberty, girls begin making fertile eggs available for procreation and boys begin producing sperm: The sexual energy shifts from the purpose of creating a healthy, viable man or woman to its new purposes—procreating new life and/or transforming human consciousness. Thus, what really occurs at puberty is not the onset of sexuality per sė but the onset of new possibilities of procreative and dissipative sexual activity. From puberty onward, we are required to do one of three things: practice the conscious regeneration of sexual communion, experience the slow ebb of misspent sexual energy, or make babies.

We make a terrible error in thinking of sex only in terms of genital intercourse and procreativity. We then compound the error by rationally denying children's sexual reality. Children are neither asexual nor presexual. If anything, they may be considered *hyper*sexual: they are relatively open and fluid systems of vital sexual energy; they are virtually compelled toward meaningful, energetic connection with others (genuine sexual peace); they find great delight in their own bodies; and, until we teach them otherwise, they experience life as a continuous current of vibratory pleasure.

So why do we teach children otherwise? If we ourselves are sexually suppressed and pleasure denying, we will tend to pass suppression and denial on to our children through any number of behaviors ranging from total avoidance of their bodies to incestuous violations of them. All of these behaviors are abusive, for they all teach children to suppress and deny sexual pleasure, and thus life itself. The sexual reality of a family thereby determines the vital growth of its children and the prevailing sexual reality of its society.

If we are to support our children in remaining sexually alive and joyfully embodied, we must learn to feel positively at ease in the presence of their ever-expanding sexual energies. This, in turn, means we must feel positively at ease with our own ever-expanding sexual energies. Hence the need, as stressed throughout this book, to vigorously pursue and reverse our personal patterns of dominant/submissive behavior. Ultimately, all such personal work carries us through an exploration and transformation of our primary family systems.

Beyond the Traditional Family

To become fully self-supporting involves becoming your own person—having your own physical, sexual, emotional, intellectual and spiritual boundaries. To do this we must leave our family of origin.

—*John Bradshaw*[5]

How do we transform the family? We can start by greatly expanding our whole sense of what is to be a family, opening our minds beyond the narrow confines of the fundamentalist's "traditional" family. As Robin Morgan writes: "Anthropology and history reveal a vast repertory of family forms that disappear, reappear, coexist, and differ within and across cultures, including blood relationships, kinship systems, language alliances, loyalty groups, households, tribes, networks, clans, communes, the 'stem' family, the 'conjugal' family, the 'pioneer' family, exogamous and endogamous families, and many more. Even the so-called American Family was always more various than we are led to believe, exuberantly reflecting different racial, ethnic, class, and religious patterns."[6] Though many of these family forms were (and some still are) the perfect building blocks of patriarchal societies, it is illuminating nonetheless to ponder such a full spectrum of human relations: There are so many ways to be a family.

Morgan offers a good working definition of family as "a combination of endurance, affection, resilience, and some bond (economic, philosophical, cultural, or chosen) deliberately acknowledged to be larger than the individual elements participating within it."[7] I would add to her definition the obvious bonds of blood and genetics. And I would expand her use of the word *affection* to encompass an infinity of physical, mental, and emotional exchanges—positive and negative—between family members.

This is a purposefully broad definition, allowing for a myriad of family forms, tried and untried. A living partnership culture requires a richly diverse ground from which to grow. Our experience of family must open to include a wide range of personal interactions.

A key lesson from ecology applies here. The healthiest ecosystems are those that display the greatest diversity of interrelating species. An old-growth forest, for instance, thrives precisely because of its complex and extensive web of differently equal relationships. Thousand-year-old Douglas firs, rotting trunks and branches, spotted owls, truffles, voles, deer, microbacteria, salmon runs, flowers, mosses, and even occasional forest fires all are bonded to one another and inextricably linked through a continuum of vital exchanges. All endure as partners, for mutual benefit, in an active balance of living and dying and living again. In nature, a wide array of family forms is positively adaptive. Thus, the healthiest ecosystems are profuse, complex, richly diverse, and always changing families.

Human agriculture, somewhat to the contrary, with its propensity toward planting mono-crops and single-species tree farms, has experienced an unending struggle with infestation, disease, soil erosion, and drought. The lesson, slow in coming, is that the intentional restriction of diversity is innately unhealthy. However appealing to logic and the need to control events it may be to plant single crops in neat and orderly rows, it is an ill-fated undermining of natural processes. The mono-cropping farmer tries to dominate nature, forcing his will upon a much older and wiser organic will of rich and ever-evolving diversity. He toils to plant and harvest a rigidly circumscribed and unchanging agri-family— the antithesis of natural diversity—and then wonders at his hard and too often fruitless task.

Patriarchal attempts to rigidly circumscribe the human family can only lead to similar results. When human relationships are forced into neat and orderly rows with no allowances for change, evolution, experimentation, spontaneity, individuality, freedom, difference, or diversity, then the human spirit surely suffers and the family becomes a torpid field of infestation and disease. The patriarch, rightly appalled at the resulting direction of society, cries out for greater rigidity in the family, just as the mono-cropper applies larger and larger doses of poison to his ailing crops. Both utterly fail to see the contaminating effects of their chronic drives for total dominion.

If we are to grow into a dynamic partnership culture, our definition and experience of family must become broad, flexible, and actively oriented toward diversity. We must grow beyond the constricted family of patriarchal fundamentalists and see that a healthy, functional family can arise out of any bond that is sustained through time and empowered with vital energetic exchanges and the mutual recognition of relatedness. A family, truly, is any two or more creatures who find themselves partners in meeting the continuing challenge of life.

The single mother raising her child on her own is as valid, relevant, and potentially healthy a family as the "traditional" father, mother and two kids. So is the gay or lesbian couple spending their years together, or the communal household of "unrelated" singles, or the unmarried couple "living in sin," or the husband and wife with no children, or the dual-home divorced parents with kids shuttling back and forth on different weekends, or the little old lady with a houseful of cats and plants, or the large extended family with grandparents, parents, uncles, aunts, cousins, nephews, nieces, and always new babies gathering for regular celebrations.

A summer camp can become a family, as can a retirement home, an English class, a twelve-step group, or a baseball team. Most workplaces have the potential to engender family (just ask the Japanese), as do political campaigns, social service groups, churches, military units, and labor unions. Community barn-raisings, protest marches, victory celebrations, and large-scale catastrophes all can create instant and remarkably unforgettable families.

Moreover, all of the above family forms, and too many others to mention, can and should have loose and flexible boundaries. A vital family is always open to receiving new members, often through bonds and exchanges that are different and untried. A friendly mailman, stopping in for tea and a chat, may over the years become a member of a family, as may a child's playmate who spends countless hours in a household. Pets of all sorts become dear family members, as do farm animals, climbing trees, and even wild creatures with their familiar cycles of coming and going. The possibilities are truly infinite: Anyone who gives a little time to bonding with a family and sensing the vital experience of relatedness becomes included in that family.

Of course, all of these family forms already exist within our current patriarchal culture. However, too often there is no recognition of the multifarious nature of the family or of the depth to which patriarchal values are ingrained throughout our various family systems. We must realize that the dominator's call for a return to the traditional family is but an instinctual reaction against the essentially uncontrollable character of diverse systems, for dominators thrive on rigid uniformity. Rather than straining to contain our family experiences within a single set of relationships, we should recognize the host of potential families always coming into our lives, each with its own benefits and burdens and energetic exchanges.

As we begin to embrace and appreciate the many families in our lives, we must simultaneously begin the work of decontamination, for the dominator virus has infected all of our familial relationships. Families are the ground from which society grows, and in patriarchal culture, families are both incubators and host bodies for the dominator virus. Even in households without an active male presence, patriarchal patterns of relationship are usually passed along. The process of clearing all of our family systems of dominant/submissive relationships is a primary task in creating a partnership culture.

Pseudo-Families and Vital Families

The end of "man" and "woman" opens the way for the eventual creation of a family as wide as all humankind, that can weep together, laugh together, and share the common ecstasy.   —George Leonard[8]

In some way, all living things are connected. So runs a basic assertion of our world's oldest philosophies and metaphysical systems, with agreement from the latest suppositions of ecology, quantum physics, and human electric exploration. All of life is an interconnected and holo-related web in which every living being is in fundamental relationship with every other living being. I am connected to Eskimo hunter is connected to Amazon rainforest is connected to Parisian artist is connected to Indian Ocean is connected to snail darter is connected to Russian folksinger is connected to spotted owl is connected to my wife of fifteen years is connected to you.

In essence, then, we are all one big interrelated family, though I may experience my wife as more "my" family than any other person or being. Family is thus a way of thinking about and sensing the quality of our connectedness with others. We are connected to all living beings, but some connections are stronger, more vital, and more actively present in our individual lives. We experience "our" families through our strongest living connections. Moreover, the health of a family at any point in time is a reflection of the current quality of its connections, for families, like all interactive living systems, tend to decline when their various parts (individual members) experience separation and disconnection.

Three meaningful views into a family's quality of connectedness are offered by our definition of family: *A family is two or more individuals who share an enduring bond, who engage in some degree of energetic exchange, and who actively choose the benefits and burdens of larger relationship.* A bond is a special connection that a family has; energetic exchange is what a family does via its connections; and the benefits and burdens of larger relationship arise from the choice to be so connected.

First, at the heart of any family is an enduring bond—some manner or sense of meaningful connectedness between individuals. This connectedness may be the simple bond of blood relationship, the practical bond of a financial contract, or the more abstract bond of a shared philosophy. It may be a sexual, racial, ethnic, religious, class, patriotic, geographical, historical, or spiritual bond, or some combination of diverse connections. It may be an entirely antagonistic bond, such as the bond of incest, or the bond between master and slave, or the bond that sometimes grows between kidnapper and hostage or between long-time enemies. Whatever its nature, the bond develops between individuals and then is sustained through time so that the individuals have some enduring (though not always recognized) connection. As long as any such bond is vitally present, the foundation of a family exists.

Second, a family system involves some active energetic exchange between family members. The phrase energetic exchange, as I am using it here, refers to a broad continuum of events involving the energy of thoughts, the energy of emotions, and the energies of money, sex, food, learning, and common enterprise. Thus, to simply think about others from time to time is to exchange energies with them. To love or hate, trust or distrust, care or resent, stand by or abandon others is to exchange energies with them. To raise children or be raised by parents is to continuously exchange the most intimate of energies with them. All financial transactions are energy exchanges. Working together toward a shared goal brings a merging and blending of creative energies, as does the simple sharing of meals. And every sexual act, even the merest kiss or the lightest touch, allows an exchange of vital energies.

Third, a family grows from each member actively choosing the benefits and burdens of larger relationship. With the bonds and energetic exchanges of family come assets and liabilities that a private individual does not have. One family member's gain or loss becomes another member's gain or loss. Individual commitments and responsibilities overlap and intertwine as each family member is subsumed within the shared experience of relatedness. An individual's sense of self expands to include others, for better and for worse, and his or her perceptions and behaviors are affected by the consequences of larger relationship. Ultimately, the intentional choice to be in relationship with others represents the most critical determinant of a healthy family.

When all three of these factors are present—bonding, energetic exchange, and the choice of larger relationship—then a vital family system exists. It may be a fairy tale family, held together with bonds of love, marriage, birth, and land, enlivened with positive emotional exchanges, good sex, and common goals, and thoroughly blessed with mutual commitment and a delight in being partners in life. It may be a totally dysfunctional family, bound together by fears, doubts, and financial dependencies, addicted to negative emotional exchanges, abusive sex, and daily grinds, and forever cursed with the feeling of being hopelessly trapped in each other's affairs. Most families fall somewhere in between these extremes, with bonds that both empower and imprison, energetic exchanges that both nurture and poison, and a consistent though often conflicted experience of the benefits and burdens of larger relationship.

When any of the three factors is absent, there is something less than a vital family system. For instance, we may have regular financial transactions with another at a level that clearly involves us in each other's assets and liabilities, but if we have no enduring bond and could walk away from and forget the relationship at any moment, then that is not a vital family system. Or, we may be bonded through blood and years of shared childhood experiences with another, but if there is no longer any energetic exchange—no calls, no cards, no physical contacts—then that is not a vital family system. Or, most difficult to understand, we may experience a lasting bond and engage in regular energetic exchanges with another, but if we do not feel ourselves genuinely involved in each other's lives, and we are no longer intentionally choosing the benefits and burdens of larger relationship, then that is not a vital family system.

A vital family, as I am defining it, must have an enduring bond, some degree of continuing energetic exchange, and a shared choice of the benefits and burdens of larger relationship. Any relationship that is lacking in these three elements is something less than vital and will tend toward dissolution and irrelevance for the individual. When we apply this definition to all of our relationships, we may be surprised to find that some relationships we have always thought of as "family"—especially those with our families of origin—simply do not measure up and may be better thought of as "pseudo-families." At the same time, we may discover active and vital family systems in relationships that we have been taking for granted or undervaluing.

Once again, I must stress the need for a soft and flexible boundary between what we experience as a family and what we do not. The very nature of a vital, thriving family is that it is always growing and open to change. The notion of a rigidly defined and structured family system that never changes is inherently unhealthy. Thus, a birth family may devitalize over the years into a pseudo-family and then revive again around some compelling event, becoming more a family than it ever was before. A wonderful marriage of twenty years may dissolve quite suddenly into separation and irrelevance. And new families potentially lie in all of our relationships if bonds exist, if regular giving and taking occurs, and if mutual choices for larger relationships arise.

This definition is not meant to diminish or trivialize the special nature of our conjugal, nuclear, and extended families. Clearly, the strongest bonds are those of blood, genetics, shared experiences, and common property. These are the bonds that give our husband and wife, parent and child, sibling, and in-law relationships such unique significance.

Still, there is more to a vital family than such bonds, however strong and enduring they may be. Both the quantity and quality of our energetic exchanges are of great importance, as are our continuing choices to be or not be related. The powerful bonds of conjugal, nuclear, and extended families can easily overshadow all other relationships. When this happens, we may fail to recognize and benefit from other potential families in our midst. At the same time, we may expect more from our "traditional" family members than they are capable of providing, which may lead to chronic conflict and frustration.

The third aspect of our definition—the choice to be in larger relationship—is often overlooked in conjugal, nuclear, and extended family relations. Being bonded by a vow made years ago or being born into each other's lives, does not mean that we are actively choosing to be in relationship now. We are connected to all of life and thus could potentially experience vital, family intimacy with any other human being. Marrying another person, or giving birth to another person, or being born to another person, or living in the same household as another person all certainly increase the possibility that we will mutually choose larger relationship with that person and sustain that choice throughout our lives. But then again, we may not. Our continuing challenge is to honestly assess the current state of all our relationships, recognizing those people who make up our real families and encouraging more intimate connection with others we choose to become more familial with.

One final point of clarification: What I am defining as a "vital" family is not necessarily a healthily functioning partnership. As I have made clear throughout this book, patriarchal patterns of relationship are replete in our world, infecting virtually all families with the dominator virus. Vital families are those in which the bonds are strong and mutually felt, there are vigorous and ongoing energetic exchanges between all members, and there is a clear and active choice to be in one another's lives. While there is great aliveness, intensity, and ardor in such families, there may also be great extremes of dominant/submissive relationship. Indeed, vital families usually provide the strongest sustenance for the dominator virus.

Pseudo-families, on the other hand, are relationships in which we experience only very weak connections—the bonds are fragile; the energetic exchanges are diminishing in quality and quantity; and the choice to share in the benefits and burdens of larger relationship is waning. Though such families are surely rooted in patriarchy, they have much less impact on our present lives than our more vital families. And though we would do well to elevate all of our relationships to vital and healthy partnerships, pseudo-families are difficult to work with: when the choice to be in a relationship is not vigorously alive, our ability to transform the relationship is greatly hindered.

This is especially critical to understand in regard to families of origin. For children, parents and siblings and older caregivers form intensely vital families. However, to whatever degree these families are poisoned with patriarchal values and behavior, they will tend toward dysfunction and, for some individuals, disconnection. Such families of origin often degrade into pseudo-families. This can cause painful dilemmas for the individuals, because their most dysfunctional patterns of relationship are rooted in families that are no longer psychoemotionally available for transformation. It is crucial for such individuals to "leave home" in search of new families where needed healing can unfold.

It is within the vital family systems in our present lives that our personal transformations into living partnership can and must occur. These transformations may include some or all of the members of our families of origin, perhaps even the people who hurt us most, or they may not. We carry our toxic childhood conditioning with us into every new relationship. Therefore, all new relationships, especially those that remain vital over time, are opportunities to do our deepest and most important healing. It is the people closest to us now—those who comprise our most vital families—who touch us at the core of our psychoemotional conditioning. It is in these families that patriarchy can be seen, felt, and finally transformed to partnership.

Personal Reflections

Think about the people in your life, from early childhood to this present moment. Who are the people you have called family? Who are your family members now?

A family is two or more people who share an enduring bond: With whom do you share an enduring bond? What bonds are most important to you: the bond of blood relationship? the bond of shared philosophy? the bond of financial transaction? the common bonds of race? religion? ethnicity? nationality? class? ideology? geography? history? Which bonds seem to be strengthening with the passing of time? Which seem to be weakening?

A family is two or more people who engage in some degree of energetic exchange: Who are the people you think about the

most? *Who do you see most often? Who do you communicate
with on a regular basis? Who arouses strong positive or negative
emotions? Who do you do business with? Who do you have
regular physical contact with? Who do you share common goals
with? Who are you sexually attracted to? Which energetic
exchanges are growing more frequent with time? Which are
lessening?*

*A family is two or more people who are actively choosing the
benefits and burdens of larger relationship: Who do you really
want in your life, for better and for worse? Who do you feel most
freely attracted to? Do they seem freely attracted to you? With
whom are you choosing to share the benefits and burdens of life?
Are they choosing to share these with you?*

*Who has occurred to you the most in answering the above
questions? These are the people who make up your vital family
system and who are most available to you for psychoemotional
growth and transformation. Look for patterns of dominant/
submissive behavior in these relationships. How can you engender partnership instead?*

NINE

"Humanature"

To survive,
our minds must taste redwood
and agate, octopi,
bat, and in the bat's mouth,
insect. It's hard
to think like a planet.
We've got to try.

—*James Bertolino*[1]

In Australia, children's outdoor play is being increasingly restricted. When they do go outdoors, they are advised to wear wide-brimmed hats and scarves around their necks, especially during the summer. They do this to protect themselves from the sun. The hole in the ozone layer, still but a bothersome theory to many people around the world, is already an indisputable and life-altering catastrophe for Australians.

One statistic frames the whole story: 75 percent of Australians past the age of sixty have had some form of skin cancer. The primary cause of such cancer is excessive ultraviolet radiation. The depletion of ultraviolet-shielding ozone has only been a problem for some thirty years, so older, cancer-stricken Australians were not even exposed until they were adults. Moreover, the problem is getting exponentially worse every year, so it does not take an environmental extremist to sound the alarm for Australia's children. An entire generation is at grave risk of illness, the likes of which humans have never before encountered and have only just begun to address.

I recently watched a panel of political commentators discuss this problem. The moderator, a well-respected journalist for PBS, had just returned from Australia and was reporting the basic facts as I have outlined them above. To my growing dismay, he gave his report with a "gosh, what'll it be next" smile, as if he was discussing the latest advance of killer bees or some outrageous new Hollywood movie. The ensuing conversation neatly side-stepped any regard for Australia's children. The conclusion, sagely intoned by all involved, was that we should not expect things to improve too quickly since there was a lot of money involved in ozone-depleting industries.

All of this took me back several years to the Reagan-era bureaucrat who suggested that we respond to ozone depletion by wearing straw hats and sunglasses. At the time, it was such a ludicrous comment that I wrote what I thought was a satire of a future in which we will all be "outfitted in our most stylish straw hats and shades, plus yellow slickers to counter acid rain, gas masks to counter smog, and latex chastity belts to ward off the possibility of AIDS." We may still find a chuckle or two in such words, but I rather doubt they are laughing Down Under. For Australians, the nightmare vision of toxic sunlight is already real.

I write the words *toxic sunlight* and think of children every-where. I think of my own childhood and of long summers playing in the sun, my skin a dark brown by late August, my normally brown hair bleached blond. Now we must say to children, "Only so many hours a day," and "Only if you put your sunscreen on," and "Don't forget to wear your hat." In the time it took me to turn from ten to forty, human industry has corrupted our fundamental relationship with the sun. True, the straw hat and sunscreen industries are doing better, but do we really want toxic sunlight and the changes it will force on our world? Is this the evolution that we want?

Though there are still many questions about the long-term effects of ozone depletion, there is general agreement that plant, animal, and human biological functions will be altered by it, and probably not for the better. Even if we step out on a dubious limb and propose that such a change in our planet's biosphere could actually cause positive changes for humans (for we are adaptable creatures), we can hardly be certain. The fact remains that whatever the long-term effects of ozone depletion turn out to be, they are being caused by a series of entirely mutable human choices. Ozone depletion is not necessary. Every ozone-depleting chemical still in use today could be replaced with something better. Perhaps it would be more expensive, but it would be infinitely better when we consider the future direction of human society.

An underlying factor in many of the ecological crises of our day is that we are utterly failing to consider the future direction of human society. We behave as if our actions have no long-term consequences whatsoever. Our governments and corporations have difficulty thinking beyond the next public opinion poll or quarterly financial statement, much less intelligently planning ten, twenty, or thirty years into the future. We buy into the false choice of "ecology versus economy," and then shrug with hopeless resignation as our world is meanly driven by short-term economic demands. We are told to have faith in free-market mechanisms despite countless examples of purely selfish market decisions that have led to monumental eco-abuse.

Even worse, we seem blithely unaware of our contributions to our own evolutionary process. We quarrel over various ecological problems as if the main question were how much more damage the planet can reasonably sustain. (The planet, evolutionary wonder that it is, will go on adapting to our most foolish excesses.) We should be asking, Who are we becoming as a result of this continuing environmental degradation? What changes in human nature are unfolding as a result of the sudden, massive, and inhospitable changes in the environment? Is this the evolution we want?

Do we want children who grow up afraid of the sun? Do we want children who grow up breathing smog and eating lead and drinking DDT from their mothers' breasts? Do we want children who never swim in oceans that were long ago polluted and never hike in forests that were long ago destroyed? Have we given any thought at all to the psychoemotional reality of such children and to who they will "naturally" become as adults? We are not just tinkering with their environment; we are blindly affecting their DNA, brain cells, and body chemistry. We are skewing their view of the world and how it works, their whole sense of human nature, and their primary patterns of relationship. As such children mature, theirs will be a rather different world, for they will be rather different humans. And they and their world, however different, will be vitally influenced by choices we are making today.

It is time for us as humans to consciously accept responsibility for the evolution of our world. Evolution is adaptation to the prevailing environment; human actions can powerfully affect the prevailing environment and thereby positively or negatively influence evolution. It is past time for humans everywhere to *get* this and to begin making obvious choices in favor of a benign and balanced environment that will inspire the best of human nature.

Though we have all become somewhat immune to the dire warnings of environmental experts, in Australia and so many other eco-abused hotspots around the globe, we are facing the truth. The time for meaningful action is upon us. We must gladly take up the tiller of human evolution. If there is anything that can be done to reverse the degrading logic of environmental abuse and to foster common sense, now is the time to get out and do it. Don't forget to wear your hat.

Partnership with Nature

A missionary was walking in Africa when he heard the ominous padding of a lion behind him. "Oh Lord," prayed the missionary, "Grant in Thy goodness that the lion walking behind me is a good Christian lion." Then, in the silence that followed, the missionary heard the lion praying too: "Oh Lord," he prayed, "We thank Thee for the food we are about to receive."
                                              —*Cleveland Amory*[2]

The greatness of a nation can be judged by the way its animals are treated.
                                              —*Gandhi*

> While we ourselves are the living graves of murdered
> beasts, how can we expect an ideal condition on earth?
> —*George Bernard Shaw*

Creating human partnership with nature will be no easy reversal given the immense dimensions of Judeo-Christian, corporate-industrial civilization. The abuse of nature runs so deeply in every civilized person's life that it seems, well, perfectly natural. Indicative of our relationship to nature is something intrinsic to our daily existence: food. As both John Robbins in *Diet for a New America* and Jeremy Rifkin in *Beyond Beef* have concisely and emphatically (if depressingly) documented, the daily diet of modern culture demands a monumental abuse of animals and land that, like any other eco-abuse, is unequivocally circling back to threaten human health and viability.[3]

Neither of these books is an easy read. Both authors shine a glaring light of awareness on the animal-based diet of modern men and women and make impassioned pleas for all of us to move toward more vegetarian food choices. They methodically trace the ethical, nutritional, social, political, and ecological consequences of widespread meat production and consumption. They back all of their suppositions with long lists of mind-numbing facts and statistics, many taken from U.S. government studies, that underscore the enormous degree to which the common carnivorous diet is negatively impacting and misdirecting our world.

The Surgeon General reports that 68 percent of all American deaths are diet related. Eighty-five percent of U.S. topsoil loss is directly associated with raising livestock. Sixty-one percent of all herbicides used in the United States are sprayed on grains used as feed for cattle and other livestock, and meat is the major source of pesticide residues in the Western diet. The organic waste generated by a typical 10,000-head feedlot is equivalent to the human waste generated in a city of 110,000. One half of the Earth's land mass is grazed by livestock, and grain consumption by livestock is growing twice as fast as grain consumption by people. Five-hundred thousand animals are killed for meat every hour in America, and slaughterhouses have the highest rates of employee turnover. If

Americans were to reduce their meat consumption by only 10 percent, it would free over twelve million tons of grain annually, more than enough to adequately feed every one of the sixty million people who will starve to death on the planet this year.[4]

Robbins and Rifkin are unrelenting in their expositions of the plain facts behind the industrial diet of modern men and women. Their books, as I have said, are difficult reading, for what is more fundamental to our daily pursuit of happiness than eating food? Who really wants to know that our lifelong food choices are seriously injuring our bodies, our societies, and our planetary ecology? Who really wants to feel the horrors of industrial factory farms, with their animals crowded into narrow stalls and cages, fattened up with steroids, crying out in constant suffering, and kept alive with heavy doses of antibiotics until their assembly-line slaughter? Who really wants to lift "the veils of deception that hide and perpetuate the darker side of our society's eating habits"?[5]

Yet, if we really want to responsibly influence the evolution of human society, we cannot ignore something as basic and far-reaching as our daily food choices. Mundane and inconsequential as eating may seem, every breakfast, lunch, and dinner reflects personal choices that have great social, political, and ecological ramifications. The modern, industrial, animal-based diet is human social evolution at its worst.

The violent mistreatment of livestock, which is sanctioned by every meat eater who cannot say where and how their piece of meat was raised and slaughtered, is as culturally degrading and denial-bound as was slavery in Jefferson's time. (I am not saying that the suffering of a human slave is equivalent to the suffering of a cow or chicken, but that society's infliction of such unnecessary suffering leads in each case to similar cultural degradation.) The modern human, biting into dead flesh, is no more capable of feeling the animal that once lived than was Jefferson capable of seeing a whole human being in any of his slaves. That such a dietary choice is also drastically depleting our soil, misdirecting the resources of forests, grain, and water, and causing a poisonous accumulation of wastes is further indication of patriarchal abuse run amok while shrouded in stuporous mass denial.

Is this a call to radical vegetarianism? Yes, unless we can return to small-scale farming that will allow people to participate as active partners in the life span of hamburger from calf to plate. The intimate connection with nature exhibited by many indigenous cultures when their people gratefully take an animal's life for food is a far cry from our supermarket purchase of plastic-wrapped meat or our gobbling down of fast-food burgers. Anytime we pay others to butcher living beings (be they enemies, cows, or whatever) in our names, we demean ourselves, our butchers, and the differently equal creatures we have chosen for such violent and always dubious sacrifices.

Vigorous arguments have been raised against the "diet for a new planet" that Robbins, Rifkin and others are advocating. It is true that humans have been eating meat for a long time. It is true that the capacity to add meat to one's diet has long been considered a step toward good nutrition and a sign of social advancement. It is true that animal husbandry has long been the pursuit of sincere, intelligent, and positively motivated people. It is true that ham and egg breakfasts, cheeseburger lunches, and turkey dinners have been the daily fare of the dominant human culture for so long that they seem unquestionable. It is true that an enormous degree of human livelihood is tied up in maintaining the status quo of the meat eater's diet.

However, similar arguments were raised for the continuation of slavery. We had to shake off the blinders of denial to see that slavery demanded an unconscionable abuse of differently equal humans that could no longer be justified. The key to a genuine environmental revolution—one that will positively alter all aspects of the human relationship with nature—is the widespread human recognition that unnecessary abuse of any other life form must be stripped of all denial, honestly questioned, and, in most all cases, brought to an end.

Of course, all creatures live at the expense of others, for all creatures eat other creatures lower on the food chain. I am not proposing a world in which eating no longer happens, nor am I proposing that we should feel guilty when we slap a mosquito or step on an ant. It may be that some people *need* to eat meat. I am not suggesting a rigid set of environmental commandments—Thou Shalt Not Eat Meat!—that dictate our every action. Instead, we must willingly develop a state of consciousness that guides us toward an increasingly healthy partnership with nature as well as with other humans.

This state of consciousness, which can lead us through our complex daily choices regarding diet, energy use, and other aspects of our relationship with nature, is one that sees all suffering as deeply harmful when it is inflicted unnecessarily. Though the meat industry tells us otherwise, innumerable studies over the past fifty years (along with millions of happy vegetarians) have virtually all come to the same conclusion: carnivorous eating is not at all necessary for human health, while vegetarianism is healthy and environmentally benign. To the extent that eating meat is unnecessary, the meat eater's diet is an inevitable source of dominator a-buse and self-inflicted injury.

A central law of the Iroquois Nation was that a people should take no action without first considering its impact on the next seven generations. This law can be especially helpful in making the many eco-choices of modern life. It is a way of thinking that takes our short-term needs and places them in a larger and more intelligent context. Asking, "Is this really necessary?" from the perspective of our great-great-grandchildren's grandchildren provides us with a wise and discerning guide for all of our actions. It generates a powerful light of awareness and brings the true costs of any abuse of the environment, other humans, or ourselves—for there really is no difference—into sharp focus.

"I sense those beings of future times hovering," writes Joanna Macy, "like a cloud of witnesses. . . . The imagined presence of these future ones comes to me like grace and works on my life."[6] What if these beings of the future graced every dinner table, were given a seat at corporate board meetings, were consulted before any trees were cut, were listened to before the production of a single ounce of forever-poisonous atomic waste? What if "a cloud of witnesses" oversaw our choices, commented on the consequences, and offered the most heartfelt of encouragement for the challenges ahead? When we had difficulty answering the question, Is this really necessary? we would need only ask these witnesses. Even if we heard no immediate answer, the fact that we had asked, listened, and sincerely wanted to know would offer us a clear light of awareness that could wisely guide our actions.

"For then," writes Macy, "thou shalt be in league with the beings of the future, and the generations to come after shall be at peace with thee."[7] If we include the needs of future generations in all our deliberations and decisions, we will be true partners with these generations, and from such a partnership will come the wisdom and compassion to rediscover our capacity for living partnership with nature. For then "human beings will experience joy when other life forms experience joy and sorrow when other life forms experience sorrow. . . . We will grieve when living beings, including landscapes, are destroyed."[8]

That is the *feeling* of an all-embracing partnership culture. We have fallen very far from such all-empathic feeling, and we very much need to recover it again. A critical step is to realize that every act of dominating abuse—against any other life form, human or otherwise—becomes a self-inflicted wound, even unto death. It is no longer inevitable, if it ever was, that we suffer on in such self-destructive foolishness. Why then should we suffer on?

Getting There

The rescue of the environment must become the central organizing principle for civilization.
—*Al Gore*[9]

In June of 1992, more than thirty-five thousand people from all over the world gathered in Rio de Janeiro for the historic Earth Summit (The United Nations Conference on Environment and Development). Nearly two hundred nations were represented at the conference, and more than one hundred heads of state attended. There were also activists from hundreds of nongovernmental organizations, as well as representatives of many of our world's surviving indigenous peoples.

This unprecedented gathering of human beings was inspired and motivated by a growing, collective recognition that the current relationship between the natural environment and human development is simply unsustainable. Though there was a wide range of opinions on the primary causes of our planet's environmental problems, it was clear to everyone that if human development continued along its present course for much longer, a worldwide collapse of ecological viability would result, with catastrophic consequences for thousands of species of life, including Homo sapiens.

To an environmentalist and practicing partner such as myself, the Earth Summit was a dream come true. It brought together men and women from north, south, east, and west, uniting capitalists and socialists, industrial people and tribal people, international VIPs and grassroots activists to examine and address the environmental crises of our age. It gave genuine hope that some urgent problems may at last be solved.

I believe that *whenever people sincerely attempt to address environmental problems, they are inevitably compelled toward practicing partnership.* Any healthy ecosystem is a complex, dynamically balanced interrelationship of diverse yet essentially equal members—it is a partnership. If humans are to further develop in this world without wreaking irreversible damage, we must do so as willing and able partners with all other species. And—the more difficult task—we must also do so as partners with people of all other races, religions, ethnic groups, nations, and political or economic philosophies.

From the all-encompassing global problems of ozone depletion and climate change to the more local concerns of recycling, water quality, and waste disposal, our search for environmentally sustainable solutions always leads us to the same basic insights: All people are essentially connected; all people must have equal access to the necessities of life; and all local and personal actions ripple out to effect the whole world, just as all global and political events continuously influence each individual. For better and for worse, we are all in this together, and our only hope for success is to learn to act as partners. The Earth Summit was a bold, if belated, movement toward truly global partnership.

However, the Earth Summit also demonstrated that the dangerous logic of domination is still a primary factor in human affairs. Many people came to the summit as separate "tribes" of indigenous peoples, special interest groups, corporations, nation-states, or regional, political, or economic blocs that were primarily concerned with the real or imagined demands of their own tribal survival. Because of this, the summit was often split into acrimonious debate and seemingly irreconcilable conflict. As certain tribes pursued their own needs with blatant disregard to the needs of others ("I'm not going to let a bunch of environmental extremists take away one American job!" whined a petulant president), the worst of environmental excesses became nonnegotiable "rights" such as the right to continue producing the petrochemicals responsible for global climate change, the right to clearcut forests, or the right to go on causing mass species extinction.

As the Parable of the Tribes predicts, as long as any tribe chose an antagonistic, dominator, "my needs are all that matter" approach at the summit, all other tribes were dragged down to the same level of interaction. This was the great failing of the U.S. delegation: Instead of using its world-leader position to forge the way toward a truly new world order of international cooperation, the Bush administration fostered an atmosphere of distrust, disconnection, and endless competition. Instead of turning America's great material wealth and advantage toward positive global evolution, the president—his head stuck deep in oil-rich sand—angrily defended and trenchantly advocated continuing with business as usual.

We cannot continue with business as usual. America is 10 percent of the world's population, consuming some 40 percent of its resources and producing nearly 50 percent of its wastes. Such figures, alarming as they are, do not begin to reflect the ecological impacts of America's chronic financial commitment to sustaining the worldwide arms race or of its ever-colonializing interference in the affairs of less-developed nations. From the environment's perspective, America is the most dominant and most ecologically abusive nation on Earth. Given the existence of the dominator virus, it follows that most of the world is forced to emulate America's development, however irrational, globally unviable, and ultimately suicidal such emulation may be.

Still, I see more reason for optimism than pessimism in the current world situation. Though the road to personal and planetary partnership is clearly a rocky one, I strongly believe we will get there. I base my optimism on the growing worldwide acceptance of environmental common sense and on the changes occurring in the power dynamics described by the Parable of the Tribes. These changes will eventually allow the necessities of environmentalism to carry us to widespread living partnership.

The greatest change, as I have stressed throughout this book, is the transformation of our most intimate relationships. The creation of dynamic and egalitarian balance between women and men—sexual peace—is a primary step toward the creation of peace between different tribes. Though we are obviously still a long way from common and collective sexual peace, there is no question that the most vital work of expanding personal and political awareness is well underway.

We have several generations of feminist thinkers, writers, and activists to thank for holding a sharply focused light on the abuses and denials of patriarchal civilization. All of the doctrines of patriarchal inevitability have been thoroughly discounted, and feminist models of cooperative wholeness are being widely disseminated. Most importantly, the ancient law of power—he (or she) who is bigger should rule; she (or he) who is smaller should submit—has been revealed for the misery-producing lie that it is. As more and more men and women personally reject the inner urgings of viral domination, the political forces of domination are challenged, weakened, and reversed.

I also find great encouragement in the increasing attention people throughout the world are bringing to children's reality. The supposed normalities of dominator pedagogies are being seriously questioned for the first time in history as the connection between abused children and dysfunctional adults is made painfully clear. We may not always know how to relate to our children as equal partners, but there is a growing awareness that wielding power-over them—physically, mentally, or emotionally—is often a form of abuse. That awareness, coupled with the love that most parents easily feel for their children, is enough to guide the evolution of partnership families.

At the political level, we are gradually shifting from a world of separate and purely self-interested tribes to a global network of interconnected tribal relationships. The Parable of the Tribes describes a situation in which an aggressor tribe moves against a neighboring tribe, forcing it to become mutually aggressive, to submit, or to move away. All three responses effectively spread the dominator virus. Central to this dynamic is the fact that the two tribes are entities that are entirely separate—from each other and from all other tribes. This keeps the outcome of any confrontation quite predictable: the stronger and more violent tribe naturally wins, making military strength and the capacity to commit violence adaptive human values.

One solution to this problem that has long been tried by smaller and weaker tribes is the formation of alliances. Several small tribes, united as one, can effectively stand together against a large aggressor tribe. History gives us many examples of such alliances that were quite successful, lending credence to the philosophy of "peace through strength." With time, however, all such alliances have fallen apart, been challenged by an even larger aggressor, or have themselves become aggressive. The "peaceful alliance" solution to the parable is still a forced reaction to violent aggression. Thus, it is inevitably infected with the dominator virus and carries the patriarchal seeds of its own dysfunction.

The great shift that is now happening (much too slowly, it seems) is that the myriad tribes of our world are coming to recognize their essential connectedness, their holo-relatedness, not as a defense against violence but as a simple fact of life. We are all connected—energetically, biologically, environmentally, economically, historically, genetically, and spiritually. We are now and always have been connected, and the common and collective recognition of this fundamental reality is the dynamic resolution to the Parable of the Tribes.

Diverse tribes may always come into conflict with one another, but such conflicts are not always doomed to aggression, violence, and patriarchal domination. When there is a basic recognition of holo-relationship and mutual respect, conflict instead becomes the moving thrust of evolutionary change. We need not seek an end to all conflict, nor a world in which everybody thinks, believes, and acts the same. Rather, we must create a planetary commitment to nondominating conflict resolution as a primary human practice and adaptive tribal value.

We are experiencing profound changes in human relationship: a dynamic resolution of the ancient battling between the sexes; a movement from poisonous pedagogies to partnership parenting; and a worldwide recognition of tribal and environmental interconnectedness. Together, these profound changes in human relationship give inspiration and form to the great evolutionary leap our species is now attempting. The Parable of the Tribes is itself transforming: it now warns that there will be no human survival unless we *all* choose peace. Even more importantly, the underlying justification for the parable—that people are different and unequal and thus forever doomed to giving and receiving abuse—is finally being seen for the destructive nonsense it truly is and always was.

The concept that we are all differently equal—the central organizing principle of our current age—has long been the central organizing principle of both feminism and environmentalism. This is why each of these movements has been so critical to the positive transformation of our world. As feminism and environmentalism gradually merge into a unified worldview ("humanaturalism"?), both the vision of planetary partnership and the path to take us there are becoming clearer and more compelling. We will, again and at last, live as differently equal partners—with each other and with all other species—because such living is the central organizing principle of planet Earth.

Still, even in the midst of optimism, there is no denying that we are wandering in uncharted realms as we seek the long-lost grail of human partnership. There is still more shadow than light on the path before us. We will need each other to find the way. If we are to get there—and I am certain that we will—we will need each other to find the way.

Original Blessing

I see a change. It is vested in the greatest rise in expectations that the world has ever seen. It is so far-reaching in its implications that one might call it evolution entering into time, the evolutionary potential asserting itself. It needed a certain critical mass, a certain merging of complexity, crisis, and consciousness to awaken. Now it is happening.

—*Jean Houston*[10]

Blessed are the peacemakers: for they shall be called the children of God.　　　　　　　—*Matthew 5:9*

Can human beings change? Can we really shift, at our most fundamental level, from being creatures of habitual abuse to being creatures of peace and harmony? Can women and men find a healthy balance that allows the diverse natures of the two sexes to be mutually vital in the co-creation of our world? Can sexual energy become a freely circulating, healing balm for all people? Can children of all nations reasonably expect to be treated as precious human equals by the forces of family and culture? Can armies everywhere begin the work of converting their organizational and productive capacities to peaceful purpose? Can the plants, animals, and ecosystems of Earth anticipate the coming of a humanity that enthusiastically embraces the task of sustainable stewardship? (Hu*woman*y has long been ready.) Will we really change in such profound ways?

The prisoners, defenders, and promoters of patriarchy will all answer, "No. Sorry, but no. These are nice enough thoughts, but they are impossible to manifest in reality, for humans are inevitably born into Original Sin. Humans are essentially sinful. It is our common and unalterable nature to inflict and suffer the most inhumane of abuses. Our task is to accept and live with such abuses, rather than to idealistically tilt at notions of sweeping transformation."

Original Sin is God the Father's curse on all humans for the innocent transgressions of the curious Eve and the willing Adam. Original Sin is an inherent weakness that forever drives us into foolish and demonic behavior. Original Sin is our instinctive, kill-or-be-killed, competitive nature. It is our animalistic self, our untamable emotions, our most unfathomable doubts and fears, and our undeniable pains. Original Sin is the long, violent saga of human history. Original Sin is penis envy, poisonous pedagogy, and techno-birthing. It is the always and forever war between the sexes, the irreconcilable differences between men and women, and the ever-natural tendency of all humans toward domination and submission. Original Sin is the dangerous logic of power-over: it is the dominator virus now loose in the world for so long that it seems incurable.

Original Sin is used to rationally explain our insane world and affairs: People are sinners and animalistically driven wretches who are simply incapable of doing any better. Certainly, the world has known its share of wretches, and has suffered through an unending torrent of wretched deeds. No, warn the dominators, there will be no great change in human nature: People are basically and unavoidably sinful and thus will always need the stern and abusive ways and means of patriarchal civilization.

The counterargument that I have been developing throughout these pages states that humans are not born sinners, are not fundamentally wretched, and are in fact designed for pleasure, play, and genuine partnership and communion with others. As the Dominican scholar Matthew Fox has so eloquently written, it is not Original Sin that we are born to, but Original Blessing. "We enter a broken and torn and sinful world—that is for sure. But we do not enter as blotches on existence, as sinful creatures, we burst into the world as 'original blessings.'"[11] We are then conditioned, trained, and adapted to sinful and wretched behavior. It is this almost universal conditioning to abusive relationship—this sec-ondhand sin—that I have been calling the passing on of the dom-inator virus. Planetary transformation will occur when more and more of us move beyond the manufactured sins of patriarchy to touch, feel, express, and share the eternal power-with of our Original Blessing.

Original Blessing is the tingling joy and holy spirit that pul-ses through Everychild: vast, wild, and miraculous. It is the inef-fable light in a baby's eyes, beaming wise, Buddha-like, and with infinite grace. Our Original Blessing carries all the power we need to move worlds: it is truth enough to unite all nations, and love enough to heal all wounds. Our Original Blessing is the memory and promise of Paradise: It is information about our primary design written deeply into our DNA, much deeper than the post-original sins of patriarchy. "Each of us inevitable," sings Whitman, tasting the Original Blessing. "Each of us limitless. . . . Each of us here as divinely as any is here."[12] Original Blessing is our inherent and incorruptible divinity, a spiritual current that forever connects us to all of creation.

Original Blessing is also our continuing co-creative responsi-bility: It is an always humanizing obligation that we give and receive blessings. Every gratefully inhaled breath carries blessings for the breather, and every freely exhaled breath offers blessings to the world. To reach across our imagined divisions with a gentle, heartfelt touch is a blessing, as is every smile tendered in the face of human hardship. Every conscious conception, every birth with-out violence, every act of joyful nurturance, and every honest communication offers new and vital blessings. Original Blessing is the common practice of sexual communion and the collective practice of sexual community. We are blessed, to the very core our beings, in every moment of genuine partnership, and out of such moments, the future of our planet will unfold.

The conscious perception of our essential holo-relationship with all living creatures may be the greatest of blessings, for it carries us back into true partnership with God. Whatever the reasons for our fall from grace, we have since lived in a continuing condition of estrangement from the Creator, and thus from all of Creation. Far from the garden of all-encompassing partnership, we have wandered too long in the valley of domination and submission, a race of battered and abused children forever fearing the next angry expression of God's will. Now, as we nibble at the fruits of partnership and sense our vital connections to all of life, we are discovering that God is not inevitably angry and abusive. Instead, it is our conditioned disconnection from the Creator—and the differently unequal relationship that results—that is the true source of our unhappiness, pain, and predisposition toward abuse.

Perhaps as we shift from our long, frustrating project of making peace to a new project of resolutely living peace, we will evolve from being the children of God to finally becoming our Creator's consort, bride, and equal partner. Perhaps, as many have suggested, God *is* a Father. Our task, then, as women and men together, is to become the Mother: the fountain of life, the glorious flesh, and the eternal nurturance and celebration of manifest Creation. Who knows what will come of such a holy union? Now it is happening. Let us offer and receive its blessings.

Notes

Chapter One

1. Thomas Berry, *The Dream of the Earth* (San Francisco: Sierra Club Books, 1988), p. 143.

2. Riane Eisler, *The Chalice and The Blade* (San Francisco: Harper & Row, 1987), p. xvii.

3. Starhawk, *Truth or Dare* (New York: Harper & Row, 1987), p. 9.

4. Eisler, *The Chalice and The Blade*, p. 105.

5. Thomas Berry, *The Dream of the Earth*, p. 150.

6. Though patriarchal culture has arisen independently in different parts of the world and through different religions, Judaism, Christianity, and Islam exemplify patriarchal religion and, taken together, exert enormous power in our world. Thus, I will confine my discussion to the Bible and its effects.

7. Merlin Stone, *When God Was a Woman* (New York: Harvest-HBJ, 1976), p. xviii.

8. Eisler, *The Chalice and The Blade*, p. 124.

9. Ibid., p. 125.

10. Robin Morgan, *The Anatomy of Freedom* (Garden City, NY: Anchor Press, 1982), p. 9.

11. Catherine A. MacKinnon, "Feminism, Marxism, Method and the State: An Agenda for Theory," *Signs: A Journal of Women in Culture and Society*, vol. 7, no. 3, Spring 1982.

12. Barbara Ehrenreich and Deidre English, *Complaints and Disorders* (Westbury, NY: The Feminist Press, 1973), p. 20.

13. Simone de Beauvoir, *The Second Sex* (New York: Alfred A. Knopf, 1952), p. 38.

14. William Irwin Thompson, *The Time Falling Bodies Take to Light* (New York: St. Martin's Press, 1981), p. 155.

15. Gerda Lerner, *The Creation of Patriarchy* (Oxford: Oxford University Press, 1986), p. 36.

16. Ibid., p. 22.

17. Thompson, *The Time Falling Bodies Take to Light*, p. 134.

18. Sherry Ortner, "Is Female to Male as Nature Is to Culture?" in *Women, Culture, and Society*, ed. Michelle Rosaldo and Louise Lamphere (Stanford, CA: Stanford University Press, 1974), p. 67.

19. Lerner, *The Creation of Patriarchy*, p. 212.

20. Ibid., p. 228.

Chapter Two

 1. Guy Murchie, *The Seven Mysteries of Life* (Boston: Houghton Mifflin Company, 1978), p. 513.

 2. Andrew Bard Schmookler, *The Parable of the Tribes* (Berkeley: University of California Press, 1984), p. 232.

 3. George Leonard, *The Transformation* (Los Angeles: J.P. Tarcher, 1972), p. 158.

 4. Lori Heise, "Crimes of Gender," *World Watch*, March 1989, p. 18.

 5. "The Killing Numbers," *Ms.*, September/October 1990, p. 45.

 6. Malcolm X, as quoted by Wendell Berry in *The Hidden Wound* (San Francisco: North Point Press, 1989), p. 1.

 7. Jeffrey Weeks, as quoted by Jamake Highwater in *Myth and Sexuality* (New York: New American Library, 1990), p. 6.

 8. Jamake Highwater, *Myth and Sexuality* (New York: New American Library, 1990), p. 5.

 9. Ibid., p. 6.

10. Joseph Chilton Pearce, *Magical Child Matures* (New York: Bantam Books, 1985), p. 45.

11. Frederick Leboyer, *Birth Without Violence* (New York: Alfred A. Knopf, 1976), p. 31.

12. Michael Sky, *Breathing* (Santa Fe, NM: Bear & Company, 1990), p. 49.

13. Joseph Chilton Pearce, *Magical Child* (New York: Bantam Books, 1977), p. 44.

14. See Frederick Leboyer, *Birth Without Violence* (New York: Alfred A. Knopf, 1976); Joseph Chilton Pearce, *Magical Child* (New York: Bantam Books, 1977); Suzanne Arms, *Immaculate Deception* (Boston: Houghton Mifflin, 1975); Desmond Morris, *Babywatching* (New York: Crown Publishers, 1991); Thomas Verney, *The Secret Life of the Unborn Child* (New York: Simon and Schuster, 1981); and Jessica Mitford, *The American Way of Birth* (New York: Dutton, 1992).

15. Leboyer, *Birth Without Violence*, p. 30.

16. Alice Miller, *For Your Own Good* (Toronto: Collins Publishers, 1984), p. 58.

17. Ibid., p. 17.

18. Ibid., p. 7.

19. Ibid., p. 16.

20. John Bradshaw, *Bradshaw on: The Family* (Pompano Beach, FL: HCI, 1988), p. 49.

21. Sonia Johnson, *Wildfire* (Albuquerque, NM: Wildfire Books, 1989), p. 18.

22. Victoria Woodhull, *The Victoria Woodhull Reader*, ed. Madeleine B. Stern (Weston, MA: M&S Press, 1974), p. 8.

23. Andrea Dworkin, *Right-Wing Women* (New York: G.P. Putnam, 1983), p. 69.

24. Sam Keen, *Fire in the Belly* (New York: Bantam Books, 1991), p. 39.

25. Sam Keen, "Faces of the Enemy," *New Age Journal*, March 1991, p. 47.

26. Rachel Carson, *Silent Spring*, quoted by Theodore Roszak in *Person/Planet* (New York: Anchor Books, 1979), p. 317.

Chapter Three

1. Joseph Campbell, quoted in Highwater, *Myth and Sexuality*, p. 36.

2. Barbara Hand Clow, *Liquid Light of Sex* (Santa Fe, NM: Bear & Company, 1991), p. 167.

3. Eisler, *The Chalice and The Blade*, p. 3.

4. Ibid., p. 1.

5. Marija Gimbutas, *Whole Earth Review*, Spring 1989, p. 121.

6. Eisler, *The Chalice and The Blade*, p. 2.

7. Ibid., p. 5.

8. Riane Eisler, *Reweaving the World*, ed. Irene Diamond and Gloria Feman Orenstein (San Francisco: Sierra Club Books, 1990), p. 25.

9. James Mellaart, *Çatal Hüyük* (New York: McGraw-Hill, 1967), p. 11.

10. Eisler, *The Chalice and The Blade*, p. 11.

11. Mellaart, *Çatal Hüyük*, p. 225.

12. Ibid., p. 225.

13. Nicolas Platon, *Crete* (Geneva: Nagel Publishers, 1966), p. 178.

14. Ibid., p. 148.

15. Ibid., p. 148.

16. Eisler, *The Chalice and The Blade*, p. 31.

17. Ibid., p. 8.

18. Marija Gimbutas, *The Gods and Goddesses of Old Europe, 7000–3500 B.C.* (Berkeley: University of California Press, 1982), p. 17.

19. Marija Gimbutas, *The Early Civilization of Europe* (Monograph for Indo-European Studies 131, University of California at Los Angeles, 1980),

chap. 2, p. 17. As quoted in Eisler.

20. Clow, *Liquid Light of Sex*, p. 167.

21. Lerner, *The Creation of Patriarchy*, p. 147.

22. Eisler, *The Chalice and The Blade*, p. 24.

23. Lerner, *The Creation of Patriarchy*, p. 30.

24. Stone, *When God Was a Woman*, p. 182.

25. Black Elk, quoted in Richard Heinberg, *Memories and Visions of Paradise* (Los Angeles: Jeremy Tarcher, 1989), p. xxiv.

26. Gloria Orenstein, *Reweaving the World*, ed. Irene Diamond and Gloria Feman Orenstein (San Francisco: Sierra Club Books, 1990), p. 21. Quoted by Brian Swimme from a personal communication.

27. Richard Heinberg, *Memories and Visions of Paradise* (Los Angeles: Jeremy Tarcher, 1989), p. 14.

28. Joseph Campbell, *The Hero with a Thousand Faces* (Princeton: Princeton University Press, 1973), p. 4.

29. Jean Houston, *Search for the Beloved* (Los Angeles: Jeremy Tarcher, 1987), p. 101.

30. Heinberg, *Memories and Visions of Paradise*, p. 16.

31. Thompson, *The Time Falling Bodies Take to Light*, p. 13.

32. Heinberg, *Memories and Visions of Paradise*, p. 15.

33. Ibid., p. 69.

34. Ibid., p. 18.

35. Ibid., p. 58.

36. J.V. Luce, *Lost Atlantis* (New York: McGraw-Hill, 1969).

37. Heinberg, *Memories and Visions of Paradise*, p. 240.

38. Richard Katz, *Boiling Energy* (Cambridge: Harvard University Press, 1982), p. 32.

39. The exclamation point before "Kung" is suggestive of a clicking sound common in their language.

40. Richard Lee, *Man the Hunter* (Chicago: Aldine, 1968), p. 40.

41. Katz, *Boiling Energy*, p. 20.

42. Lorna Marshall, *The !Kung of Nyae Nyae* (Cambridge: Harvard University Press, 1976), p. 245.

43. Katz, *Boiling Energy*, p. 26.

44. Ibid., p. 28.

Chapter Four

1. Fritjof Capra, *The Turning Point* (New York: Bantam Books, 1983), p. 72.

2. Willis Harmon, *Global Mind Change* (Indianapolis: Knowledge Systems, Inc., 1988), p. 10.

3. Ibid., p. 7.

4. Joseph Campbell, *The Masks of God*, vol. 2 of *Oriental Mythology* (New York: Viking, 1962), p. 39.

5. Highwater, *Myth and Sexuality*, p. 99.

6. Joseph Campbell, *The Masks of God*, vol. 4 of *Creative Mythology* (New York: The Viking Press, 1968), p. 101.

7. Heinberg, *Memories and Visions*, p. 79.

8. Campbell, *Creative Mythology*, p. 20.

9. Highwater, *Myth and Sexuality*, p. 55.

10. Heinberg, *Memories and Visions*, p. 87.

11. Chuang Tzu, *Sources of Chinese Tradition*, ed. Wm. Theodore de Bary et al. (New York: Columbia University Press, 1960), p. 70. Quoted in Heinberg, *Memories and Visions*, p. 95.

12. Heinberg, *Memories and Visions*, p. 96.

13. Thompson, *Falling Bodies*, p. 156.

14. Eisler, *The Chalice and The Blade*, p. 43.

15. Ibid., p. 43.

16. Ibid., p. 45.

17. Stone, *When God Was a Woman*, p. 66.

18. Eisler, *The Chalice and The Blade*, p. 45.

19. Schmookler, *Parable of the Tribes*, p. 21.

20. Ibid., p. 20.

21. Ibid., p. 21.

22. Ibid., p. 22.

23. Ibid., p. 21.

24. Ibid., p. 266.

Chapter Five

1. Murchie, *Seven Mysteries of Life*, p. 158.

2. Ibid., p. 159.

3. Deepak Chopra, *Quantum Healing* (New York: Bantam, 1989), p. 248.

4. Murchie, *Seven Mysteries of Life*, p. 172.

5. Gloria Steinem, *Revolution from Within* (Boston: Little, Brown and Company, 1992), p. 314.

6. Adolph Hitler, *Mein Kampf*, quoted by Miller in *For Your Own Good*, p. 161.

7. Miller, *For Your Own Good*, p. 284.

8. Ibid., p. 243.

9. Thomas Jefferson, *Notes on the State of Virginia*, ed. William Peden (Chapel Hill, NC: University of North Carolina Press, 1955), p. 163.

10. Fawn H, Brodie, *Thomas Jefferson* (New York: Norton, 1974), p. 160.

11. Robin Morgan, *The Anatomy of Freedom* (Garden City, New York: Anchor Press, 1982), p. 224.

12. Bradshaw, *The Family*, p. 78.

13. Miller, *For Your Own Good*, p. 277.

14. Starhawk, *Truth or Dare*, p. 85.

15. Brian Swimme, "How To Heal a Lobotomy," *Reweaving the World*, ed. Irene Diamond and Gloria Feman Orenstein (San Francisco: Sierra Club Books, 1990), p. 15.

16. Ronald Reagan, during his State of the Union address, 1988.

17. Antero Alli, *Angel Tech* (Phoenix: Falcon Press, 1986), p. 95.

Chapter Six

1. Christopher Fry, from the play *A Sleep of Prisoners* in *Three Plays* (London: Oxford University Press, 1960), p. 209.

2. Niro Markoff Asistent, *Why I Survive AIDS* (New York: Simon & Schuster, 1991), p. 75.

3. Ibid., p. 5.

4. Ibid., p. 24.

5. Ibid., p. 215.

6. Larry Dossey, *Space, Time & Medicine* (Boulder, CO: Shambhala, 1982), p. 222.

7. Michael Murphy, *Jacob Atabet* (Millbrae, CA: Celestial Arts, 1977), p. 212.

8. Chopra, *Quantum Healing*, p. 257.

9. Fred Alan Wolf, *The Body Quantum* (Macmillan Publishing Company: New York, 1986), p. 285.

10. Murphy, *Jacob Atabet*, p. 95.

11. "The Killing Numbers," *Ms.*, September 1990, p. 45.

12. Heidi Vanderbilt, "Incest," *Lear's*, February 1992, p. 52.

13. Ibid., p. 53.

14. Michael Renner, "Swords into Plowshares," *Utne Reader*, May 1990, p. 44.

Chapter Seven

1. Schmookler, *Parable of the Tribes*, p. 54.

2. Morris Berman, *Coming to Our Senses* (New York: Bantam Books, 1990), p. 128.

3. George Leonard, *The Silent Pulse* (New York: E.P. Dutton, 1978), p. 34.

4. Wolf, *The Body Quantum*, p. 110.

5. Richard Gerber, *Vibrational Medicine* (Santa Fe, NM: Bear & Company, 1988), p. 101.

6. Wolf, *The Body Quantum*, p. 193.

7. Chopra, *Quantum Healing*, p. 6.

8. See Richard Grossinger's *Planet Medicine* (Boulder, CO: Shambhala, 1980), pp. 90-91, for a fascinating discussion of voodoo death.

9. Gerber, *Vibrational Medicine*, p. 44.

10. Christopher Hills, "A Gift from the Light Force," *Enlightener*, vol. 12, no. 1 (1992), p. 3. Published by Light Force, Inc., Santa Cruz, CA.

11. Walt Whitman, from "Songs of Parting" in *Leaves of Grass* (New York: The New American Library of World Literature, Inc., 1954), p. 378.

12. Capra, *The Turning Point*, p. 72.

13. Ibid., p. 72.

14. Gerber, *Vibrational Healing*, p. 148.

15. Chopra, *Quantum Healing*, p. 127.

16. Whitman, from "Song of Myself" in *Leaves of Grass*, p. 49.

17. David Bohm, *Wholeness and the Implicate Order* (London: Routledge and Kegan Paul, 1980), p. 174.

18. Whitman, from "Assurances" in *Leaves of Grass*, p. 346.

19. Leonard, *The Silent Pulse*, p. 77.

20. Richard Leviton, "The Holographic Body," *East West*, August 1988, p. 47.

21. Whitman, from "A Song of Joys" in *Leaves of Grass*, p. 162.

22. Da Free John, *The Love of the Two-Armed Form* (Middletown, CA: The Dawn Horse Press, 1978), p. 82.

23. Mantak Chia and Maneewan Chia, *Cultivating Female Sexual Energy* (Huntington, NY: Healing Tao Books, 1986), p. 33.

24. Margo Anand, *The Art of Sexual Ecstasy* (Los Angeles: Jeremy Tarcher, 1989), p. 5.

25. Da Free John, *Two-Armed Form*, p. 249.

26. Ibid., p. 23.

Chapter Eight

1. Leboyer, *Birth Without Violence*, p. 62.

2. Leonard, *The Silent Pulse*, p. 201.

3. Pearce, *Magical Child*, p. 72.

4. Ibid., p. 73.

5. Bradshaw, *The Family*, p. 190.

6. Morgan, *Anatomy of Freedom*, p. 186. See also Karen Sacks, *Sisters and Wives* (Westport, CT: Greenwood Press, 1979), and Peggy Powell Dobbins, *From Kin to Class* (Berkeley: Signmaker Press, 1981).

7. Morgan, *Anatomy of Freedom*, p. 186.

8. Leonard, *The Transformation*, p. 199.

Chapter Nine

1. James Bertolino, *Like a Planet* (Anacortes, WA: Stone Marrow Press, 1993), p. 20.

2. Cleveland Amory, quoted by John Robbins in *Diet for a New America* (Walpole, NH: Stillpoint, 1987), p. 201.

3. See John Robbins, *Diet for a New America* (Walpole, NH: Stillpoint, 1987); *That All May Be Fed* (San Francisco: Earthsave, 1992); and Jeremy Rifkin, *Beyond Beef* (New York: Dutton, 1992).

4. All statistics from *What's the Beef & Who Pays?* (Santa Cruz, CA: Earth Save Foundation, 1992).

5. John Robbins, *That All May Be Fed* (New York: William Morrow, 1992), p. 13.

6. Joanna Macy, *World as Lover, World as Self* (Berkeley: Parallax Press, 1991), p. 220–221.

7. Ibid., p. 225.

8. Arne Naess, from an interview in *Deep Ecology*, ed. Bill Devall and George Sessions (Layton, UT: Gibbs M. Smith, Inc., 1985), p. 75.

9. Albert Gore, *Earth in Balance* (Boston: Houghton Mifflin, 1992), p. 269.

10. Jean Houston, *The Possible Human* (Los Angeles: J.P. Tarcher, 1982), p. 212.

11. Matthew Fox, *Original Blessing* (Santa Fe, NM: Bear & Company, 1983), p. 47.

12. Walt Whitman, "Salut au Monde!" in *Leaves of Grass,* p. 135.

Suggested Reading

The Nature of Patriarchy

Beauvoir, Simone de. *The Second Sex*. New York: Alfred A. Knopf, 1952.

Berry, Thomas. *The Dream of the Earth*. San Francisco: Sierra Club Books, 1988.

Clow, Barbara Hand. *Liquid Light of Sex*. Santa Fe, NM: Bear & Company, 1991.

Diamond, Irene, and Gloria Feman Orenstein. *Reweaving the World*. San Francisco: Sierra Club Books, 1990.

Dinnerstein, Dorothy. *The Mermaid and the Minotaur*. New York: Harper & Row, 1976.

Dworkin, Andrea. *Right-Wing Women*. New York: G.P. Putnam, 1983.

Ehrenreich, Barbara, and Deidre English. *Complaints and Disorders*. Westbury, NY: The Feminist Press, 1973.

Eisler, Riane. *The Chalice and The Blade*. San Francisco: Harper & Row, 1987.

Faludi, Susan. *Backlash: The Undeclared War against American Women*. New York: Crown, 1991.

French, Marilyn. *Beyond Power*. New York: Summit Books, 1985.

Heise, Lori. "Crimes of Gender." *World Watch*, March 1989.

Johnson, Sonia. *Wildfire*. Albuquerque, NM: Wildfire Books, 1989.

Keen, Sam. *Fire in the Belly*. New York: Bantam Books, 1991.

"The Killing Numbers," *Ms.*, September/October 1990.

Lawlor, Robert. *Earth Honoring*. Rochester, VT: Park Street Press, 1989.

Lerner, Gerda. *The Creation of Patriarchy*. Oxford: Oxford University Press, 1986.

MacKinnon, Catherine A. "Feminism, Marxism, Method and the State: An Agenda for Theory." *Signs: A Journal of Women in Culture and Society* 7, no. 3, Spring 1982.

Morgan, Elaine. *The Descent of Woman*. New York: Stein and Day, 1972.

Morgan, Robin. *The Anatomy of Freedom*. Garden City, New York: Anchor Press, 1982.

Rosaldo, Michelle, and Louise Lamphere, eds. *Women, Culture, and Society*. Stanford, CA: Stanford University Press, 1974.

Starhawk. *Truth or Dare*. New York: Harper & Row, 1987.

Steinem, Gloria. *Revolution from Within*. Boston: Little, Brown and Company, 1992.

Stone, Merlin. *When God Was a Woman*. New York: Harvest-HBJ, 1976.

Thompson, William Irwin. *The Time Falling Bodies Take to Light*. New York: St. Martin's Press, 1981.

Woodhull, Victoria. *The Victoria Woodhull Reader*. Edited by Madeleine B. Stern. Weston, MA: M&S Press, 1974.

Our Partnership Past

Campbell, Joseph. *The Hero with a Thousand Faces*. Princeton: Princeton University Press, 1973.

———. *The Masks of God*. Vol. 4, *Creative Mythology*. New York: The Viking Press, 1968.

Gimbutas, Marija. *The Gods and Goddesses of Old Europe, 7000–3500 B.C.* Berkeley: University of California Press, 1982.

The Early Civilization of Europe. Monograph for Indo-European Studies 131, University of California at Los Angeles, 1980.

Heinberg, Richard. *Memories and Visions of Paradise*. Los Angeles: J.P. Tarcher, 1989.

Highwater, Jamake. *Myth and Sexuality*. New York: New American Library, 1990.

Houston, Jean. *Search for the Beloved*. Los Angeles: J.P. Tarcher, 1987.

Luce, J.V. *Lost Atlantis*. New York: McGraw-Hill, 1969.

Mellaart, James. *Çatal Hüyük*. New York: McGraw-Hill, 1967.

Platon, Nicolas. *Crete*. Geneva: Nagel Publishers, 1966.

Sitchin, Zecharia. *Genesis Revisited*. Santa Fe, NM: Bear & Company, 1991.

Wilber, Ken. *Up from Eden*. Boulder: Shambhala, 1983.

A Partnership Present

Katz, Richard. *Boiling Energy*. Cambridge: Harvard University Press, 1982.

Lee, Richard. *Man the Hunter*. Chicago: Aldine, 1968.

Marshall, Lorna. *The !Kung of Nyae Nyae*. Cambridge: Harvard University Press, 1976.

Changing Paradigms

Capra, Fritjof. *The Turning Point*. New York: Bantam Books, 1983.

George, Demetra. *Mysteries of the Dark Moon*. San Francisco: Harper, 1992.

Harmon, Willis. *Global Mind Change*. Indianapolis: Knowledge Systems, Inc., 1988.

Houston, Jean. *The Possible Human*. Los Angeles: J.P. Tarcher, 1982.

Leonard, George. *The Transformation*. Los Angeles: J.P. Tarcher, 1972.

Russell, Peter. *The Global Brain*. Los Angeles: J.P. Tarcher, 1983.

Waring, Marilyn. *If Women Counted*. San Francisco: Harper & Row, 1988.

Poisonous Pedagogy

Alli, Antero. *Angel Tech*. Phoenix: Falcon Press, 1986.

Bass, Ellen, and Laura Davis. *The Courage to Heal*. New York: Harper & Row, 1988.

Bradshaw, John. *Bradshaw on: The Family*. Pompano Beach, FL: HCI, 1988.

———. *Healing the Shame That Binds You*. Deerfield Beach, FL: Health Communications, 1988.

Miller, Alice. *For Your Own Good*. Toronto: Collins Publishers, 1984.

———. *The Drama of the Gifted Child*. Toronto: Collins Publishers, 1981.

Pearce, Joseph Chilton. *Magical Child Matures*. New York: Bantam Books, 1985.

The Dominator Virus

Brodie, Fawn M. *Thomas Jefferson*. New York: Norton, 1974.

Chopra, Deepak. *Quantum Healing*. New York: Bantam, 1989.

Kohn, Alfie. *No Contest: The Case Against Competition*. Boston: Houghton Mifflin, 1986.

Murchie, Guy. *The Seven Mysteries of Life*. Boston: Houghton Mifflin Co., 1978.

Schmookler, Andrew Bard. *The Parable of the Tribes*. Berkeley: University of California Press, 1984.

———. *The Illusion of Choice*. Ithaca, NY: University of New York Press, 1992.

The Light of Awareness

Asistent, Niro Markoff. *Why I Survive AIDS*. New York: Simon & Schuster, 1991.

Berman, Morris. *Coming to Our Senses*. New York: Bantam Books, 1990.

Campbell, Peter A., and Edwin M. McMahon. *Bio-Spirituality*. Chicago: Loyola Press, 1985.

Crum, Thomas F. The Magic of Conflict. New York: Touchstone, 1987.

Dossey, Larry. *Space, Time & Medicine*. Boulder, CO: Shambhala, 1982.

Renner, Michael. "Swords into Plowshares." *Utne Reader*, May 1990.

Schindler, Craig, and Gary Lapid. *The Great Turning*. Santa Fe, NM: Bear & Company, 1989.

The Human Electric

Acharya, Pundit. *Breath, Sleep, the Heart and Life*. Clearlake Highlands, CA: The Dawn Horse Press, 1975.

Achterberg, Jeanne. *Imagery and Healing: Shamanism and Modern Medicine*. Boston: Shambhala, 1985.

Becker, Robert. *The Body Electric*. New York: William Morrow and Company, 1985.

Bohm, David. *Wholeness and the Implicate Order*. London: Routledge and Kegan Paul, 1980.

Da Free John. *Conscious Exercise and the Transcendental Sun*. Middletown, CA: The Dawn Horse Press, 1977.

————. *The Enlightenment of the Whole Body*. Middletown: The Dawn Horse Press, 1978.

Dossey, Larry, M.D. *Space, Time & Medicine*. Boulder, CO: Shambhala, 1982.

Gerber, Richard. *Vibrational Medicine*. Santa Fe, NM: Bear & Company, 1988.

Grossinger, Richard. *Planet Medicine*. Boulder, CO: Shambhala, 1980.

Gunther, Bernard. *Energy Ecstasy and Your Seven Vital Chakras*. Los Angeles: The Guild of Tutors Press, 1978.

Leonard, George. *The Silent Pulse*. New York: E.P. Dutton, 1978.

Leviton, Richard. "The Holographic Body." *East West*, August 1988.

Wolf, Fred Alan. *The Body Quantum*. New York: MacMillan, 1986.

Sexual Communion

Anand, Margo. *The Art of Sexual Ecstasy*. Los Angeles: Jeremy Tarcher, 1989.

Chia, Mantak, and Maneewan Chia. *Cultivating Female Sexual Energy*. Huntington, NY: Healing Tao Books, 1986.

Da Free John. *The Love of the Two-Armed Form*. Middletown, CA: The Dawn Horse Press, 1978.

Feuerstein, Georg. *Sacred Sexuality*. Los Angeles: J.P. Tarcher, 1992.

Henderson, Julie. *The Lover Within*. Barrytown: Station Hill, 1986.

Gentle Birth and Sexual Children

Arms, Suzanne. *Immaculate Deception*. Boston: Houghton Mifflin, 1975.

Leboyer, Frederick. *Birth Without Violence*. New York: Alfred A. Knopf, 1976.

Liedloff, Jean. *The Continuum Concept: Allowing Human Nature to Work Successfully*. Reading, MA: Addison-Wesley, 1991.

Mitford, Jessica. *The American Way of Birth*. New York: Dutton, 1992.

Morris, Desmond. *Babywatching*. New York: Crown Publishers, 1991.

Pearce, Joseph Chilton. *Exploring the Crack in the Cosmic Egg*. New York: The Julien Press, 1974.

———. *Magical Child*. New York: Bantam Books, 1977.

———. *The Crack in the Cosmic Egg*. New York: The Julien Press, 1971.

Silverstein, Samuel. *Child Spirit*. Santa Fe, NM: Bear & Company, 1991.

Sky, Michael. *Breathing*. Santa Fe, NM: Bear & Company, 1990.

Verney, Thomas. *The Secret Life of the Unborn Child*. New York: Simon and Schuster, 1981.

"Humanature"

Devall, Bill, and George Sessions. *Deep Ecology*. Layton, UT: Gibbs M. Smith, Inc., 1985.

Fox, Matthew. *Original Blessing*. Santa Fe, NM: Bear & Company, 1983.

Gore, Albert. *Earth in Balance*. Boston: Houghton Mifflin, 1992.

LeShan, Lawrence. *Alternate Realities: The Search for the Full Human Being*. New York: Ballantine, 1976.

Lovelock, J.E. *Gaia: A New Look at Life on Earth*. Oxford: Oxford University Press, 1979.

Macy, Joanna. *World as Lover, World as Self*. Berkeley: Parallax Press, 1991.

Rifkin, Jeremy. *Beyond Beef*. New York: Dutton, 1992.

Robbins, John. *Diet for a New America*. Walpole, NH: Stillpoint, 1987.

———. *That All May Be Fed*. San Francisco: Earthsave, 1992.

Seed, John. *Thinking like a Mountain*. Philadelphia: New Society Publishers, 1988.

Sheldrake, Rupert. *A New Science of Life*. Los Angeles: J.P. Tarcher, 1982.

Shepard, Paul. *Nature and Madness*. San Francisco: Sierra Club Books, 1982.

Swimme, Brian. *The Universe Is a Green Dragon*. Santa Fe, NM: Bear & Company, 1985.

Watson, Lyall. *Supernature*. New York: Bantam, 1973.

Index

About the Author

Michael Sky is a holistic healer, teacher, and firewalking instructor. Since 1976, he has maintained a private practice as a therapist and bodyworker focusing on breath, life energy, and the resolution of suppressed emotions. He travels throughout the United States and Japan leading workshops in the exploration of breathing, firewalking, bodywork, ritual, and the effective practice of partnership.

Michael has facilitated firewalking workshops for more than four thousand people since 1984. He is the author of *Dancing with the Fire* (Bear & Company, 1989), a comprehensive exploration of the scientific, psychological, and spiritual teachings of fire, and *Breathing* (Bear & Company, 1990), a definitive book on the use of breath for therapeutic and spiritual benefits. He and his wife, Penny Sharp, publish the nationally distributed progressive and environmental newsletter *Dragonfly Quarterly* and live on a small green island in the Pacific Northwest.

The author may be contacted at the following address:

Michael Sky
P.O. Box 1085
Eastsound, WA 98245